Picture That! From Mendel to Normandy

Picture That! From Mendel to Normandy

Picture Books and Ideas, Curriculum and Connections—for 'Tweens and Teens

Sharron L. McElmeel

LIBRARIES UNLIMITED

An Imprint of ABC-CLIO, LLC

A B C ❧ C L I O

Santa Barbara, California • Denver, Colorado • Oxford, England

Library of Congress Cataloging-in-Publication Data
McElmeel, Sharron L.
   Picture that! from Mendel to Normandy : picture books and ideas, curriculum and connections for 'tweens and teens / Sharron L. McElmeel.
       p. cm.
   ISBN 978-1-59158-588-6 (hard copy : alk. paper)
   1. Pictures in education. 2. Picture books. 3. Reading (Secondary) 4. Content area reading. I. Title.

LB1043.67M35 2009
373.133′52—dc22   2009010645

13   12   11   10   09   1   2   3   4   5

This book is also available on the World Wide Web as an eBook.

Visit www.abc-clio.com for details.

ABC-CLIO, LLC
130 Cremona Drive, P.O. Box 1911
Santa Barbara, California 93116-1911

This book is printed on acid-free paper ∞

Manufactured in the United States of America

For: E. J.—and Michael, Deborah, Thomas, Steven, Matthew, and Suzanne; and Michael, Jade, Aubrey, Tarrah, Jessie, E.J., Kylie, Kaydence, and Marissa.

Contents

1

Picture It, Read It ... Make Connections

Library media specialists in schools have long known that value can be added to the curriculum with the use of picture books. While some books are meant for the very young, there are many picture books that are both sophisticated in approach and in content. The many layers of each of these books can be peeled back and fully appreciated only by readers who have the necessary schema to recognize the nuances of the content and to make connections to enhance their learning and understanding.

Kirsten Joy Pratt-Serafina has written environmentally focused books such as *A Walk in the Rainforest* and *The Forever Forest: Kids Save a Rainforest*. Her large, colorful illustrations attract the youngest of readers, but the information—details about the flora and fauna of the forest—give older readers much to contemplate. Each of Pratt-Serafina's books opens the reader to the possibility of becoming active in saving the world—or at least contributing to making the world a more environmentally friendly place. This possibility will be directly meaningful to many older readers in ways that younger readers will not recognize.

The value of picture books can enhance the understanding of curriculum topics presented to older students. As more and more picture books are being published with more sophisticated themes, and with the emergence of graphic novels as an accepted genre, classroom teachers are taking a closer look at the value of illustrated texts—and picture books as a valuable addition to the resources for building knowledge and schema about a topic.

> "'What is the use of a book', thought Alice, 'without pictures or conversations?'"—Lewis Carroll in *Alice in Wonderland*

> "One of the great things about books is sometimes there are some fantastic pictures." — George W. Bush

Making the Best Use of This Book

In intermediate, middle, and high schools where picture books are not readily available for browsing, it might be difficult to identify books that would fit into content-area classrooms and literature-related activities. The citations in this book are intended to provide titles and suggestions for making that identification somewhat easier—easier to request from lower-level libraries, public libraries, or to investigate through electronic sources. With titles and author's names in hand, we hope to spark some additional interest in picture books and to provide some connections that will be the seed for the development of lesson plans to complement units of studies already in place—units with identifiable goals and standards that might be obtained more efficiently and effectively with the addition of a picture book to the resources used in instructional activities. No list however, could be an end-all list. In the quick list chapter, we have actually included a space for folder notes. In the chapters where book titles are dealt with in a more detailed manner, we have left plenty of white space so notes can be added for future convenience. Each of these measures is an effort to ensure that this book will be used frequently and not just as a reference book but also as an ongoing and interactive resource that will contain user notes about successes and uses for each of the picture books cited. I would like this book to become not only a reference book but also a resource that includes your professional notes as well.

If this resource book is owned by a library or other sharing unit, the white space might be used to list the library's call number or another title that might be owned by the library and which would be an excellent collaborative read. An individual who owns this book personally will want to note the source of books located and used, and a note or two regarding how the title might fit into the curriculum and lessons being taught. Additional titles and ideas could be added—somewhat of a working notebook of which the published text is only a start.

In addition, more detailed plans for specific lessons using the book (be sure to include goals and objectives that address skills and standards for your district) might be stored in a corresponding file folder along with:

> You cannot write for children. They're much too complicated. You can only write books that are of interest to them.
> —Maurice Sendak

- Notes about the author and the author's sources for the story
- Materials and colored pictures for thematic bulletin boards—perhaps book jackets
- A paperback copy of the book (very handy for those unexpected situations)
- Masters for prepared visuals—overhead transparencies, graphic organizers, and so forth
- Bookmarks with lists of collaborative reads—young adult novels, information books, poetry, and such

These folders can be numbered and referenced in the resource book and will be convenient for planning from semester to semester.

Picture Books and the Curriculum

Where do picture books fit into the secondary classroom? The answer is *everywhere*.

Using picture books to introduce a topic, to build a schematic background for content-area studies, and to develop higher-level thinking skills—to integrate a piece of well-written literature with content-area subject matter, is part of an efficient and effective methodology in classrooms populated with readers beyond the primary grades. Often, using a picture book can provide a short and focused stimulant and synopsis of a topic that will promote discussion and further investigation into the topic. Personal narratives provide a glimpse into the human factors present during historical periods. Other texts can provide a context through which to investigate mathematical concepts, science topics, geography (landform and locations for example), and language-arts skills.

Beatrix Potter's *The Tale of Peter Rabbit* (first published in 1902 by Frederick Warne Publishers) and *The Tale of Benjamin Bunny* (Warne, 1904), for example, were used in a tenth-grade classroom to help readers understand the function of sequels; that is, a literary work whose narrative continues that of a preexisting work. In *The Tale of Benjamin Bunny*, the two cousins, Peter and Benjamin, return to Mr. McGregor's garden to recover the clothing that Peter lost on a previous trip to the garden as portrayed in *The Tale of Peter Rabbit*. Benjamin Bunny's appearance as the father of the bunny children in *The Tale of the Flopsy Bunnies* (Beatrix Potter; Warne, 1909) became a good example of a companion book—a book that follows a previous title in terms of time, but does not necessarily continue the narrative (plot) of a previous work. These short and quick reading books can be easily read in one sitting and the concept discussed, whereas to read a longer narrative would be too time consuming to illustrate the concept. Once the concept of a sequel is cemented into the students' understanding, other longer narratives can be discussed in terms of details in each book that makes one book a sequel or a prequel to another title. Such knowledge can open up a whole area of discussion regarding the status of older classics (Are the books in C. S. Lewis's Narnia chronicles sequels or companion titles? And what evidence supports your answer?) or the status of newer titles such as the Harry Potter series.

Books by James Stevenson, such as *The Great Big Especially Beautiful Easter Egg* (Greenwillow, 1983), often employ flashback scenes and are effective in helping readers to understand this literary technique. Using both the narrative and illustrations, the sections that flashed back in time were clear and woven seamlessly into the book's plot.

The brief nature (thirty-two to forty pages) of most picture books promotes the sharing of ideas and information without getting bogged down with lengthy narratives. A literary technique can be modeled and information discussed as a prelude to longer narratives and more detailed curriculum-focused texts.

In recent years, many readers have become enamored with the books written and illustrated by Patricia Polacco. Polacco's *Pink and Say* has become a mainstay for those introducing a curriculum unit focused on the Civil War. The book tells the story of a friendship between Sheldon Curtis (Say) and Pinkus Aylee (Pink), one white boy, an injured soldier, and one African American boy, a Union soldier who rescues Say from the battlefield. Say, taken to Pink's mother, is nursed back to health. But when marauders come to Pink's home and kill his mother, the two boys flee only to be captured and taken to Andersonville prison. In a very dramatic and sad conclusion, Pink is hanged within hours of arriving. Say survives and honors Pink's memory in a moving connection to Pink. The fact that Pink had once touched Abraham Lincoln's hand serves as a connecting theme in the narrative. *Pink and Say* is a powerful introduction to the topic of the Civil War and Andersonville Prison.

Patricia Polacco's *The Butterfly* serves a similar function as Polacco tells the story of a great aunt's childhood in Nazi-occupied France during World War II. Monique forms a friendship with a Jewish girl, Servrine, when she discovers that Servine and her family have been living for months in the family's basement, protected by Monique's mother. A neighbor's chance sighting of the two girls at the window causes Sevrine's family to flee the oppression of the Nazis and their racism.

Some of the links, such as the curriculum connections to Polacco's books, are quite obvious; it simply takes someone who has the inspiration to read the books aloud and conduct a thoughtful discussion of the information that each book shares. In *Pink and Say*, Polacco touches on the role of African Americans in the Civil War, as well as the role that young men (and boys) played in the war. A discussion of that element of the war is a natural lead-in to books written specifically for the older reader. The role of boys in the Civil War is examined in depth in *The Boys' War: Confederate and Union Soldiers Talk About the Civil War* by Jim Murphy (Clarion, 1990), a 128-page book that uses the diaries and journals of young soldiers to present the Civil War and the role that boys (some as young as nine) played in the war. Andersonville Prison figured into the death of many Union soldiers. Its tragic and controversial existence is chronicled in Edward F. Roberts's *Andersonville Journey: The Civil War's Greatest Tragedy* (originally published by White Mane Publishing in 1998 and republished in 2007 in paperback by Burd Street Press). Both books are solid and mature reading selections for secondary readers. Picture books can be used very successfully to segue into lengthier, more involved titles on the same subject. Picture books can inspire and whet a reader's appetite for more information.

When I moved from a position as a library media specialist in an elementary school to the library department chairperson in a large high school, the district's library media coordinator assured me that I would find the two levels "not that different; the students are a little bigger, but they will be much the same." He was right. What I wasn't prepared for is that I would be totally familiar with much of the literature. Poems and stories I had known in the elementary school had found their way into the high school library and curriculum. On the poetry shelves I found poems by Christina Rossetti (1830–1894) and William Blake (1757–1827) and stories by Lewis Carroll (pseudonym of Charles Lutwidge Dodgson [1832–1898]), the author of *Alice in Wonderland* and *Through the Looking Glass*. Rossetti was known to me as the poet who wrote poems such as:

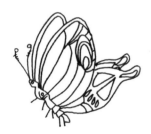

Brown and furry
Caterpillar in a hurry,
Take your walk
To the shady leaf, or stalk,
May no toad spy you,
And the birds pass by you;
Spin and die,
To live again a butterfly.

In the elementary school, I had used that poem many times as a companion to Eric Carle's *The Very Hungry Caterpillar* (Philomel, 1963). In the high school, Rossetti's poems were found in *Poems of Christina Rossetti* by Christina Rossetti (Gramercy, 1994). There were other favorites, including "Goblin Market" and "Up-Hill" and romantic Victorian verses.

William Blake became a favorite in elementary schools after the Newbery Award-winning *A Visit to William Blake's Inn: Poems for Innocent and Experienced Travelers* by Nancy Willard (Harcourt, 1981) was introduced to readers. In the elementary school, we went searching for poems by the poet who inspired Willard's work and found *Songs of Innocence* and *Songs of Experience* by William Blake (Dover Publications, 1992). In the high school, the process reversed itself; we found Blake's book on the shelves and then turned to Nancy Willard's title to bring readers to a fuller understanding of the motifs and images that Blake used in his poetry. We found angels, stars, the moon, and the sun. The Christina Rossetti poems we selected were more sophisticated, but we also found the simpler titles were great preludes to the poems of Paul Fleischman in his *Joyful Noise: Poems for Two Voices* (HarperCollins, 1988) and *I Am Phoenix: Poems for Two Voices* (HarperCollins, 1985).

When our elementary students read Franklyn Branley's *Journey Into a Black Hole* they were introduced to a sophisticated concept and a new vocabulary: mass, gravity, X-rays, and atoms, for example. High school advanced-placement science students knew the vocabulary and had a passing knowledge of the concept, but this illustrated introduction of black holes helped to clarify the theory and prepared them for the in-depth treatment the scholarly works our high school library held.

High school (and middle school) readers enjoyed the many stories of Dr. Seuss—much like their elementary counterparts. But the secondary readers found interest in the fact that a great and familiar story was really a window into the complexities of World War II. They learned about parodies as they read *Horton Hears a Who* by Dr. Seuss (Random House, 1954) and realized that the "Whos" symbolized the Japanese people seeking democracy. The phrase, "a person's a person no matter how small" took on new significance and meaning. Older readers realized that the title story in Seuss's *Yertle the Turtle and Other Stories* (Random House, 1958) presented a parody of the Nazi regime under Hitler.

Using Illustrated Stories with Older Readers

While younger readers enjoy picture books for both their illustrations and narrative, older readers might be given the text in a different form and sometimes without illustrations or with other illustrative matter. For example, *Nadia the Willful* by Sue Alexander (Knopf, 1983) was first published as a picture book. Later the narrative was included in an anthology of literature selections for seventh-grade students. "Casey at the Bat," a poem by Ernest Lawrence Thayer, has been put into dozens of picture books, but is often read by older students, especially in middle-school literature anthologies. With the older readers, the poem becomes a point of exploration of the time and era and material for reader's theater.

> A book that is enjoyed only by children is a bad children's story. The good ones last. A book that is not worth reading at age fifty is not worth reading at age ten.
> —C. S. Lewis

Picture books that are characterized by brevity (usually thirty-two pages) and with pictures on each page do not necessarily have a low reading level or immature interest level. More and more picture books are actually written for a more mature audience. And others have nuances and layers of meaning that are understood by and more appropriate for older students. In many cases, younger students do not have the background of understanding to comprehend the more complex layers of meaning.

When introducing longer or more sophisticated texts with a specific concept, it is helpful to use picture books or poems—simpler, shorter, more focused texts—to activate and refine prior knowledge. Picture books (and poems) in the classroom have many uses. Picture books afford the teacher short and concise materials with which to fuse literacy into their daily lessons while building an awareness of the language and the joy and cadence of the words.

> The book to read is not the one which thinks for you, but the one which makes you think.
> —James McCosh

And as Cynthia Leitich Smith has pointed out on her Web site <http://www.cynthialeitichsmith.com>, picture books can be used to make older readers aware of various literary techniques. She said, "... *Jingle Dancer* (HarperCollins, 2000) is built around the number four—Jenna goes in four directions to four women to collect four rows of jingles and then dances as the fourth jingle dancer at the powwow—rather than the more commonly used number three."

Picture books, especially biographies and informational books, are great prompts for introducing a topic and providing enough information to lead curious learners to other, more involved texts about the topic or person—sources that will allow (and encourage) more in-depth study. The content can easily build a schema for further study and a springboard to more research.

Read *Dear Mr. Rosenwald* by Carole Boston Weatherford (Scholastic, 2006) and then find out just who Mr. Rosenwald was and how much of the story Weatherford tells is from history. How did Mr. Rosenwald fit into the pages of history? And how did his role in building schools contribute to the culture of the United States and what impact did his philosophy of philanthropy have on future generations? How does his work and ideas compare with other philanthropists of the times?

Many stories can become texts for dramatic interpretations and in-class performances of various types. The books also become models for teens in their future role as parents. The illustrations in picture books are among some of the finest art being created today. Some of the illustrators are the best artists of our time. Artists such as E. B. Lewis, Leo and Diane Dillon, James Ransome, Jeni Reeves, Chris Raschke, Mary Azarian, David Wiesner, and dozens of others not only have gained acclaim as children's book illustrators but also have shown their work in galleries and museums. Their work can help to teach artistic illustrative styles.

> The best effect of any book is that it excites the reader to self activity.
> —Thomas Carlyle

Picture books can be used to help teach literary devices: foreshadowing, flashbacks, and so forth; and to teach elements of literature, plotting, characterization, and how to convey ideas simply.

Selecting and Using Picture Books

There are some overriding criteria that I feel are very important when selecting picture books for readers of any age. Criteria certainly should follow selection guidelines for any literature format; but of primary concern to me is that picture books used have an absence of stereotypic images or material. It is also important that the narrative is well-written and that the illustrations enhance the understanding of the text or are reflective of the narrative. Above all, the text and illustrations must be accurate in their portrayal of historic and current events, people, and places.

Since few of us are experts in every topic included in literature, professional reviews are very important in assessing books in relation to the criteria laid out for selection. *School Library Journal, Kirkus Reviews, Library Media Connection, Publishers Weekly, The Horn Book,* and other professional journals include reviews of children's books. Few, however, assess books for use across grade/age levels, so it will be up to individual educators to read, select, and connect specific titles to opportunities for surrounding their students in learning and literacy. Even our suggestions here will not be appropriate for all classes in all communities, but there are many possibilities.

Reading a picture book aloud to a group is an effective way to share it; sometimes the book can be read as a short story without sharing the illustrations, as the text stands alone. But in most picture books, the illustrations add much to the interpretation of the book and its content. Using a document camera to show the illustrations projected on a large screen serves to showcase them without violating copyright. Another useful technique is to make the book available either before or after the formal presentation of it (I generally prefer making it available for further exploration after I present it). Allow students a chance to read the book for themselves individually or as a pair or in small groups, employing a closer look at the illustrations. Later revisit the book as a large group and discuss any enhancement of meaning or connections they have made to both the book and the topic on which the class is focusing.

Often, looking at a group of picture books as a thematic unit can yield many details for discussion. For example, gather several picture books about World War II and have a read-in on a selected day. Allow ample time for students to read and discuss informally, with a focused question such as, "What do you know about World War II after reading this book?" Later that day or the next day, discuss as a large group the information students were able to glean from the books read and how those facts fit with the material and information being presented in the class textbook or formal curriculum materials.

History Is a Story Well Told

Especially in the area of history, traditionalists have focused on a collection of dates and events that can be repeated as fact. But history is much more—it is not a 600-page textbook, it is the stories of individual people and events that carry the real understanding of the time in history. Those seeking engagement in history are looking for stories—the best stories of the real human experience are the stories of individuals. Picture books are a perfect venue for bringing to the forefront the history of individuals, the average, everyday people—those whose names do not show up in textbooks. It is these stories that bring history alive.

In a similar but perhaps a less dramatic manner, picture books can focus on inventions, people, and events in other areas of study. A biography of an important but lesser-known scientist might shine the spotlight on the procedure used, the invention itself, or the creativity and perseverance of those who have an idea and bring the final solution to society. Picture books can also serve to introduce more involved topics in more manageable slices to provide the general information that will allow readers to begin to build greater layers of understanding and meaning. Other content areas are served in much the same manner.

The main section of this book has as its purpose to use picture books to provide educators with a seed of inspiration for using these books within their curricula. The full indexing in this book's appendices will aid in locating material to fit into classroom/library goals and standards. Each main entry in this book features a brief suggestion on its Idea Shelf to provide a basic thought about using the book to stimulate further exploration and learning. The Quick List will provide more titles and allow educators to move forward with developing even greater opportunities for literacy connections.

Read, share, enjoy, and explore.

2

Satchel Paige: Don't Look Back
by David A. Adler

Idea Shelf

Satchel Paige could not change the color of his skin, but with his patience and perseverance, he was able to change the way others viewed him and those of his race. He managed to overcome prejudices to show that blacks were capable of anything anyone else could do. Read this book aloud and discuss Paige's personal character traits or use it as a prelude to a discussion of the civil rights era.

Adler, David A. (2007) *Satchel Paige: Don't Look Back.* Illustrated by Terry Widener. Harcourt, Inc. ISBN-13: 978-0-15-205585-1; ISBN-10: 0-15-205585-1.

Bookshelf

Annotation

Satchel Paige was the best pitcher in baseball during his lifetime, but it took him more than twenty-five years to reach the major leagues. He was African American, and the color of his skin kept him out of the big leagues. Born in 1906, he was the seventh of eleven children. He earned his nickname, at the age of seven, when he devised a way to carry several bags (satchels) for travelers at the train station in Mobile, Alabama. He also hung out at the ballpark. He didn't own a baseball so he practiced with rocks. At the age of twelve, he was arrested for stealing and sent to a reform school in Mount Meigs, Alabama. He stayed there five years—but he was warm and fed, something that was good. After he was released, he sought a position with a local baseball team and was immediately offered a job. For the next twenty-five years he pitched for whatever team paid him the most. At the end of the season, his all-black team often played against all-star teams from the big leagues. Such greats as Joe DiMaggio, Ted Williams, and Dizzy Dean acknowledged Satchel's talent. He knew his time would come if he could just stay in the game long enough—and his time did come. In 1947, Jackie Robinson broke the color barrier by becoming the first African American to play in the major leagues. Paige's offer came in 1948, when he was forty-two years old. He continued to pitch in the major leagues as late as 1965—when he was fifty-nine years old. In 1971, Paige was inducted into the Baseball Hall of Fame at Cooperstown, New York. He died on June 8, 1982—one month short of seventy-six years old. A final page provides a time line of the highlights of Satchel Paige's life and source notations.

Curriculum Link: Sports, Heroes, African American History, Famous Firsts, Jim Crow Laws, Biographies, Baseball

Background

LeRoy "Satchel" Paige (1906–1982) was the oldest rookie ever to enter the [major baseball leagues]. When he made a special appearance with the Kansas City Athletics in 1965, he became the oldest man to ever play Major League Baseball. In addition to his induction into the Baseball Hall of Fame he earned many other honors. Information about Paige can be located on the Official Satchel Paige Web site at <http://www.satchelpaige.com>.

Extension Ideas

1. Make a time line of Satchel Paige's life.
2. Research the first five African Americans to have played Major League Baseball. Write a short profile of each highlighting any recognition they received, such as Hall of Fame membership and so forth.
3. Write an article: "The Rise of African Americans in Major League Baseball and Its Contribution to the Demise of the Negro Leagues."
4. Read more books about Satchel Paige and then prepare a faux interview transcript with "Satchel Paige" by your favorite sportscaster.
5. Create a baseball card for Paige or any African American player in the major leagues during the early days of their participation.
6. Discuss the Jim Crow laws and their ramifications on the African American community.

Books to Explore

Cline-Ransom, Lesa. (2000) *Satchel Paige*. Illustrated by James E. Ransom. Simon & Schuster.

Fox, William Price. (2005) *Satchel Paige's America*. Fire Ant Books.

Paige, LeRoy. (1993) *Maybe I'll Pitch Forever*. Afterword and contributions by David Lipman. University of Nebraska Press. (Originally published in 1962.)

Ribowsky, Mark. (1994) *Don't Look Back: Satchel Paige in the Shadows of Baseball*. Simon & Schuster.

Sterry, David. (2001) *Satchel Sez: The Wit, Wisdom, and World of Leroy "Satchel" Paige*. Three Rivers Press.

Sturm, James. (2007) *Satchel Paige: Striking Out Jim Crow*. Illustrated by Rich Tommaso. Jump at the Sun/Hyperion.

Other Media

Solarz, Ken. (2008) *Only the Ball was White*. DVD. 30 minutes. MPI Home Video. Includes interviews with many famous Negro League players: Roy Campanella, Paul Winfield, Satchel Paige, Effa Manley, Buck Leonard, and others.

3

An Egg Is Quiet
by Dianna Aston

Vertebrates include five groups of animals: mammals, birds, reptiles, amphibians, and fish. This book is an excellent beginning introduction to the characteristics of some of the animals that lay eggs. Provide a brief book-talk to introduce the book and then make it available for individual browsing. In a follow-up discussion, focus on the characteristics of the animal groups and what was learned about these groups from this book. Make a list.

Idea Shelf

Aston, Dianna. (2006) *An Egg Is Quiet.* Illustrated by Sylvia Long. Chronicle Books. ISBN-13: 978-0-8118-4428-4; ISBN-10: 0-8118-4428-5.

Bookshelf

Annotation

A pictorial representation of eggs of all shapes and sizes, from a black-necked stilt to a California thrasher; to the ladybird beetle and the tubular eggs of a dogfish; to Atlantic salmon and the sooty tern. All of the eggs are quiet until they hatch; then the "egg is noisy!" Many of the eggs are pictured in actual size, although in some cases, it is noted that the representations are larger than actual size. The pictures of the birds/reptiles on the final double-page spread, however, are not actual size.

Curriculum Link: Egg-laying animals, Birds, Physics of flight.

Background

Birds are a unique type of animal, but all have common characteristics. All birds have a backbone and feathers. Their body functions are faster than those of other animals. A bird's breathing is faster, its heart beats faster, and its body temperature is higher. Like mammals, birds are warm-blooded and are egg-laying animals like most fish and reptiles. A bird's bill or beak is a tool of defense. All birds have wings but not all can fly. Ornithology is the scientific study of birds.

Extension Ideas

1. Draw the egg and the bird/reptile/insect that lays it as a life-sized object.
2. How big is the black-necked stilt that is shown with the spotted egg that hatches the noisy birds?
3. Research the size of the bird and its egg and create graphs and charts to compare and contrast their sizes.
4. Is there a correlation between the size of the animal and the size of the egg? Is there a pattern in regard to size of egg? For example, the bigger the bird, the bigger the egg? Or do birds with long legs have smaller eggs, etc.?
5. Investigate the mysteries of birds' feathers. Not all are the same. Feathers do not cover the entire body of most birds (even though they appear to do so), and there are six types of feathers: powder-down feathers, bristle feathers, filoplume feathers, down feathers, semiplume feathers, and contour feathers. Not all birds have each of these types of feathers. Feathers have hollow stems and a basic structure that allow for flight. The color of feathers is very important to the mating process.
6. Several other bird-related topics might be explored: beaks, hydrodynamics, and/or the work of Swiss mathematician and physicist Daniel Bernoulli (1700–1782). Caution: Information about Bernoulli and his work, available in the English language, is scarce.
7. Explore Bernoulli's Principle. The principle is named after Daniel Bernoulli, who discovered that air moving quickly creates high pressure in the direction in which it travels. The faster the air moves, the less pressure is exerted in other directions. A discussion of this principle is in *Bill Nye the Science Guy's Consider the Following*, pp. 8–10.

Books to Explore

Burton, Robert, and Stephen Kress. (2002) *The Audubon Backyard Birdwatcher: Birdfeeders and Bird Gardens*. Thunder Bay Press.

Dunn, Jon L., and Jonathan Alderfer. (2006) *National Geographic Field Guide to the Birds of North America, Fifth Edition*. National Geographic.

Nye, Bill. (2000) *Bill Nye the Science Guy's Consider the Following*. Hyperion.

4

Gregor Mendel: The Friar Who Grew Peas
by Cheryl Bardoe

Gregor Mendel's work became the foundation for modern-day genetics. Use this book to introduce the idea of genetics and heredity—creating charts for eye color and other visible characteristics in the pattern of those illustrated by Smith in this book. Ask students to survey their ancestors for eye color (for example) and then create charts showing the pattern of eye color passed down to children and grandchildren.

Idea Shelf

Bardoe, Cheryl. (2006) *Gregor Mendel: The Friar Who Grew Peas*. Illustrated by Joseph A. Smith. Abrams Books for Young Readers. ISBN: 0-8109-5475-3.

Bookshelf

Annotation

Gregor Mendel grew up in a poor home but because of his thirst for knowledge, his family sacrificed to send him to boarding school. But when his father was injured, the family could no longer support his studies. Gregor was faced with a decision: he had to choose to feed his mind or his soul. For a while he was able to fend for himself but eventually realized that if he became a monk at the abbey, he would be able to eat and study. He conducted experiments with peas and proved his hypothesis—he created hybrid plants and conducted controlled studies. He applied scientific methodology to help discover the patterns and variables in the behavior of plants and animals and how those traits are passed from generation to generation. His thorough records documented all of his findings, but when they were published in 1866, few paid attention. Scientists did not seem to uncover his writings or to realize how astonishing his discoveries were until the turn of the century, several years after Mendel's death in 1884.

Curriculum Link: Science, DNA, Biology, Gregor Mendel, Genetics

Background

In the nineteenth century, Johann Mendel (1822–1884) was born in an area now known as the Czech Republic. (Mendel took the name Gregor when he entered the abbey.) His father was a farmer in a small village. The townspeople had already learned about grafting two types of apple trees to produce a better apple and breeding two kinds of sheep to produce a sheep with thicker wool. Mendel was curious and eager to learn. After he became a friar—a monk at the Abbey of St. Thomas in Brno—he was surrounded by scholars and thousands of books and could immerse himself in the study of nature. His work with peas is often cited as the foundation of genetics; Mendel himself is referred to as the "father of modern genetics."

Extension Ideas

1. Use this book to discuss the scientific method, theory, hypothesis, controlled studies, and conclusive results. Develop a study with plants—how much water one requires, how much sunlight, what makes a plant grow faster, and so forth. Develop the theory and hypothesis and then set out to prove (or disprove) the hypothesis.
2. This book is a great example of a biography that focuses on an event or accomplishment. Research any personality that is of interest and write a short biographical account of his/her major contribution to the world.
3. Use these two simple poetry books by J. Patrick Lewis to stimulate writing about another scientist:
   Science-Trickery: Riddles in Science. Harcourt, 2004.
   Arithme-Tickle: An Even Number of Odd Riddle-Rhymes. Harcourt, 2002.
4. Investigate more in-depth information about Mendel and his experiments and findings.

Books to Explore

Edelson, Edward. (2001) *Gregor Mendel: And the Roots of Genetics.* Tandem Library.
Henig, Robin Marantz. (2001) *The Monk in the Garden: The Lost and Found Genius of Gregor Mendel, the Father of Genetics.* Mariner Books.
Klare, Roger. (1997) *Gregor Mendel: Father of Genetics.* Enslow Publishers.
Mawer, Simon. (2006) *Gregor Mendel: Planting the Seeds of Genetics.* Harry N. Abrams, Inc.

5

Now & Ben: The Modern Inventions of Benjamin Franklin
by Gene Barretta

Begin a unit focusing on inventions by introducing Benjamin Franklin and his many inventions.

Idea Shelf

Barretta, Gene. (2006) *Now & Ben: The Modern Inventions of Benjamin Franklin.* Henry Holt and Company. ISBN: 0-8050-7917-3.

Bookshelf

Annotation

Clever illustrations on the first few pages foreshadow the many inventions created by Benjamin Franklin. Barretta lists various significant inventions, one by one. A brief text accompanied with illustrations further illustrates the ideas. Franklin's accomplishments are many:

- Illustrations in newspapers/political cartoons
- Bifocals
- Electricity (implications for use)
- Lightning rods
- Long arm/grabber
- Swimming flippers
- Charted the Gulf Stream
- Benefits of vitamin C
- Glass harmonica (a now-rare musical instrument)
- Franklin stove
- Library chair

- Writing chair
- Rocking chair
- Odometer for vehicles
- Hospital
- Library
- Post office
- Fire department
- Sanitation department

Many documents: the Constitution, the Treaty of Alliance with France, the Treaty of Peace with England, and the Declaration of Independence

---

Curriculum Link: Inventions, Inventors, Benjamin Franklin

Background

Benjamin Franklin is known as a patriot, a founder of the United States of America, a signer of the Constitution, and an inventor. To pursue very basic information about him, visit *The World of Benjamin Franklin* page on the Franklin Institute's Web site at <http://www.fi.edu/franklin/>.

Extension Ideas

1. Investigate Franklin's role in each of the inventions included in Baretta's book.
2. Write a paragraph telling others about the invention you have chosen; or show information about the invention in a visual presentation.

Books to Explore

Editors of *Time for Kids*. (2005) *Time for Kids: Benjamin Franklin: A Man of Many Talents*. HarperCollins.

Fleming, Candace. (2003) *Ben Franklin's Almanac: Being a True Account of the Good Gentleman's Life*. Schwartz/Atheneum.

Franklin, Benjamin. (1984) *Autobiography of Benjamin Franklin*. Buccaneer Books, Inc.

Fritz, Jean. (1976) *What's the Big Idea, Ben Franklin?* Putnam Publishing Group.

Tucker, Tom, and Richard Loehle. (1998) *Brainstorm! The Stories of Twenty American Kid Inventors*. Sunburst.

Van Vleet, Carmella. (2007) *Amazing Ben Franklin Inventions You Can Build Yourself*. Nomad Press.

6

Nauvoo: Mormon City on the Mississippi River
by Raymond Bial

Every community has a history. Nauvoo has a more unusual history than most. Read selected portions of this book aloud and then share stories of your community or other nearby cities. Put the book in a reading center for further browsing. Investigate the historical records for your own town/city/neighborhood. When was the city/town built or your unique neighborhood established? By whom? Why was it established where it was? What were the first buildings? How has the community evolved over the years? Arrange to interview citizens and then record the findings by writing the story of the community. The story could be presented as a written article or presented in a visual manner: a movie documentary, a PowerPoint presentation, or museum-like exhibit. This is a great research project to involve readers in local history.

Idea Shelf

Bial, Raymond. (2006) *Nauvoo: Mormon City on the Mississippi River.* Houghton Mifflin. ISBN-10: 0618-39685-3; ISBN-13: 978-0618-39685-6.

Bookshelf

Annotation

Bial provides a good overview of the religion, the history of persecution, and historical events during the mid-1800s, tracing the history of the Church of Jesus Christ of Latter-day Saints (Mormons) from 1839 to 1846, when they lived in Nauvoo. Photographs in the book help establish historical accuracy.

Curriculum Link: Religious Persecution, Mormons, Mormon Trail, Westward Movement, John Smith, Brigham Young, Nauvoo, Illinois

Background

Members of the religious group the Church of Jesus Christ of Latter-day Saints fled to safety from Missouri to Illinois, where they established the community of Nauvoo in 1839. Their history (and persecution) began years earlier in 1823, with revelations given to Joseph Smith. The church itself was formally established in 1830 in New York State. Eventually the group, led by Joseph Smith, settled in Ohio, but left because of persecution. They traveled to Missouri where the governor was, seemingly, welcoming of the several groups of Mormons who were moving there. Hostility caused by the Mormons' belief that they were the "chosen people" and their opposition to slavery caused them to leave the area around Independence and move to Far West, Missouri. But mobs began to attack the Mormon settlements and what came to be known as the Missouri Mormon War began. In 1838, the governor reversed his support and issued an "Extermination Order" declaring that Mormons should be exterminated or driven from the state. Attacks on Mormons intensified—in one attack, eighteen men and boys were killed. Suffering many hardships, the Mormons fled to Nauvoo, Illinois, hoping for a better life. The exiles seemed to be welcomed warmly in communities in Iowa and Illinois along the Mississippi River. It was Nauvoo that became one of the most well-known Mormon settlements of the day.

Bial's story focuses on the settlement in Nauvoo. By 1846, Nauvoo was the tenth-largest city in the United States, as populous as Chicago. By 1844, the people in Illinois had become distrustful of the Mormon community and controversy was arising among the Mormons themselves. However, the settlement continued to thrive. Illinois governor Thomas Ford sent letters to John Smith and his brother Hyrum. The two brothers felt it important to flee across the river, fearing for their lives. They later returned where they were immediately jailed and eventually murdered by a mob that rushed the jail, despite the governor's personal assurance that they would be safe there. Turmoil followed, and after months of threats and attacks, Brigham Young led approximately 14,000 Mormons on a forced migration across the frozen Mississippi River and into Iowa. An area near Council Bluffs, Iowa, was the staging ground for the long trip west to Salt Lake City, Utah—a land no one wanted. Nauvoo was inhabited by a communal group, and more recently has been the site of restoration by the Mormons who have rebuilt the temple and restored a dozen or more of the original homes.

Extension Ideas

1. Investigate the movement of other groups to the west. Explore the history and passage of the Mormon Trail and other well-known trails.
   a. The Oregon Trail
   b. The Applegate Trail
   c. The Beckwourth Trail
   d. The Bozeman Trail
   e. The California Trail

    f. The Cherokee Trail

    g. The Nevada Emigrant Trail

    h. The Nez Perce Trail

    i. The Pony Express

    j. The Smoky Hill Trail

    k. The Butterfield Overland Dispatch

    l. The Butterfield Overland Mail

    m. The Chisholm Trail

    n. Coronado and the Lost Cities of Gold

    o. The Escalante Trail: The Legend of Everett Ruess

    p. The Gila Trail

    q. The Goodnight-Loving Trail

    r. The Karl Bodmer Trail

    s. The Lewis and Clark Expedition

    t. Military roads of the Old West

    u. The Overland Trail Pages

    v. The Santa Fe Trail

    w. Trails to the Gold Rush

    Who were the people who used these trails? When were the trails used? During what period of time was each trail in use? What hardships did the travelers encounter? Can you show the trail on a U.S. map?

2. What is the history of your city? Or another city in your state?

Books to Explore

Dary, David. (2000) *The Santa Fe Trail: Its History, Legends, and Lore*. Knopf.

Dary, David. (2005) *The Oregon Trail: An American Saga*. Oxford University Press.

Francis, Dorothy Brenner. (2003) *Courage on the Oregon Trail*. Perfection Learning.

Hill, William E. (2004) *The Lewis and Clark Trail Yesterday and Today*. Caxton Press.

Landau, Elaine. (2006) *The Mormon Trail*. Children's Press.

Simmons, Marc. (1986) *On the Santa Fe Trail*. University of Kansas Press.

7

Across the Blue Pacific: A World War II Story
by Louise Borden

Idea Shelf

After sharing this book, adopt a soldier (and his/her family), whether in a war zone or providing support at home. Write letters, send packages to the soldier and his/her unit, and share the soldier's story with your school community.

Borden, Louise. (2006) *Across the Blue Pacific: A World War II Story.* Illustrated by Robert Andrew Parker. Houghton Mifflin Books for Children. ISBN-10: 0-618-33922-1; ISBN-13: 978-0618-33922-8.

Bookshelf

Annotation

In 1944, men are going away to World War II and across the Pacific. A young girl's fourth-grade class sent letters overseas to soldiers or sailors that they knew. Lieutenant Ted Walker had lived next door to the young girl on Orchard Road. Everyone looked forward to the days when Lieutenant Walker came home on leave. All the children loved him. During the school year, they wrote letters. The children found out that Lieutenant Walker was on a ship in the Pacific—a submarine, the *USS Albacore*. Days go by, the holidays come and go, no one has heard from Lieutenant Walker. On December 12, 1944, the Walkers received a letter. The letter said that Ted Walker was "missing in action." The children went on with their school days, and often shared stories of Lieutenant Walker—"remember when." His mother worked in her garden—alone. The war ended in 1945 but Lieutenant Walker was not coming home. Years have passed now and the narrator knows that the important thing is that "stories are passed down" from neighbor to friend and that "stories that are important enough to keep." In an author's note, Louise Borden shares that the facts in the story are based on her own uncle Theodore Taylor Walker's World War II service—service that was on the *USS Albacore*. Like the Ted Walker in the book, the author's uncle did not return from the war. After the war, the family found out that the submarine had been blown up in the Sea of Japan when it hit a mine. Walker perished with eighty-five other crewmembers, all of whom are honored at the Submarine Memorial in Honolulu, Hawaii.

Curriculum Link: World War II, Letter Writing, Family Stories

Background

Many schoolchildren have written letters to soldiers in the World Wars, the Korean Conflict, the Vietnam War, and more recently during the wars in Afghanistan and Iraq. Many also participated in sending packages to soldiers, especially those overseas.

There is evidence that a Japanese patrol boat actually verified the sinking of the *USS Albacore* on November 7, 1944. The *Albacore* struck a mine while underwater near Esan Misaki, off the south coast of Hokkaido.

Those who investigate the *USS Albacore* will find that on August 1, 1953, Doris Stanton Jowers, the widow of one of the enlisted men lost on the first *Albacore*, christened a newly built *USS Albacore*. The "new" *Albacore* was the 120th submarine built at the shipyards of Portsmouth, Maine.

Extension Ideas

1. Participate in writing letters to soldiers serving overseas or stateside away from their families.
2. Interview someone in your family who served in the military. Write one anecdote about that person's story. Decide if your anecdote is serious, sad, humorous, or a "call to action."
3. Discuss the elements of a friendly letter. If you do not have a member of the military to write to, write to a veteran. There are many veterans' homes throughout the states that might distribute your letters. Locate veterans' homes in your state by visiting the National Association of State Veterans Homes Web site at <http://www.nasvh.org/>.
4. Investigate the history of the *USS Albacore*.
5. Investigate other events that took place on November 7, 1944, in addition to the sinking of the *USS Albacore*.
6. Locate the spot where the *USS Albacore* actually sank. Show it on a map of that region.

Books to Explore

Largess, Robert P., and James L. Mandelblatt. (1999) *U.S.S. Albacore: Forerunner of the Future*. Portsmouth Marine Society.

8

Call Me Marianne
by Jen Bryant

Idea Shelf

Use this book as a stimulus to getting involved in poetry, especially the poetry of Marianne Moore, and encouraging students to write their own poetry. Give students a blank notebook and invite them to observe and write anecdotal notes (poetry or prose) about what they have observed.

Bryant, Jen. (2006) *Call Me Marianne*. Illustrated by David A. Johnson. Eerdmans Books for Young Readers. ISBN: 0-8028-5242-4.

Bookshelf

Annotation

Call Me Marianne is the fictional encounter of Marianne Moore, a poet, with a young boy who also enjoyed the zoo. The two first notice one another on a Saturday bus ride to the zoo. Jonathan is reading an article, "Exotic Lizards Have New Home in the Zoo," that he has clipped from the *New York Times*. He notices a woman dressed all in black (with a tricornered hat) reading the same article. They both get off the bus at the city zoo. When the woman's hat blows off, Jonathan retrieves it and they have a friendly exchange and spend time looking at various exhibits together. Before they leave for the day, Jonathan finds out that Marianne Moore is a poet and in turn he inquires about "being a poet."

"Being a poet," she says, "begins with watching." She explains that noticing details and writing them down allows her to shuffle the ideas all around like the pieces of a puzzle. She describes her process of revision and tells him that some poems take a long time and others a much shorter time to write—"Every poem is different—just like those lizards."

Before she leaves the zoo, she gives Jonathan a notebook that she has with her and he is left sitting on a bench in the zoo observing animals and writing in his new notebook.

Curriculum Link: Marianne Moore, Poetry, Animal Poems

Background

Marianne Moore (November 15, 1887–February 5, 1972) was a popular poet in the 1900s. Her first book was published in 1921, and more followed. She was particularly fond of animals and often used them in her poetic writings. Animals and their behavior frequently served as metaphors for human behaviors that she wanted to address. After moving to New York City in 1921, Moore attended zoology lectures at the New York Public Library and at the Museum of Natural History. She was a frequent visitor to the zoo. In fact, she visited so often that *Life* magazine featured her in an article "Life Goes on a Zoo Tour with a Famous Poet" (Vol. 35, no.12; September 21, 1953; pp. 202–207).

Born near St. Louis, Missouri, on November 15, 1887, Moore was raised in the home of her grandfather, a Presbyterian pastor. After his death in 1894, Moore, her mother, and her brother stayed with other relatives, and in 1896, they moved to Carlisle, Pennsylvania. She attended Bryn Mawr College and received her BA in 1909. Following graduation, Moore studied typing at Carlisle Commercial College, and from 1911 to 1915, she was employed as a schoolteacher at the Carlisle Indian School. She taught typing and bookkeeping for four years at the U.S. Industrial Indian School in Carlisle. One of her pupils was the famous Native American athlete Jim Thorpe.

In 1918, Moore and her mother moved to New York City, and in 1921, she became an assistant at the New York Public Library. She began to meet other poets, such as William Carlos Williams and Wallace Stevens, and to contribute to *The Dial*, a prestigious literary magazine. She served as acting editor of *The Dial* from 1925 to 1929. Along with the work of other members of the Imagist movement, such as Ezra Pound, Williams, and Hilda Doolittle, Moore's poems were published in the *Egoist*, an English magazine, beginning in 1915. In 1921, two of Moore's friends, Hilda Doolittle and Robert McAlmon, published Moore's first book, *Poems*, without her knowledge.

Extension Ideas

1. Visit a zoo (either on a field trip or a virtual visit—the Columbus [Ohio] Zoo and Aquarium has an informative Web site at <http://www.colszoo.org/>) and write notes about what is observed. Use the notes to create a paragraph or a poem.
2. Read poems by Moore and choose a favorite to read to others.
3. In *Call Me Marianne*, Moore shared some initial suggestions for being a poet. Keeping her suggestions in mind, try writing a poem or two.
4. Moore had friendships with fellow poets, T. S. Eliot, Ezra Pound, Elizabeth Bishop, and E. E. Cummings. Find poems by each and choose favorite poems to include in a personal anthology of poems: "The Poems of Marianne Moore and Friends."

5. Using Moore's poems and pictures you create or find in magazines, create a collage representing three or four poems by Moore. The collage should attempt to capture the mood, theme, and meaning of her poems.

Books to Explore

Miller, Christine. (1995) *Marianne Moore: Questions of Authority*. Harvard University Press. The author places Moore's work in context of historical, literary, and family environments that shaped her life and work.

Moore, Marianne. (1994) *Complete Poems* (Twentieth-Century Classics). Penguin Classics. This book contains 320 pages of poems from Moore's lifetime.

Moore, Marianne, and Grace Schulman. (2005) *The Poems of Marianne Moore*. Penguin Classics. Previously unpublished poems are now included in this comprehensive collection of poems; it includes poems that Moore suppressed in her own collection.

9

Journeys for Freedom: A New Look at America's Story
by Susan Buckley and Elspeth Leacock

Studying U.S. history? Choose a month—twenty school days, and read one story per day from America's past. Put the event on a time line and use the story as a springboard to further reading or discussion. Additional stories from America's history are available in Susan Buckley's and Elspeth Leacock's companion title *Kids Make History: A New Look at America's Story*. (See chapter 10.)

Idea Shelf

Buckley, Susan, and Elspeth Leacock. (2006) *Journeys for Freedom: A New Look at America's Story*. Illustrated by Rodica Prato. Houghton Mifflin Books for Children. ISBN: 0-618-22323-1.

Bookshelf

Annotation

From the beginning of our history, those settling on the land in what is now the United States had been on a journey for freedom. The twenty stories collected in this volume tell the true tales of several of those journeys.

1. "To Providence—1631" Roger Williams and Mary Williams left Massachusetts (for religious reasons) and settled in Providence (now Providence, Rhode Island).
2. "Le Grand Dérangement—1755" When the British overtook the Acadian region of Nova Scotia, they insisted that the Acadians give up their Catholic religion and also swear allegiance to the king of England. When they refused, the Acadians were forced into the lower level of a British ship, sailed across the Atlantic Ocean, and deposited on the shores of Maryland. Elizabeth Brasseux and her children were among those exiled to Maryland. Eventually they were welcomed into the French colony of Louisiana and sailed there from Maryland on March 2, 1767.

Here at last they were free to speak French, be Catholic, and to live as Acadians. (Some 7,000 Acadians were removed by the British and resettled; others fled to Canada, France, and French islands in the Caribbean.)

3. "On the Forbidden Path—1760" Teedyuscung, a Delaware Indian chief, wanted freedom for his people even though he entered into a treaty meaning his people were destined to lose their land, much of the Ohio Valley, within three years. The Delawares (Lenni Lenape, as they prefer to call themselves) lost their ability to live on their land.

4. "Soldier in Disguise—1782" Robert Shurtliff Sampson was the brother who died before Deborah Sampson was born. So when she wanted to fight in the Revolutionary War, she disguised herself as a man and volunteered as Robert. On May 20, 1782, Sampson enlisted in the Fourth Massachusetts Regiment of the Continental Army.

5. "Called by the Voice of America—1789" This story details the first days of the presidency of George Washington as the ceremonial procession and events took place in New York City on April 23, 1789.

6. "Buying Freedom—1795" Frank McWhorter, an African American slave earned money to purchase the freedom of his wife, Lucy, and eventually his children and all of his grandchildren—a total of fifteen family members. During the time that his efforts took to free his family, he and Lucy moved from Kentucky to Illinois (a free state) and founded a town. Free Frank established the town of New Philadelphia. (McWhorter called himself Free Frank for all the years of his freedom.)

7. "Give Us Freedom—1839" This is the tale of the revolt on the *Amistad*. Spanish men purchased forty-nine men and four children in Cuba and loaded them on the *Amistad*. The captives managed to take over the ship and order that the ship sail back to Africa. The ship ended up in Long Island, New York, and when the government seized the boat, a legal battle ensued. Eventually the men and children were released and allowed to return to Africa. Later, one of the children, Margru, returned to America, studied at Oberlin College, and then returned to Africa to become a principal of a school.

8. "A Thousand Miles for Freedom—1848" This is the story of William and Ellen Craft, who masqueraded as an invalid white man (Ellen) and her man slave (William) to escape slavery. They traveled by train from Savannah to the free state of Pennsylvania. Philadelphia was very close to slave states so they continued on to Boston. But when the 1850 Fugitive Slave Bill was signed into law, the Crafts fled to England, where they remained until 1869, several years after the end of the Civil War. When the Crafts returned to Georgia, they set up a cooperative farm for freedmen.

9. "Walking to Zion—1856" Details the journey of the McBrides, Mormons who traveled from Scotland to the United States, where they lived near Iowa City for weeks. Other Mormons helped them launch their trip, with all of their worldly goods in a pushcart, to Zion. Four hundred twenty-six members of the Church of Jesus Christ of Latter-day Saints survived the pushcart trip four months after the trip began, on November 30, 1856.

10. "For Honor, Duty, and Liberty—1863" This is the story of Henry Gooding and the all-black 54th Massachusetts Volunteer Infantry that fought in the Civil War. Gooding died in Andersonville on July 19, 1864. A series of his letters was published in the *New Bedford Mercury* between March 1863 and February 1864.

11. "Gold Mountain—1865" Ah Goong and his story of immigration from China to San Francisco and his work on the Transcontinental Railroad.
12. "Flight of the Nez Perce—1877" When settlers coveted the Nez Perce's Wallowa Valley (Northwest Territory), the government gave the valley to them and demanded that the Nez Perce leave. Battles followed, and eventually Chief Joseph and 200 of his followers were sent to a reservation in Oklahoma. Others, including Wetatonmi, Chief White Bird, and approximately 200 other Nez Perce fled to Canada.
13. "The Promised Land—1894" This story recounts the travels of Russian Jewish children who, with their mother, follow their father from the "Pale of Settlement"—near Polotzk, a place where Russian Jews were forced to live, to America.
14. "Going North—1924" White southerners did not like the fact that African American sharecroppers (who worked for a meager part of the crops they raised) were going in great numbers up north, where there were better jobs and a more equitable life. Mildred Mack was just a child when her father slipped out in the dark of night to board a train and head north. Weeks later, his wife and children had to devise a plan to slip out of North, a town in South Carolina, and make their way secretly to Newark, New Jersey, where Mildred's father was waiting for them. Mildred Mack spent the rest of her life in Newark.
15. "The Road to California—1934" During the Depression, Flossie and James Haggard suffered immeasurable farming losses and then their barn burned. The family was forced to join the exodus to California and hopefully find some opportunities to survive.
16. "Saved … —1939" This is the story of Isi Veleris's flight, with his mother, from the Nazis during World War II. Only through the kindness of others who befriended and hid them were mother and son temporarily saved. The Nazis invaded France, and mother and son were ultimately packed off to await being sent to Auschwitz. When the Swiss Red Cross demanded the freedom of some boys taken from their castle, Isi's mother made plans. She arranged for the Swiss to return for Isi; the next day she was sent to Auschwitz. But her plans had saved her son. Isi eventually came to the United States but is now back in France, where he is a photographer.
17. "Walk Together, Children—1965" This story details the march from Selma to Montgomery, Alabama, in support of civil rights. It is told from the vantage point of fifteen-year-old Lynda Blackmon.
18. "La Peregrinación—1966" César Chávez's efforts to create the National Farm Workers Association (now the United Farm Workers of America) are compellingly told in this story.
19. "Losing China—1966" Nien Cheng was imprisoned for six years during the Cultural Revolution. Freed, finally, after President Richard Nixon visited China, Cheng never again felt free there. On September 20, 1980, she traveled to the United States and still lives in Washington, D.C. (The Cultural Revolution lasted from 1966 until 1976.) Cheng told her story in *Life and Death in Shanghai*.
20. "Welcome to America—1988" Peter Malual is but one "lost boy" of the Sudan. Fleeing from Sudan to Ethiopia, and then forced back to Sudan by the civil unrest in Ethiopia, he was finally helped by the Red Cross to enter a safer refugee camp in Kakuma, Kenya. While living in the refugee camp in Kenya, Malual, at the age of eighteen (after twelve years of having no home: fleeing or in refugee camps) was chosen to come to the United States on May 15, 2001.

Curriculum Link: Sudan, Lost Boys, Civil War, Civil Rights Movement, Freedom, Ethiopia

Background

The fight for freedom has taken many forms throughout the world's history. In the United States, the most discussed fight is the fight against slavery during the Civil War era. However, slavery and loss of freedom has taken other forms throughout the history of the world. Today there are many instances of child labor in countries with emerging economies, and there are many accounts of young people (especially females) being sold into sexual slavery. There are instances of immigrants being brought to the United States illegally and then held hostage in fear of being exposed as illegal.

Extension Ideas

1. Discuss the term "freedom" and what it really means.
2. Investigate whether there are people in today's world that no longer have their freedom. What are their circumstances, and how can those without freedom gain their personal liberation and be truly free?
3. Investigate more information about the "Lost Boys of the Sudan." How old would they be today, and what is the "rest of the story." Share the information gathered through a written or visual presentation. Be creative: Could you locate a former Sudan refugee and interview him? Could you find enough images to create a museum type exhibit.
4. Write an article for your local (or for a national) newspaper making readers aware of the exploitation of minors that is occurring in the United States and across the world. Focus on child labor or actual slavery situations.

Books to Explore

Bok, Francis. (2004) *Escape from Slavery: The True Story of My Ten Years in Captivity and My Journey to Freedom in America*. St. Martin's Griffin. A young boy from Sudan is taken into slavery in 1986.

Lester, Julius. (1998) *From Slave Ship to Freedom Road*. Illustrated by Rod Brown. Dial. Graphic but accurate illustrations of the Middle Passage.

McCormick, Patricia. (2006) *Sold*. Hyperion. A contemporary tale of sexual slavery.

10

Kids Make History: A New Look at America's Story
by Susan Buckley and Elspeth Leacock

Young people have a long history of their involvement in the history of the United States. Choose a month and each day, read one story from America's past. Put the event on a time line and use the story to lead to further reading or discussion. Focus the discussion on the contribution made by young citizens to the culture of their country. Additional stories from America's history are available in Susan Buckley's and Elspeth Leacock's companion title *Journey for Freedom: A New Look at America's Story.* (See chapter 9.)

Idea Shelf

Buckley, Susan, and Elspeth Leacock. (2006) *Kids Make History: A New Look at America's Story.* Illustrated by Randy Jones. Houghton Mifflin. ISBN-10: 0-618-22329-0; ISBN-13: 978-0-618-22329-9.

Bookshelf

Annotation

Children in the history of the United States—twenty stories.

1. "Powhatan's Favorite Daughter—1607" This is the story of Pocahontas and her family's life in the village of Werowocomoco. Pocahontas's father was Powhatan, the ruler of the Algonquian people, the chief of chiefs.
2. "James Towne Boy—1608" Sam Collier, a boy with the explorers, John Smith, and 107 other settlers came from Britain to Virginia, arriving in December 1606. "James Towne" was established but destroyed by a fire and rebuilt as new settlers arrived.
3. "Evil in the Air—1692" Ann Putnam was at the center of accusations against many women in Salem. She accused the women of practicing witchcraft. Eventually the town leaders, after hanging many "witches," decided that they should not

listen to the accusations of girls like Putnam. In 1706, once she was grown, she asked for forgiveness.

4. "Kidnapped—1743" This details the fate of one boy, Peter Williamson, who was kidnapped (as were hundreds of other boys during the 1740s) from the streets of Aberdeen, Scotland, and sold into service as an indentured servant in America.

5. "Yankee Doodle Soldier—1776" Joseph Plumb Martin joined the Continental Army in 1776, as a fifteen-year-old boy. He fought until the war's end.

6. "The House on the Hill—1838" John Rankin Jr., a twelve-year-old member of the family who regularly helped fleeing slaves in their home in Ripley, Ohio, helped a brave woman and her child to move on to the next Underground Railroad station.

7. "Never Take No Cutoffs" The Reed and Donner families set out in April 1846 to trek westward to California. The group was trapped for more than four months in an early snowstorm on what has become known as Donner's Pass. Virginia Reed was one of the few survivors. She was twelve when the journey began.

8. "Pony Rider—1854" For two years, Nick Wilson lived with the Shoshone and later, after returning to his family, he heard about the Pony Express. He was one of many riders who delivered mail during the few months before the telegraph and stagecoach lines put the Pony Express out of business.

9. "Pull-Up Boy—1860" Six-year-old Marty Myers began to work at the Sligo Iron Works in Pittsburgh. He was proud to be learning a trade next to his father. The workdays were ten hours.

10. "Working for Freedom—1863" Susie Shaw was just thirteen when she left Savannah, Georgia, and was taken by Union soldiers to St. Catherine Island. From there, she stayed with one of the first regiments of black soldiers to fight in the Civil War. She taught them to read, helped them take care of their clothes, and nursed them to health when they contracted smallpox or got wounded. She remained with the troops until the war ended in 1865.

11. "Pioneer Girl—1868" This summarizes the travels of Laura Ingalls Wilder from her birth home on the prairie to the shores of Silver Lake in Dakota Territory.

12. "Three Blows—1875" Fourteen-year-old George Fred Tilton slipped away from his home in Martha's Vineyard in Massachusetts and stowed away on a whaling ship, the *Union*. After hiding for two days, he revealed himself and was put to work. He spent more than a year at sea, but when he returned home, he owed more than his pay.

13. "A Most Wonderful Sight—1893" Jane, a thirteen-year-old, recounts her adventures at the Chicago World's Fair.

14. "High Jinks at the White House—1902" Tales from the White House during the days President Theodore Roosevelt, Edith Roosevelt, and their family of six children occupied the residence.

15. "Low Bridge!—1909" This story details the travels of the Garrity family down the Erie Canal using mules as they moved from one lock to another.

16. "Riding the Orphan Train—1926" Orphan children and those whose parents could not care for them were boarded onto trains on Long Island, New York. The three boys in this story were taken to the Midwest, where families who wished for a child (either as a true member of the family or as an extra hand in the household or on the farm) could offer to give the child a home. The boys ended up in different families.

17. "Sunday Morning at Pearl Harbor—1941" Nine-year-old Joan Zuber was in Hawaii when Pearl Harbor was bombed. She and other members of her family were taken to safety after witnessing much of the devastation.
18. "On the Circuit—1955" Francisco Jiménez was a sixth-grader and knew that education was a way to change his life. As his family moved from place to place, he attended many different schools. His family members were migrant workers and eventually the work resulted in his father developing a bad back so the family decided to stay in Santa Maria. Then immigration officials came and sent them back to Mexico. He prayed that he could return to Santa Maria but knew that his education was the one thing no one could take away.
19. "It's About Freedom—1963" Malcolm Hooks was part of the Birmingham sit-ins in the Holiday Inn and other peaceful protests.
20. "9/11: The Day the Towers Fell—2001" Jukay was in a classroom on the north side of Stuyvesant High School in lower Manhattan when the planes hit the World Trade Center. After his school was evacuated and he had reached safety at a friend's apartment, Jukay volunteered to help in the Red Cross office that fed rescue workers and helped care for the few survivors who arrived.

Curriculum Link: Children and their Impact on Social History: Wars, Inventions. and so forth

Background
Children have made significant marks on our society. The Civil War is often referred to as the Boy's War. Inventors, such as Louis Braille and Margaret Knight, have made marks as child inventors. More recently, through organizations such as Youth Service America, children have spearheaded a number of humanitarian efforts worldwide. Many individual youths have created projects of their own initiative.

Extension Ideas

1. Investigate the Youth Service America organization's Web site at <http://ysa.org/>. Discuss what the youth in your group might be able to accomplish on Global Youth Service Day.
2. Read about other teens and their efforts to contribute to their society, and discuss what *you* can do to contribute to society.
   Clayton Lillard and his "backyard crew" repair bicycles to give to those who are too poor to own one.
      Owen, Linda. (2004) "Clayton Lillard: Teen Humanitarian." *Today's Christian*, <http://www.christianitytoday.com/tc/2004/004/23.40.html>.
      Clayton's Backyard Crew—Clayton Lillard. (2007) <http://www.claytons backyardcrew.com.>
   A group of 100 teens is working on an environmental project in California.

Luna, Kenny. (October 16, 2007) "Teen Green: Local Teens Making a Difference." TreeHugger.com, <http://www.treehugger.com/files/2007/10/theyre_a_recent.php>.

Jennifer Tao, is a Moraga, California, teen community volunteer.

ABC7 News (January 19, 2007) "Teen Volunteer is a Community Leader." <http://abclocal.go.com/kgo/story?section=news/abc7_salutes&id=4952990>.

Jennifer Lentine and sixteen other Philadelphia teens volunteer in their community.

Katalinas, Theresa. (April 28, 2008) "Teens Making a Difference." PhillyBurbs.com. <http://abclocal.go.com/kgo/story?section=news/abc7_salutes&id=4952990>.

Read about Milwaukee area Jewish Teens' Social action day and their activities at <http://www.cjlmilwaukee.org/Teens/cjlteens_news.htm>, *News from CLJ Teens* on the Coalition for Jewish Learning Web site.

Oprah Winfrey, in partnership with Craig Kielburger of the Free the Children organization, is sponsoring an initiative to involve young people through their schools or as individuals. Educators who are interested in a school group club and involvement may choose to join the O Ambassadors as a group but there are also opportunities for individuals to get involved. Log onto <http://www.oambassadors.org> and see what opportunities await you.

If these articles are no longer available, search the Internet for recent articles using the phrase "Teens make a difference."

And locate information about the Teens Make a Difference Day and establish an initiative in your community.

Books to Explore

Kielburger, Craig, and Marc Kielburger. (2002) *Take Action! A Guide to Active Citizenship.* Jossey-Bass.

Kielburger, Craig, and Marc Kielburger. (2008) *Me to We: Finding Meaning in a Material World.* Fireside.

Lynette, Rachel (2008) *Craig Kielburger: Free the Children.* KidHaven Press.

Major, Kevin. (1999) *Free the Children: A Young Man Fights Against Child Labor and Proves that Children Can Change the World.* HarperPerennial.

Zieman, Nancy Luedtke, and Gail Brown. (2003) *Creative Kindness: People and Projects Making a Difference and How You Can, Too.* Krause Publications.

11

Pop's Bridge
by Eve Bunting

This is one story of one bridge in one city. Introduce the idea of investigating the stories of well-known structures in your community. Write or tell the story (fiction or nonfiction).

Idea Shelf

Bunting, Eve. (2006) *Pop's Bridge.* Illustrated by C. F. Payne. Harcourt Children's Books. ISBN-10: 0-15-204773-5; ISBN-13: 978-0152-04773-3.

Bookshelf

Annotation

A mile-wide span from San Francisco to California's Marin County was accessible only by ferry until Joseph Baermann Strauss convinced civic leaders to build a bridge—a suspension bridge that he designed. This is the fictionalized tale of the bridge's beginnings and its construction that took place between January 1933 and May 1937, when the bridge was officially opened. The bridge had cost over $34 million, and several lives had been lost. The accident described in the book really did occur.

Curriculum Link: Construction, Golden Gate Bridge, Local History, San Francisco, Suspension Bridges

Background

A well-known bridge, the Golden Gate Bridge is the subject of Bunting's fictionalized account of an accident that did happen, although Bunting mentions a dozen men fell with only two surviving while other sources mention thirteen men falling with two surviving. The accident occurred on February 17, 1937, near the end of the construction period.

And while Joseph Baermann Strauss was given credit for building the bridge, it is now thought that the major designer was actually Charles Alton Ellis, whom Stauss fired before the bridge was constructed.

Extension Ideas

1. Investigate the role each of these men had in the building of the bridge.
   Joseph Baermann Strauss (1870–1938)
   Irving Morrow (1884–1952)
   Charles Alton Ellis (1876–1949)
   Leon Moisseiff (1872–1943)
2. Learn more about the building of the Golden Gate Bridge by using this resource: Public Broadcasting System. "American Experience: Golden Gate Bridge." <http://www.pbs.org/wgbh/amex/goldengate/>.
3. Learn more about the types of bridges that are commonly constructed at Public Broadcasting System/NOVA Online: Super Bridge—Build a Bridge (2000) at <http://www.pbs.org/wgbh/nova/bridge/build.html>.
4. Take pictures of bridges in your area. Collect as many pictures as you can and post them on a board of bridges. Write about each bridge. What kind of bridge is it? Who built it? When was it built? Are there any local stories about the bridges you have pictured? For suggestions about how to conduct local research, consult this source:
   Martin, Jacqueline Briggs, and Sharron L. McElmeel. (November/December 2001). "Kids Search: Social Studies Research and Local Resources." *Library Talk.* 14:5, pp. 14–15, <http://www.mcelmeel.com/writing/kidssearch.html>.

Books to Explore

Johmann, Carol A., et al. (2000) *Bridges: Amazing Structures to Design, Build & Test.* Williamson Publishing Company.

12

The Sensational Baseball Song: Take Me Out to the Ball Game
by Jim Burke

Sing a rousing rendition of "Take Me Out to the Ball Game," eat some Cracker Jack, and read this story.

Idea Shelf

Burke, Jim. (2006) *The Sensational Baseball Song: Take Me Out to the Ball Game.* Illustrated by Jim Burke. Lyrics by Jack Norworth. Introduction by Pete Hamill. Little, Brown Young Readers. ISBN: 0-316-75819-1.

Bookshelf

Annotation

This book chronicles a legendary game between the New York Giants and the Chicago Cubs—a game that would decide the National League pennant. Due to the failure of Fred Merkle to touch second base, the Cubs retrieved the baseball and executed a play that resulted in an out and invalidated the Giants' winning run. The game ended in a 1–1 draw and was rescheduled for October 8, 1908, a game that the Cubs won. The Giants, however, considered themselves "the real champions."

Curriculum Link: Baseball, "Take Me Out to the Ball Game," Jack Norworth, World Series

Background

The tale is told through historical notes and the lyrics of the popular song are accompanied by boldly painted scenes from the game itself. The song's lyrics, stanza by stanza, are printed in large type while notes about the era and times are featured in a box in smaller type.

This book is a tribute to the song written in 1908 and to many things associated with baseball. The boxed copy includes historical references to:

1. Christy Mathewson (and statistics of his legendary play)
2. Polo Field, Jack "The Giant Killer" Pfiester—Mathewson's archrival in the 1908 World Series
3. Nicknames in baseball
4. Pitching styles
5. Umpire signals
6. Popcorn and peanuts (Cracker Jack)
7. Electronic scoreboard (invented by George Baird)
8. Joe Tinker (Chicago's Ace shortstop)
9. The introduction of various baseball accessories—batting helmets and the catcher's shin guards.

Notes that might be helpful:

- Christy Mathewson (Matty) was known as "the Christian Gentleman" and was also a great college football player and a superb checkers player who once beat world champion Newell Banks.
- "Baseball" was written as "base ball."
- "Sou" in the lyrics refers to a small amount of money.
- Fred Merkle—"to merkle" has come to be an expression that means "to never appear."

Extension Ideas

1. In a clever montage on the end pages, baseball card style illustrations show a "beau," "Casey (a fan)," "Bucknell (a dog)," "Big Six—Mathewson," "Tinker," and in a tip of the hat (nod of acknowledgment) to the author of the song lyrics, he also includes Jack Norworth and to Albert Von Tilzer, who wrote the music. On the back end papers, an additional baseball card appears—although it is labeled "Merkle, NY. NAT'L," there is no picture in the frame (explain why). Explain the significance of the other illustrations in the montage.
2. Investigate the origin of the following items:
   a. Cracker Jack
   b. Electronic scoreboard
   c. Batting helmets
   d. Catcher's shin guards
   e. The term "hot dog"
3. The end papers of this book celebrate the connections to baseball. Think of any other topic that interests you and create a montage of symbols inspired by that interest.
4. Neither Jack Norworth nor Albert Von Tilzer had been to a ball game before Norworth wrote the lyrics and Tilzer wrote the music to "Take Me Out to the Ball

Game." Investigate the other music and lyrics written by Norworth and music by Tilzer.

5. Norworth wrote the first version in 1908 and a second version in 1927. Compare and contrast the two versions. In general, the chorus is the same in each version. Generally, now only the chorus is sung—few if anyone actually sings the verses.

6. The 100th anniversary of "Take Me Out to the Ball Game" was celebrated on May 2, 2008. The U.S. Postal Service issued a stamp in honor of the anniversary. Investigate how one gets a stamp designed and issued to honor a particular event or person.

7. Learn more about the origin of the song on the Library of Congress's page "Take Me Out to the Ball Game: Article Brief Display: Performing Arts Encyclopedia." <http://lcweb2.loc.gov/diglib/ihas/loc.natlib.ihas.200153239/default.html>.

Books to Explore

Thompson, Robert, et al. (2008) *Baseball's Greatest Hit: The Story of "Take Me Out to the Ball Game."* Hal Leonard; Har/Com edition.

13

Akira to Zoltán: Twenty-Six Men Who Changed the World
by Cynthia Chin-Lee

Idea Shelf

Introduce students to the lives of exemplary men by reading aloud each of these men's stories—one a day for twenty-six days. Use each as a springboard to further research and discussion. Alternate with the stories of women told in Chin-Lee's companion book, *Amelia to Zora: Twenty-Six Women Who Changed the World*. (See chapter 14.)

Chin-Lee, Cynthia. (2006) *Akira to Zoltán: Twenty-Six Men Who Changed the World*. Illustrated by Megan Halsey and Sam Addy. Charlesbridge. ISBN-10: 1-57091-579-2; ISBN-13: 978-1570915796.

Bookshelf

Annotation

This book contains short biographies of twenty-six men—a diverse group from Akira Kurosawa to Pelé—in a variety of professions. Each entry is a one-page biographical profile detailing the subject's significant contributions. A quote from the subject is integrated into the vibrant mixed-media illustrations. Among the subjects are men in the performing arts, writers and poets, architects, political leaders, doctors, and astronauts. A bibliography provides sources for further investigation about the subjects: Mohandas Gandhi, Nelson Mandela, Langston Hughes, Diego Rivera, Greg Louganis, Octavio Paz, and Vine Deloria Jr., to name a few. A selection of luminaries provides a great cross-section across the spectrum of world culture.

Curriculum Link: Language Arts—Research, "What Makes a Great Person Great?"

Background

Each of these subjects has characteristics of a leader and of a great person. Many of these characteristics are common in all those who become noted personalities. Examine the life and accomplishments of the individuals and develop a concept about the common characteristics. Read the introduction in *Akira to Zoltan: Twenty-Six Men Who Changed the World* and use the information to help develop your list of common characteristics.

Extension Ideas

1. Choose a subject and research his life and accomplishments and develop a theory about why he has become or was a leader or great person.
   Akira Kurosawa
   Badshah Abdul Ghaffar Khan
   César Estrada Chávez
   Diego Maria Rivera
   Ellison Shoji Onizuka
   Frank Lloyd Wright
   Greg Louganis
   Hiram Leong Fong
   Ivan Petrovich Pavlov
   Jacques-Yves Cousteau
   Kahlil Gibran
   Langston Hughes
   Mohandas Karamchand Gandhi
   Nelson Rolihlanhla Mandela
   Octavio Paz
   Pelé
   Quincy Delight Jones Jr.
   Rudolf Hametovich Nureyev
   Steven Spielberg
   Tiger Woods
   U Thant
   Vine Deloria Jr.
   Walt Elias Disney
   Xavier Cugat Mingall
   Yo-Yo Ma
   Zoltán Kodály
2. Locate the place of birth for each of the twenty-six subjects and plot the locations on a world map. Research and list ten facts about their birth locations at the time the subject was born.
3. Nominate your own "great" person, prepare a one-page biographical profile for them, and create a multimedia collage to accompany the profile.

Books to Explore

Books/Web sites to explore for more information about the subjects in the book:
Akira Kurosawa
   Cardullo, Bert. (2007) *Akira Kurosawa: Interviews*. University Press of Mississippi.

Kurosawa, Akira. (1982) *Something Like an Autobiography*. Knopf.

Nogami, Teruyo. (2006) *Waiting on the Weather: Making Movies with Akira Kurosawa*. Stone Bridge Press.

Badshah Abdul Ghaffar Khan

Easwaran, Eknath. (1999) *Nonviolent Soldier of Islam: Badshah Khan, A Man to Match His Mountains*. Nilgiri Press.

César Estrada Chávez

Collins, David R. (1996) *Farmworker's Friend: The Story of Cesar Chavez*. Lerner Publishing Group.

Diego Maria Rivera

Hamill, Pete. (2002) *Diego Rivera*. Harry N. Abrams

Ellison Shoji Onizuka

National Aeronautics and Space Administration (NASA). (2007) "Astronaut Biographical Data: Ellison Onizuka." <http://www.jsc.nasa.gov/Bios/htmlbios/onizuka.html>.

Frank Lloyd Wright

Secrest, Merlye. (1998) *Frank Lloyd Wright: A Biography*. University of Chicago Press.

Greg Louganis

Louganis, Greg, with Eric Marcus. (2006) *Breaking the Surface*. Sourcebooks, Inc.

Hiram Leong Fong

Pearson Educational. (2002–2007) "Fong, Hiram Leong (1906–2004)." *Infoplease*. <http://www.infoplease.com/biography/us/congress/fong-hiram-leong.html>. Original source: Biographical Directory of the U.S. Congress, 1771–Present (U.S. Government).

Ivan Petrovich Pavlov

Sauders, Barbara R. (2006) *Ivan Pavlov: Exploring the Mysteries of Behaviors*. Enslow Publishers.

Jacques-Yves Cousteau

Zronik, John Paul. (2007) *Jacques Cousteau: Conserving Underwater Worlds*. Crabtree Publishing Company.

Kahlil Gibran

Gibran, Kahlil. (1923) *The Prophet*. Knopf.

Langston Hughes

Miller, R. Baxter. (1990) *The Art and Imagination of Langston Hughes*. University Press of Kentucky.

Mohandas Karamchand Gandhi

Gandi, Mohandas Karamchand. (1983) *Autobiography: The Story of My Experiments with Truth*. Dover Publications.

Nelson Rolihlanhla Mandela

Mandela, Nelson. (1995) *Long Walk to Freedom: The Autobiography of Nelson Mandela*. Back Bay Books.

Octavio Paz

Quiroga, Jose. (1999) *Understanding Octavio Paz*. University of South Carolina Press.

Pelé

Buckley, James. (2007) *Pelé*. DK Publishing.

Quincy Delight Jones Jr.

Jones, Quincy. (2002) *Q: The Autobiography of Quincy Jones*. Harlem Moon.

Rudolf Hametovich Nureyev

Barnes, Clive. (1982) *Nureyev*. Helene Obolensky Enterprises, Inc.

Steven Spielberg

Spielberg, Steven. (2000) *Steven Spielberg*. University Press of Mississippi.

Tiger Woods

Roberts, Jeremy. (2007) *Tiger Woods*. Lerner Publishing Group

U Thant

Firestone, Bernard J. (2001) *The United Nations Under U Thant, 1961–1971*. Scarecrow Press, Inc.

Vine Deloria Jr.

Pavlik, Steve, and Daniel R. Wildcat, ed. (2006) *Destroying Dogma: Vine Deloria Jr. and His Influence on American Society*. Fulcrum Publishing.

Walt Elias Disney

Fanning, Jim. (2000) *Walt Disney*. Chelsea House.

Xavier Cugat Mingall

Space Age Music. (2006) "Xavier Cugat." *Space Age Musicmaker*. <http://www.spaceagepop. com/cugat.htm>.

Yo-Yo Ma

Chippendale, Lisa A. (2004) *Yo-Yo Ma: A Cello Superstar Brings Music to the World* (People to Know). Enslow Publishers

Zoltán Kodály

Boosey & Hawkes. (n.d.) *Zoltán Kodály*. <http://www.boosey.com/pages/cr/composer/composer_ main.asp?composerid=2847&ttype=SNAPSHOT&ttitle=Snapshot>.

14

Amelia to Zora: Twenty-Six Women Who Changed the World
by Cynthia Chin-Lee

Idea Shelf

Use each of these stories as a springboard to research and discussion about characteristics that are possessed by successful women. Introduce students to the lives of exemplary women by reading aloud each of these women's stories—one a day for twenty-six days. Alternating with the stories of men told in Chin-Lee's companion book, *Akira to Zoltán: Twenty-Six Men Who Changed the World* will provide a balance of readings in terms of gender. (See chapter 13.)

Bookshelf

Chin-Lee, Cynthia. (2005) *Amelia to Zora: Twenty-Six Women Who Changed the World.* Illustrated by Megan Halsey and Sam Addy. Charlesbridge. ISBN-10: 1570915229; ISBN-13: 978-1570915222.

Annotation

Twenty-six women of strength, character, and leadership are featured on one-page spreads that include a two-paragraph biographical profile against a multimedia collage depicting aspects of the subject's life. The subjects are diverse and represent the arts, sports, journalism, science, and entertainment.

Curriculum Link: Language Arts—Research, "What Makes a Great Person Great?"

Background

The diversity of subjects in this book provides a wide spectrum of people who share one common trait—they are considered great leaders in their fields. What are the qualities and attributes that make each of these women great?

Extension Ideas

1. Choose a person as a subject of research. Examine their life and accomplishments and develop a concept about why this individual has become or was a leader/great person. As women, did any of these women face obstacles that were not faced by men in their field? Read the introduction of *Amelia to Zora: Twenty-Six Women Who Changed the World* and use the information to help develop a research strategy.

   Amelia Earhart
   Babe Didrikson Zaharias
   Cecilia Payne-Gaponschkin
   Dolores Huerta
   Eleanor Roosevelt
   Frida Kahlo
   Grace Hopper
   Helen Keller
   Imogen Cunningham
   Jane Goodall
   Kristi Yamaguchi
   Lena Horne
   Maya Lin
   Nawal El Sadaawi
   Oprah Winfrey
   Patricia Schroeder
   Quah Ah (Tonita Peña or Maria Antonia Peña)
   Rachel Carson
   Suu Kyi, Daw Aung San
   Mother Teresa
   Ursula K. Le Guin
   Vijava Lakshmi Pandit
   Wilma Mankiller
   Chen Xiefen
   Yoshiko Uchida
   Zora Neale Hurston

2. List ten facts about each of the subject's birth locations at the time that they were born. Plot the 26 locations on a map.

3. Create a one-page biographical profile for a "great" person of your choosing. Create a multimedia display to accompany the written profile.

Books to Explore

Amelia Earhart
   Stone, Tanya Lee. (2007) *Amelia Earhart*. DK Publishing.
Babe Didrikson Zaharias
   Freedman, Russell. (1999) *Babe Didrikson Zaharias: The Making of a Champion*. Houghton Mifflin.

Cecilia Payne-Gaponschkin
> Harvard Square Library. (2006) "Cecilia Payne-Gaposchkin: Astronomer and Astrophysicist." *Notable American Unitarians.* <http://www.harvardsquarelibrary.org/unitarians/payne2.html>.

Dolores Huerta
> Miller, Debra A. (2006) *Dolores Huerta: Labor Leader* (The Twentieth Century's Most Influential Hispanics). Lucent Books.
> Worth, Richard. (2007) *Dolores Huerta* (The Great Hispanic Heritage). Chelsea House.

Eleanor Roosevelt
> Fleming, Candace. (2005) *Our Eleanor: A Scrapbook Look at Eleanor Roosevelt's Remarkable Life.* Simon & Schuster.
> Freedman, Russell. (1997) *Eleanor Roosevelt: A Life of Discovery.* Clarion.

Frida Kahlo
> Kahlo, Frieda. (2005) *The Diary of Frida Kahlo: An Intimate Self-Portrait.* Harry N. Abrams.

Grace Hopper
> Williams, Kathleen Broome. (2004) *Grace Hopper: Admiral of the Cyber Sea* (Library of Naval Biography). U.S. Naval Institute Press.

Helen Keller
> Garrett, Leslie. (2005) *Helen Keller* (DK Biography). DK Children.

Imogen Cunningham
> Lorenz, Richard. (1993) *Imogen Cunningham: Ideas Without End, a Life in Photographs.* Chronicle Books.

Jane Goodall
> Peterson, Dale. (2006) *Jane Goodall: The Woman Who Redefined Man.* Houghton Mifflin.

Kristi Yamaguchi
> Hasday, Judy L. (2007) *Kristi Yamaguchi* (Asian Americans of Achievement). Chelsea House Publishers.

Lena Horne
> Buckley, Gail Lumrt. (1986) *The Hornes.* Knopf.

Maya Lin
> Lashnits, Tom. (2007) *Maya Lin* (Asian Americans of Achievement). Chelsea House Publishers.

Nawal El Sadaawi
> Sadaawi, Nawal El. (2002) *Walking Through Fire.* Zed Books.

Oprah Winfrey
> Garson, Helen S. (2004) *Oprah Winfrey: A Biography.* Greenwood Publishing Group.

Patricia Schroeder
> Schroeder, Patricia. (1989) *Champion of the Great American Family.* Random House.

Quah Ah
> Gray, Samuel L. (1990) *Tonita.* Avanyu Publishing.
> Note to aid further research: Quah Ah (White Coral Beads) was the Indian name given to Maria Antonia Peña when she was four years of age. As an adult, she was also known as Tonita Peña (1893–1949).

Rachel Carson
> Ehlich, Amy. (2003) *Rachel: The Story of Rachel Carson.* Illustrated by Wendell Minor. Silver Whistle.
> Kudlinski, Kathleen V. (1989) *Rachel Carson: Pioneer of Ecology (Women of Our Time).* Penguin/Puffin.

Suu Kyi, Daw Aung San
> Victor, Barbara. (2002) *The Lady: Aung San Suu Kyi—Nobel Laureate and Burma's Prisoner.* Faber & Faber (the 2002 afterword updates her release from a Burma prison).

Mother Teresa
> Langford, Joseph, MC. (2007) *Mother Teresa: In the Shadow of Our Lady.* Our Sunday Visitor.

Ursula K. Le Guin
  Slusser, George Edgar. (1997/1999) *Between Worlds: The Literary Dilemma of Ursula K. Le Guin* (Milford Series, Popular Writers of Today). Wildside Press/Borgo Press.
Vijava Lakshmi Pandit
  Note to aid further research: There seems to be no definitive book source of biographical information about this honored Indian diplomat and politician, Vijaya Lakshmi Nehru Pandit (1900–1990), the first female president of the United Nations General Assembly. There are, however, numerous encyclopedia entries and Web sites that detail her political achievements.
Wilma Mankiller
  Dell, Pamela. (2006) *Wilma Mankiller: Chief of the Cherokee Nation* (Signature Lives). Compass Point Books.
  Wallis, Michael, and Wilma Mankiller. (1993) *Mankiller: A Chief and Her People*. St. Martin's Press.
Chen Xiefen
  Hershatter, Gail. (2004) *Holding Up Half the Sky: Chinese Women Past, Present, and Future*. Feminist Press.
Yoshiko Uchida
  Uchida, Yoshiko. (1995) *The Invisible Thread: An Autobiography*. HarperTrophy/Beech Tree.
Zora Neale Hurston
  Huston, Zora Neale. (1984) *Dust Tracks on a Road: An Autobiography*. University of Illinois Press.

15

Hurricane Hunters! Riders on the Storm
by Chris L. Demarest

Idea Shelf

Use this book as a springboard for the discussion of unique and interesting careers or as a transition into a study of weather-related disasters such as the devastation caused in New Orleans and nearby areas by Hurricane Katrina in August 2005, the June 2008 floods in Iowa and other Midwestern states, or the 2004 Indian Ocean tsunamis.

Demarest, Chris L. (2006) *Hurricane Hunters!: Riders on the Storm*. Margaret K. McElderry Books. ISBN-10: 0-689-86168-0; ISBN-13: 978-0-689-86168-0.

Bookshelf

Annotation

The Fifty-third Weather Reconnaissance Squadron is informally known as "Hurricane Hunters." When storms approach land, weather forecasters predict how and when they might arrive—where the destruction might occur and how severe the storm might be. Using this information, the Hurricane Hunters help gather information about the strength and direction of the storm and send back helpful statistics to the National Hurricane Center. The Fifty-third Weather Reconnaissance Squadron is based at Keesler Air Force Base in Biloxi, Mississippi. Demarest acquaints readers with the details of the interior of the WC-130 Hercules plane that the squadron has outfitted specially to drop the dropsonde (a weather device that measures weather conditions as it is dropped from an aircraft) that send back the barometric pressure and other statistics to the National Hurricane Center. An author's note gives readers additional details and information about the Hurricane Hunters.

Curriculum Link: Hurricanes, Science, Weather

Background

Hurricane Hunters do not fly above the storm; they fly directly into it. The crew is a six-person crew: a commander, copilot, flight engineer, navigator, weather officer, and dropsonde system operator. The dropsonde is a container with a parachute on it. The device provides information about hurricane's humidity, wind, temperature, and pressure inside the storm. The data collected is then transferred to a satellite and then on to the National Weather Service.

Extension Ideas

1. Investigate the history of the Fifty-third Weather Reconnaissance Squadron.
2. The Fifty-third Weather Reconnaissance Squadron is associated with the Army but there are private "storm chasers"—one such team is lead by Warren Faidley, who has been chasing storms for more than twenty years. Find out more about him and the National Association of Storm Chasers and Spotters (NASCAS) at <http://www.stormchaser.com> and additional storm chaser information at <http://www.stormtrack.org>.
3. Make a chart of the positive outcomes from the work of hurricane hunters and storm chasers. Besides being thrilling work, what is the benefit of their work?
4. Make a "career brochure" supporting the career of weather forecasting, specifically the work of storm chasing; what skills one needs to possess, educational needs, and so forth.

Books to Explore

Davies, Jon, Robert Rath, and Jim Reed. (2008) *Storm Chasers! On the Trail of Twisters*. Farcountry Press.
Hollinshead, Mike, and Eric Nguyen. (2008) *Adventures in Tornado Alley: The Storm Chasers*. Thames & Hudson.
Reed, Jim (2007) *Storm Chaser: A Photographer's Journey*. Abrams Books.

16

This Jazz Man
by Karen Ehrhardt

Idea Shelf

At the beginning of class periods, play some well-known jazz music as students enter the classroom. After a couple of days, discuss the type of music and introduce the idea of the people behind the music. Use this book as an introduction for stimulating investigation into other types of music and the people behind that music. This provides an opportunity for readers to locate information about their favorite musicians—historical or otherwise. Use the biographical sketches here as models for writing.

Ehrhardt, Karen. (2006) *This Jazz Man*. Illustrated by R. G. Roth. Harcourt Children's Books. ISBN-10: 0-15-2005307-7; ISBN-13: 978-0-15-2005307-9.

Bookshelf

Annotation

To the tune of "This Old Man," Ehrhardt takes readers through a rhythmic introduction to jazz and nine jazz men. Brief stanzas highlight each man's contribution to jazz.

1. "plays rhythm with his thumb"
2. "makes music with his shoes"
3. "plays congas 'tween his knees"
4. "conducts through the score"
5. "plays bebop, he plays jive … blows with the band"
6. "plays solo with his sticks"
7. "plays … toot-toot! Doodly-doot!"
8. "plays keys—all eighty-eight"
9. "plucks strings that sound divine"

The final pages name and provide illuminating details about the jazz life of each of these men and give a paragraph or two about their individual accomplishments. Those highlighted are:

1. Louis "Satchmo" Armstrong (New Orleans, Louisiana)
2. Bill "Bojangles" Robinson (Richmond, Virginia)
3. Luciano "Chano" Pozz y González (Havana, Cuba)
4. Edward Kennedy "Duke" Ellington (Washington, D.C.)
5. Charlie "Bird" Parker (Kansas City, Kansas)
6. Art "Bu" Blakey (Pittsburgh, Pennsylvania)
7. John Birks "Dizzy" Gillespie (Cheraw, South Carolina)
8. Thomas Wright "Fats" Waller (Harlem, New York City)
9. Charles "Baron" Mingus (Watts, Los Angeles)

Curriculum Link: Biography, Elements of Music, Jazz, Slave Songs, Spirituals

Background

The type of music now known as jazz was played late in the nineteenth century in the New Orleans area—some point to 1895 as the year of the birth of jazz. The term "jazz" was not yet used to describe the evolving form of music. First used in sports dialogue on the West Coast around 1912, "Jazz" began to appear around 1915 in the Chicago area in connection with the new music evolving from the South. The term gradually spread to other cities and finally reached New Orleans in 1918. In 1919, the *Literary Digest* credited Bert Kelly of Chicago as first using the term "jazz band" in a commentary when referring to the New Orleans music.

According to the Public Broadcasting System's Jazz Timeline online at <http;// pbskids.org/jazz/time/1700.html>, the roots of jazz arrived in the 1700s, with Africans who came to America in chains. Forbidden to speak to one another, they developed a call-and-response element in their songs, sang spirituals and works songs, and used their strong voices to express their emotions. A century later, European music (French quadrilles, Spanish flamenco, Irish jigs, and German waltzes) began to be influenced by the strong beats of the music of the black community. A musical form, ragtime, with notes that were dragged out and rearranged to make it more energetic, was entrenched in the musical world by 1890. Missouri was the center of ragtime music. While ragtime and the blues were taking hold, the African American community in New Orleans was taking bits and pieces of the Spanish and French cultures from among the residents of the area. Soon, English, Irish, Scottish, German, and Italian immigrants migrated to the vibrant Mississippi port town. Musical traditions from all over the world began to merge, and jazz was born. By the time World War I engulfed the country, jazz had moved from being played only in the honky-tonks of New Orleans to radio, dance halls, and phonograph players in living rooms across the United States. People could afford to buy radios and frequent dance halls. It was the era of "flappers" and of music with a fast, vibrant beat—jazz.

The Great Depression brought a halt to the rapid economic growth. Jazz, however, made the Depression bearable, and since radios were now in most homes, music from the airwaves was cheap entertainment. Kansas City, however, seemed to escape many of the effects of the Depression, so unemployed musicians fled there to survive, and the Kansas City jazz scene grew and prospered. Jazz took the form of swing bands, and the big-band era emerged.

By the time World War II began in 1939, the big dance bands took a swing downward. Many musicians were being drafted into the army and there were rations on the use of plastic and gasoline. The production of records was slowed and racial prejudice set in. Black musicians struggled while white jazz musicians continued to be successful. Discrimination was highly evident, even in the military, where segregation kept blood supplies separate and African Americans were not allowed to eat where even white German prisoners of war were. African Americans began to question their service to the United States when their own freedom was not a part of American life.

After the war, television became more popular and kept more people at home as that form of entertainment competed with the music in dance halls. Elvis Presley and his rock 'n' roll style of music became popular and shrunk the audience for jazz even further. But jazz was not ready to step aside. Creative musicians continued to play and develop new ideas for making jazz even more vibrant and new roads through which to make jazz popular. The Vietnam War came and so did the civil rights movement. The African American community expressed its displeasure by ramping up the music. Blacks protested the white control of their lives and their music. Jazz became energized once again.

In addition to the jazz greats mentioned in Ehrhardt's book, the following are also notable jazz musicians:

> Miles Davis (1926–1991)—Davis was known for his musical innovations.
> Charlie Parker (1920–1955)—Parker was a creative force who developed bebop.
> Billie Holiday (1915–1959)—The only female on the list, she is said to have used her voice like an instrument.
> Ornette Coleman (1930–)—He is an innovator of music and is known as a musician in the free-jazz movement.
> Benny Goodman (1909–1986)—He was a Jewish musician who struggled to make a name for himself and became known as the "King of Swing." His band was one of the first, if not the first, to have black and white musicians play side-by-side.

Extension Ideas

1. Play some jazz selections for your students and at the conclusion of each, ask them to call out one-word descriptions of what they just heard—how it made them feel and how they would describe the music. Repeat this procedure with several selections and then introduce the term "jazz" and read Ehrhardt's book introducing jazz and jazz musicians.
2. Explore the contributions of individual musicians to the world of jazz.
3. Define the musical forms known as bebop, ragtime, blues, jazz, Zydeco, rock 'n' roll and how they connect to one another. Make a time line of various eras and list popular music during each of those eras.

4. Jazz is noted for its solos, improvisations, and the call-and-response method—where one instrument seems to answer another. Find and identify examples of these elements in jazz selections.

5. The call-and-response element has its roots in spirituals and slave songs. Investigate the spirituals sung in the early twentieth century and the religious songs that brought African Americans together. Explain how the call-and-response element in spirituals and slave songs translated into jazz. What is the essence of the call-and-response element? (Note: The song leader would sing or tap out a line [call] and listeners would repeat or tap the line back [repeat]). Jazz emulated this element, with an instrument playing a segment (often an improvisation) and another instrument would respond by playing an "answer" to the improvisation.

6. Improvisation: Remind students that every story must have a beginning, a middle, and an end. Start a story with three sentences and then tap the shoulder of the person beside you. He or she will add another two to three sentences to move the story along. About halfway through the class, there should be a middle, and then continue on to the climax and the end. Record the story and explain that it was improvisational—made up as one goes along. That is the way much of jazz develops.

7. After students investigate the life of a notable jazz musician, create a bio-poem about that musician. For an example of a bio-poem read:

The Microscope by Maxine Kumin (illustrated by Arnold Lobel; HarperCollins, 1984).

Johnny Appleseed by Stephen Vincent Benét and Rosemary Benét (illustrated by S. D. Schindler; Margaret K. McElderry, 2001)

or any of the poetry selections in this classic volume:

Book of Americans by Stephen Vincent Benét and Rosemary Benét (Farrah and Rinehart, 1933).

Books to Explore

Note that those books with an * are illustrated, often innovative, books that are short reads to put readers in the mood to learn more about jazz.

Gioia, Ted. (1998) *The History of Jazz*. Oxford University Press.

Hughes, Langston. (1982) *The First Book of Jazz*. Ecco Press.*

Lester, Julius. (2001) *The Blues Singers: Ten Who Rocked the World*. Hyperion Books for Children.*

Marsalis, Wynton. (2005) *Jazz ABZ: Collection of Jazz Portraits*. Illustrated by Paul Rogers. Candlewick.*

Miller, William, and Charlotte Riley-Webb. (2001) *Rent Party Jazz*. Lee & Low Books.*

Myers, Walter Dean. (2003) *Blues Journey*. Illustrated by Christopher Myers. Holiday House.*

Myers, Walter Dean. (2006) *Jazz*. Illustrated by Christopher Myers. Holiday House.*

Orgill, Roxane. (1997) *If I Only Had a Horn: Young Louis Armstrong*. Houghton Mifflin

Peretti, Burton. (1998) *Jazz in American Culture*. Ivan R. Dee.

Pinkney, Andrea Davis. (1998) *Duke Ellington: The Piano Prince and His Orchestra*. Illustrated by Brian Pinkney. Jump the Sun.*

Pinkney, Davis Andrea. (2002) *Ella Fitzgerald: The Tale of a Vocal Virtuosa*. Illustrated by Brian Pinkney. Hyperion/Jump the Sun.*

Raschka, Chris. (1992) *Charlie Parker Played Bebop*. Scholastic/Orchard Books.*

Raschka, Chris. (2002) *John Coltrane's Giant Steps*. Atheneum/Richard Jackson Books.*

Schroeder, Alan. (1999) *Satchmo's Blues*. Dragonfly Books.*

Shaik, Fatima. (1998) *The Jazz of Our Street*. Dial Books.*

Shapiro, Nat, and Nat Hentoff. (1966) *Hear Me Talkin' to Ya: The Story of Jazz as Told by the Men Who Made It*. Dover.

Walser, Robert. (1998) *Keeping Time: Readings in Jazz History*. Oxford University Press.

Winter, Jonah. (2006) *Dizzy*. Illustrated by Sean Qualls. Arthur A. Levine Books.*

17

Josias, Hold the Book
by Jennifer Riesmeyer Elvgren

What role does literacy have in moving countries from third world status? This book will help in developing a look at how volunteers can best assist others—"doing" for others or "teaching" others to do for themselves. This is a great debate topic.

Idea Shelf

Elvgren, Jennifer Riesmeyer. (2006) *Josias, Hold the Book.* Illustrated by Nicole Tadgell. Boyds Mills Press. ISBN: 1-59078-318-2.

Bookshelf

Annotation

This story is set in Haiti, where every member of the family must help their family survive. Each day Chrislov asks his friend Josias when he is going to "hold the book." But each day the answer is the same: Josias must tend his bean garden so that his family will have enough to eat. Each member of the family is doing their part to help the family, and Josias must do the same. However, Josias's beans are not growing. He gives the beans more water and donkey dung but still they don't do well. Each day Josias works with his beans and each day Chrislov invites Josias to "hold the book." One day, though, Josias has an idea: maybe information in a book would help him know what to do to make his beans grow. He asks his friend Chrislov, and Chrislov asks his teacher. That evening when Chrislov comes back, he has a book that tells them both that the soil is tired and that the beans should be planted elsewhere and a new crop planted in the tired garden. Josias shares the information with his father and together they decide that Josias can "hold the book" and care for the beans in the evening instead of playing soccer.

Curriculum Link: Literacy

Background

Give a hungry person a fish and you've fed him/her for one day. Teach a person to fish and you've taught him/her to feed himself/herself for a lifetime. This book shares that philosophy by emphasizing books as a means of knowledge and learning.

Extension Ideas

1. Explore ways in which young people can help others help themselves. What kinds of helping hands could we extend to others in our community? Brainstorm a list of helping-hand projects. Included might be: helping others to learn how to garden or sharing a skill or item that might help a person earn an income or become literate.
   a. Heifer Project at <http://www.Heifer.org>—Heifer International home page
   b. Ethiopia Reads at <http://www.ethiopiareads.org>—Ethiopia Reads home page
2. Select a project and figure out how your class/group might help fund or support that project.
3. Develop a service project that helps others help themselves.

Books to Explore

Clark, Sondra. (2008) *77 Creative Ways Kids Can Serve*. Wesleyan Publishing House.

Saylor, Ann, and Susan Ragsdale. (2008) *Ready-to-Go Service Projects: 140 Ways for Youth Groups to Lend a Hand*. Abingdon Press.

Wrede, James, et al. (2003) *Tween Time: Fellowship and Service Projects for Preteens*. Abingdon Press.

18

The Poet Slave of Cuba:
A Biography of Juan Francisco Manzano
by Margarita Engle

Often slavery is associated with the Civil War era, but in fact there has been and is slavery in many parts of the world and during many times. This book will help to introduce the facts about the problem of slavery—even today. Share the facts about Juan Francisco Manzano, encourage readers to think beyond slavery being a Civil War/United States issue, and then go in search of how prevalent the problem is in today's world—and how can we help obtain real freedom for all.

Idea Shelf

Engle, Margarita. (2007) *The Poet Slave of Cuba: A Biography of Juan Francisco Manzano.* Illustrated by Sean Qualls. Henry Holt. ISBN-10: 0805077065; ISBN-13: 978-0805077063.

Bookshelf

Annotation

Haunting poems give voice to the daily terror and hypocrisy of the slave system in South America. Juan Francisco Manzano (1797–1854) is punished unmercifully for reading and writing, but the punishment does not break his spirit as he strives to endure and persists in his quest for freedom. This book offers a glimpse into the life of a slave in the Caribbean and the culture of slavery in the Caribbean and South America.

Curriculum Link: History—Cuba; Slavery—North America; Slavery—South America; Biography; Poetry

Background

Juan Francisco Manzano was born in Havana and raised as a slave and later, after those who admired his poetry bought his freedom, he lived in poverty. By birth he was a slave. In 1821, while still enslaved, he managed to publish a small collection of poems and another in 1830. A biography he wrote was translated into English and, along with a few of his poems, was published in London. In 1842, a drama he authored was published. By 1844, he was implicated in a high treason trial and spent several months in prison. Manzano died in 1854 but his life overlapped that of Frederick Douglass (1818–1895), a slave in North America. Both men suffered extreme cruelties and managed by perseverance to rise as leaders. Their success included a struggle to learn to read and write.

Extension Ideas

1. Compare and contrast the life of Juan Francisco Manzano to the life of Frederick Douglass. How were their lives parallel? How did each come to influence the political structure to bring about a better life for blacks?
2. The Civil War and the Emancipation Proclamation signed by Abraham Lincoln brought about freedom for thousands of slaves in North America. How did freedom transpire for slaves in South America? What is the story of their emancipation?
3. Although many like to point out that slavery has been abolished, it in fact has not been. Throughout the world, many young people are sold (some by their own families) as slaves. Others are brought into the United States, for example, with a promise of a better life, but find themselves in virtual slavery—being forced to work to pay back travel and/or upkeep charges. The prices are so high that the worker is never able to be free. As illegal immigrants, they do not feel that they can go to the authorities. Investigate and report on the slave trade throughout the world. Research "modern-day slavery" or "human trafficking" to locate Web sites, articles, and so forth that discuss what is happening now.

Books to Explore

Contemporary:
McCormick, Patricia. (2006) *Sold*. Hyperion. (Fiction)

Historical:
Andrews, William L. (1989) *Six Women's Slave Narratives*. Oxford University Press.
Douglass, Frederick. (2004) *Narrative Life of Frederick Douglass*. Prestwick House Inc. (Originally published in May 1845 by the American Anti-Slavery Society of Boston; various publishers have republished this narrative.)
Gates, Henry Louis. (2002) *The Classic Slave Narratives*. Signet Classics.
Yetman, Norman R. (1999) *Voices from Slavery: 100 Authentic Slave Narratives*. Dover Publications.

19

The Adventures of Marco Polo
by Russell Freedman

The life of Marco Polo can be a great introduction into the lives of the explorers who brought a focus on the wider world and expanded the thinking of common people about the view of the world. Share aloud a selected chapter from this short, heavily illustrated account of Polo's life and discuss his impact on exploration and changes taking place in the world during his lifetime, the late 1200s and early 1300s.

Idea Shelf

Freedman, Russell. (2006) *The Adventures of Marco Polo.* Illustrated by Bagram Ibatoulline. Arthur A. Levine Books/Scholastic. ISBN: 0-439-52394-x.

Bookshelf

Annotation

Marco Polo has become known for two traits. During his lifetime he was often thought of as the most traveled man in the world as well as a man who told a lie as easily as he told the truth. Freedman examines Polo's life and attempts to separate the truth about Polo's life from the fabrications surrounding his exploits. Freedman's text is complemented with period illustrations by Bagram Ibatoulline and with archival, period artwork. Six short chapters present the highlights of the travels of Marco Polo. During his twenty-four-year adventure, Polo and his father and uncle traveled from Venice to the capitol of the Mongol Empire. In the Mongol Empire, the three men met Kublai Khan in Shangdu. Kublai Khan was the grandson of the Genghis Khan who had expanded the Mongol empire from what is now China to Russia and Iraq. Kublai Khan became both their friend and their mentor for the years the Polos lived in the country he ruled. It was Kublai Khan who built the city of Khanbalik (the Chinese called it Daidu, the Great Capitol), which later became the modern capital of Beijing. Highlights of the men's adventures and road to wealth and fame are included. Several legends have been circulated about Marco Polo. Freedman discounts a number of these. One has Marco Polo introducing pasta from China to Italians. However, Italians already were eating noodles, so it is untrue that Polo introduced pasta in Italy. Polo did not, in any writings, claim that he did but the legend persists. Freedman also states that the idea that Polo brought back ice cream to Venice is equally false.

Curriculum Link: Marco Polo, Explorers

Background

In 1269, Venetian merchants Nicolo and Matteo Polo returned to Venice and discovered that Nicolo's fifteen-year-old son was alone, as his mother had died. The two brothers and the young Marco soon left Venice and traveled east and in 1275 met the Great Khan. Soon Marco was in the Khan's inner circle and eventually spent seventeen years in the Mongol Empire. When they did leave in 1292 it was to escort a princess to her wedding in the Persian Gulf. Once the Polos returned to Venice, Marco joined the army, but was captured and put into prison. While in prison, he dictated his account of his travels. *Travels of Marco Polo* was first published in French and although many question its complete accuracy, it has become a classic of geographical exploration.

Extension Ideas

1. Make a list of items that Marco Polo is credited with bringing back to Europe: coal, spices, etc.
2. Create a map showing the route of the Polo's travels.
3. Create a time line of the Polo's travels.
4. Investigate the names and travels of other explorers who might have explored Europe and Asia during this period of time.

Books to Explore

Feeney, Kathleen. (2004) *Marco Polo: Explorer of China*. Enslow. This is another account of the travels of Marco Polo.

Sittman, Erik (October 17, 2006) Silkroad Foundation. "Marco Polo and His Travels." <http://www.silk-road.com/artl/marcopolo.shtml>. This is an overview of the travels of Marco Polo. Some of the information seems to contradict the facts as put forth by Russell Freedman.

Yamashita, Michael. (2004) *Marco Polo: A Photographer's Journey*. White Star. Yamashita, a *National Geographic* photographer, retraced the journey of Marco Polo and recorded it with 518 pages of photographs.

20

Honky-Tonk Heroes & Hillbilly Angels: The Pioneers of Country & Western Music
by Holly George-Warren

In conjunction with or using techniques similar to those suggested for Karen Ehr-hardt's *This Jazz Man* (see chapter 16), at the beginning of several class periods, play some well-known country music as students enter the classroom. After a couple of days, discuss the type of music and introduce the people behind the music. Use the book as an introduction for stimulating investigation into other types of music and the people behind that music. This allows readers to locate information about their favorite musicians—historical or otherwise. Use the bio-graphical sketches here as models for writing.

Idea Shelf

George-Warren, Holly. (2006) *Honky-Tonk Heroes & Hillbilly Angels: The Pioneers of Country & Western Music.* Houghton Mifflin. ISBN-10: 0-618-19100-3; ISBN-13: 978-0618-19100-0.

Bookshelf

Annotation

Just as the title indicates, the pioneers of country and western music are highlighted in this book. Each pioneer is featured with a folk-style painting and a biographical sketch on a double-page spread devoted just to that particular artist. The artists featured include:

- The Carter Family: Maybelle Carter, Sara Carter, and A. P. Carter; and later Maybelle and her daughters, June (who married Johnny Cash), Helen, and Anita.
- Jimmie Rodgers
- Roy Acuff

- Gene Autry
- Ernest Tubb
- Bill Monroe
- Bob Wills
- Kitty Wells (pseudonym of Muriel Deason)
- Hank Williams (pseudonym of Hiriam Williams)
- Patsy Cline (pseudonym of Virginia Hensley)
- Buck Owens (pseudonym of Alvis Edgar Owens)
- Loretta Lynn (born Loretta Webb)
- Tammy Wynette (pseudonym of Wynette Pugh)
- George Jones
- Johnny Cash

Curriculum Link: Music, Country Music, Biographical Sketches, Writing

Background

Emerging from the U.S. South, country music (earlier referred to as country and western) became a term used to describe several styles of music. Country music generally includes the music of fiddles, dulcimer, mandolin, guitar, or banjo—the most common instruments used. The interaction of various ethnic groups helped produce this unique blend of music that became popular in North America in the 1920s. Western movies further popularized cowboy songs or western music in the 1930s and 1940s. In the mid-1940s, honky-tonk and bluegrass music began to make an appearance; they were sometimes referred to as "folk" or "hillbilly" music. Later, the term "traditional country" would be used to describe the varied form. In the early days of country music, the bands did not include drummers; even as late as the 1950s, most drummers were kept backstage at the Grand Ole Opry in Nashville, Tennessee. However, by the 1960s, most country bands included a drummer. Electric guitars were used as early as 1938 and gradually became a popular addition to country bands. In the 1990s and the first decades of the twenty-first century, country music influenced many other forms of music, and country rock, country pop, and outlaw country became popular additions to the world of music.

Extension Ideas

1. This book highlights a list of people who are notable in a particular field. Each one has qualities that helped him/her gain the fame they achieved. List qualities that each person possesses. Discuss how these people were similar and what qualities helped them achieve notable status in their chosen field.
2. Writing: Use this book and its format to provide a model for writing biographical sketches about notable figures in any other area that students might be studying. For example: presidents of the United States (or vice presidents or first ladies), scientists of the twentieth century, current rulers of the world, and so forth.
3. Create a time line showing the popularity of country music, honky-tonk, and so forth.

Books to Explore

Carlin, Richard. (2006) *Country Music*. Black Dog & Leventhal Publishers.

Ferris, William. (2007) *Nashville Portraits: Legends of Country Music*. The Lyons Press.

Kingsbury, Paul, and Alanna Nash. (2006) *Will the Circle be Unbroken: Country Music in America*. DK Adult Books.

21

Ice Cream: The Full Scoop
by Gail Gibbons

Idea Shelf

Ice cream is a favorite food of many. Its origin can be a topic of research or provide a peek into the origin of some other favorite food. Perhaps more interesting might be the role ice cream played in other eras. In the early 1900s and well into the 1950s and 1960s, many communities were brought together by ice cream socials. This event is often used even today to raise money for charities, more than for community solidarity. Use the ice cream theme as a springboard into a look at the function of community in the 1900s, the origin of favorite foods, or mathematical calculations examining: What is the nation's favorite ice cream flavor? How much ice cream do the students in your school consume in a week? How does that compare to the country's consumption statistics?

Gibbons, Gail. (2006) *Ice Cream: The Full Scoop.* Illustrated by Gail Gibbons. Holiday House. ISBN-10: 0-8234-2000-0; ISBN-13: 978-0-8234-2000-1.

Bookshelf

Annotation

According to Gibbons, ice cream might have originated about 700 years ago when Marco Polo brought recipes for flavored ices from China. European chefs experimented with adding cream and creating a new dessert called "ice cream." Gibbons shows how liquids (such as milk) can change the state to a solid by using ice cream makers, and salt and ice, to freeze cream into the frozen dessert. Ice cream-related desserts were developed later: ice cream sandwich, ice cream soda, banana split, sundae, ice cream bar, ice cream cake, pie a la mode.

Curriculum Link: Ice Cream, How Things are Made, Statistics

Background

Facts about ice cream:

- Vanilla is the most popular flavor; chocolate the second.
- Hot chocolate fudge sauce poured over ice cream is called a hot fudge sundae.
- Sprinkles are sometimes put on the ice cream in a cone.
- Almost 10 percent of milk produced in the United States is used for ice cream.
- More ice cream is sold on Sunday than on any other day.
- Grocery stores did not sell ice cream until the 1930s.
- In 1920, a man named Harry Burt created the Good Humor Bar (a bar of ice cream covered with a chocolate coating on a stick).
- U.S. consumption of ice cream is approximately 15 quarts (14.2 liters) of ice cream per person annually.
- Ice cream sundaes were first served as a special treat on Sunday—the spelling changed when people started eating them on other days.
- 80 percent of the world's vanilla beans used for ice cream are grown in Madagascar.

Extension Ideas

1. Select another "manufactured" food/object, and using the Gibbons book as a model, write an explanation of how that food or object is created.
    Suggestions:
    - pencil
    - baseball
    - football
    - M&M's
    - tennis ball
    - Baby Ruth candy bar
    - jelly beans
    - chocolate syrup
    - glass bottle
    - peanut butter
    - jam or jelly
    - fortune cookie
    - crayon
    - chocolate-covered cherry
    - marshmallow
    - red & white candy cane
    - rubber band
    - pencil
    - caramel corn

- Post-it note
- feather duster
- candy kiss
- maple syrup
- applesauce
- chocolate chip
- candle
- blank compact disc (CD)
- lipstick

Books to Explore

Brain, Marshall. (2001) *How STUFF Works*. Wiley.

Brain, Marshall. (2002) *MORE How STUFF Works*. Wiley.

DK Publishing. (2007) *See How It's Made*. DK Children.

Harrison, Ian. (2004) *Book of Inventions*. National Geographic.

Jones, George. (1995) *My First Book of How Things Are Made: Crayons, Jeans, Guitars, Peanut Butter, and More*. Scholastic.

Langone, John. (2004) *The New How Things Work: From Lawn Mowers to Surgical Robots and Everything in Between*. National Geographic.

Rose, Sharon, and Neil Schlaer. (2003) *How Things Are Made: From Automobiles to Zippers*. Black Dog & Leventhal Publishers.

22

The Storyteller's Candle/La velita de los cuentos
by Lucía González

This book is a great introduction to another dimension of immigration and helping within our own community. Read it aloud and discuss how we can impact our community and make it a better place. What can we do?

Idea Shelf

González, Lucía. (2008) *The Storyteller's Candle/La velita de los cuentos*. Illustrated by Lulu Delacre. Children's Book Press. ISBN-10: 0892392223; ISBN-13: 978-0892392223.

Bookshelf

Annotation

When Hildamar and Santiage arrived in New York City in 1929, they felt far away from Puerto Rico and wondered how they would get along in their new home. But then a very special day arrived—into their classroom came a woman named Pura Belpré (1899–1982). She was the first Latina librarian in all of New York City and she was a gifted storyteller. She introduced the library to the children and invited them to make use of it. She told them that the library belonged to everyone, whether they spoke English, Spanish, or some other language. Her work became so important to the community that she was eventually honored when the American Librarian Association named an annual award for her. The Pura Belpré Award honors Latino authors and illustrators.

In this book, the illustrator uses interesting bits and pieces from the *New York Times* as part of the collage background that sets the tone for the events of the era. Articles show evidence of the arrival of steamships, theater productions, and news of the Three Kings' Day celebration from San Juan.

The book is written in both English and Spanish.

Curriculum Link: Pura Belpré, Latino History, Librarians, Libraries

Background

Pura Belpré was born in Puerto Rico (her birthdate has been recorded as being February 2, 1899; December 2, 1901; and February 2, 1903), where she grew up and attended the University of Puerto Rico. She came to New York City to attend the wedding of her sister Elisa, and ended up staying. At first she worked in the garment industry but soon began working as an assistant in the public library as a protégé of Ernestine Rose, the head of the Harlem library. Belpré was the first Puerto Rican to be hired by the New York Public Library. By 1926, she had begun formal studies in the area of library science and by 1929, she was actively advocating for the Spanish-speaking community and working at the 115th Street branch of the library. That branch became an important cultural center due to her work. Belpré was a writer, a collector of folktales, and a puppeteer. After her marriage in 1940 to musician Clarence Cameron White, she devoted herself full time to her writing while touring with him. After his death in 1960, she returned to the library in various capacities, all supporting literacy and the Latino culture.

Extension Ideas

1. Locate other notable names in library history. Research their stories and share how they impacted literacy in their community and how that affected a wider group of people. What connection did they have to libraries? Names to consider: Andrew Carnegie, Julius Rosenwald, Miss Breedlove, Benjamin Franklin, Melvil Dewey, Giacomo Casanova, Mao Tse-tung (or Mao Zedong), Beverly Cleary, Pope Pius XI, Laura Bush, Gold Meir, and J. Edgar Hoover.
2. Investigate and learn about Pura Belpré. List ten ways that she was an influential person in the community.
3. Investigate other influential Puerto Ricans or Latinos who have impacted the culture in the United States. What Puerto Ricans or Latinos have contributed significantly to the integration of Latinos in the United States? Writers? Inventors? Politicians? Create an informational piece (a PowerPoint presentation, an oral report, a poster, a radio interview, and so forth) that will share your newly found information and will introduce this person to your classmates.
   Here are some names of individuals to help you get started:
   - Alma Flor Ada
   - Mario Kreutzberger *(pseudonym, Don Francisco)*
   - Judith Francisca Baca
   - Sandra Cisneros
   - Rodolfo Llinás
   - Jaime Escalante
   - Antonia Novello
   - Gloria Estefan
   - Ellen Ochoa
   - Charles Patrick García

- Edward James Olmos
- Carolina Herrera
- Alex Rodríguez
- Ileana Ros-Lehtinen

4. Investigate the criteria and origin of the Pura Belpré Award. What other awards recognize the contributions of other groups of citizens? Native Americans, African Americans, and so forth. Create an informational piece (a PowerPoint presentation, an oral report, a poster, a radio interview, and so forth) that will share your newly found information and will introduce this award and its winners to your classmates.

Books to Explore

Badia, Arnhilda. (2004) *Hispanics in the USA: Making History.* Altea.
Reyes, Luis, and Peter Rubie. (2000) *Hispanics in Hollywood.* Lone Eagle.

23

John Lewis in the Lead: A Story of the Civil Rights Movement
by Jim Haskins and Kathleen Benson

Idea Shelf

This book investigates one incident in the fight for civil rights. Take a look, then investigate other pivotal moments in the movement. Use this book as a model for writing about those pivotal events.

Bookshelf

Haskins, Jim, and Kathleen Benson. (2006) *John Lewis in the Lead: A Story of the Civil Rights Movement.* Illustrated by Benny Andrews. Lee & Low Books, Inc. ISBN-10: 1-58430-250-X; ISBN-13: 978-1-58430-250-6.

Annotation

U.S. Congressman John Lewis has served in Congress since 1986. Before he was a politician, he worked tirelessly to obtain civil rights for African Americans; particularly the right to register and vote without force being used to prevent these activities. Lewis was a young boy when he first learned of the power of collective action, and as a young man studied the concept of nonviolent protest as put forth by Mohandas K. Gandhi. By the time he was twenty-three, he was speaking on the Capitol steps during the March on Washington—on the same stage as Martin Luther King Jr. when he made the famous "I Have a Dream" speech. Afterward, Lewis began to focus on obtaining real voting rights for blacks in the South. When they attempted to register and vote, they were often turned away. Those efforts culminated in a march from Selma to Montgomery to demonstrate their plight. Their first efforts resulted in a bloody confrontation—Lewis was injured, as were many other participants. The media coverage was so great that pressure was put on the state of Alabama and the federal government. The third (and successful) march began on March 21, 1965, and ended up in Montgomery, 25,000 people strong.

Twenty-one years later, the people of Georgia elected him to the U.S. House of Representatives. He is still serving in Congress today.

Curriculum Link: Civil Rights, John Lewis, Martin Luther King Jr., Rosa Parks

Background

In 1965, the three Selma-to-Montgomery marches for voting rights marked an important event in the U.S. civil rights movement. Amelia Boynton and her husband instigated the march by bringing important figures in the campaign to Selma to focus national attention on the efforts to obtain voting rights. It was only the third, and last, march that successfully made it into Montgomery. The route of the march is now commemorated as the Selma to Montgomery National Historic Trail.

Extension Ideas

1. Other dignitaries participated in the marches in addition to John Lewis. Among those attending were Dr. Martin Luther King Jr., James Bevel, and Hosea Williams. Research the background of the participants.
2. Where does the Birmingham church bombing fit on the time line? What is the relationship between the bombing and the marches?
3. Create a time line of the major events that contributed to the push for civil rights in the 1960s. Consider adding these events: lunch counter sit-ins; the Freedom Rides; the Student Nonviolent Coordinating Committee (SNCC); the voter-registration drives; the 1963 March on Washington; the Birmingham church bombings; the murders during Freedom Summer (don't miss the Chris Crowe books about the Emmet Till case); the Mississippi Freedom Democratic Party; Bloody Sunday in Selma in 1964; and the Selma-to-Montgomery marches.
4. Research how any one of the events listed in #3 impacted the overall movement toward civil rights in the 1960s.

Books to Explore

Bausum, Ann. (2006) *Freedom Riders: John Lewis and Jim Zwerg on the Front Lines of the Civil Rights Movement*. National Geographic Children's Books
Lewis, John, and Michael D'Orso. (1999) *Walking with the Wind: A Memoir of the Movement*. Harvest Books.

24

Theodore
by Frank Keating

Idea Shelf

Theodore Roosevelt was a president of the United States of America; this book profiles in thirty-two pages his life from his birth through the significant events of his presidency. Share this book; ask each student to choose a president (draw names from a hat) and then to set out to profile that president. Students should be asked to make their subject as interesting as possible. Think of a creative way to present material to fellow classmates.

Keating, Frank. (2006) *Theodore*. Illustrated by Mike Wimmer. Paula Wiseman Books/Simon & Schuster Books for Young Readers. ISBN-10: 0-689-86532-5; ISBN-13: 978-0-689-86532-9.

Bookshelf

Annotation

In a simplistic but interesting text, Keating highlights the significant events in Theodore Roosevelt's life—from his birth on October 27, 1858, to his election as vice president and his ascent to the presidency after President William McKinley's assassination. Roosevelt began life as a sickly infant, with asthma and weak eyes. But he loved reading and history and aspired to be strong and to accomplish great things. He lived in Dakota Territory, became a cattle rancher, returned to New York City, and ran for governor (and lost the election). But it was his involvement in the Spanish-American War that brought him notice and the nation's highest award for bravery in combat, the Congressional Medal of Honor. He returned to New York and was successfully elected governor, then went on to hold other offices and eventually became (at age forty-two) the youngest president of the United States. Wimmer's illustrations are realistic paintings of the president as an infant, a young boy, and an adult. His illustrations are stunning. An author's note provides a few more details.

Curriculum Link: Presidents—United States, Theodore Roosevelt

Background

Theodore Roosevelt was born into a wealthy family but struggled with health issues and suffered from extreme grief when his first wife (Alice Lee Roosevelt) and his mother died on the same day in 1884. After spending two years in the Dakotas working on his ranch, he entered politics, became governor of New York, and was elected vice president under William McKinley. With the assassination of McKinley, Roosevelt became the youngest president (at forty-two) in U.S. history. He was involved in the building of the Panama Canal, the Monroe Doctrine, trust-busting, the Sherman Act, and was awarded the Nobel Peace Prize.

Extension Ideas

1. Provide students with a list of Roosevelt's accomplishments gleaned from the picture book and preliminary research. Assign to individuals or small groups the task of investigating a specific accomplishment. Report back to the larger group (using a poster, an oral report, a dramatic play, a radio interview, and so forth) about that accomplishment. What was it? How did it impact the culture of the United States? The world?
2. Discuss Roosevelt's legacy as president. How does he measure up in terms of history?

Books to Explore

Harness, Cheryl. (2007) *The Remarkable Rough-Riding Life of Theodore Roosevelt and the Rise of Empire America*. National Geographic Children's Books.

McCullough, David. (1982) *Mornings on Horseback: The Story of an Extraordinary Family, a Vanished Way of Life, and the Unique Child Who Became Theodore Roosevelt*. Simon & Schuster.

Morris, Edmund. (2001) *Theodore Rex*. Random House.

Morris, Edmund. (2001) *The Rise of Theodore Roosevelt*. (Companion to *Theodore Rex*) Modern Library.

25

My Senator and Me: A Dog's-Eye View of Washington, D.C.
by Senator Edward M. Kennedy

Idea Shelf

There are three branches of government on the federal level (as well as on the state level): executive, legislative, and judicial. Use this book to introduce the legislative branch and the duties of a legislator—in this case, a senator in the U.S. Senate.

Kennedy, Senator Edward M. (2006) *My Senator and Me: A Dog's-Eye View of Washington, D.C.* Illustrated by David Small. Scholastic. ISBN: 0-439-65077-1.

Bookshelf

Annotation

Senator Edward M. Kennedy was first elected to the U.S. Senate when he was elected by the people of Massachusetts to complete the term of his brother John F. Kennedy, who was elected president in 1960. Senator Kennedy felt that "If you want a friend in Washington, get a dog." So that is what he did. Senator Kennedy and his wife Victoria Reggie Kennedy went to pick out a dog at a dog farm. They chose a Portuguese Water Dog, Champion Amigo's Seventh Wave—nicknamed "Splash" because he loved the water.

The author tells the story of a usual day on Capitol Hill, dealing with committees, votes, and meeting constituents, all told from the perspective of Splash. Small's illustrations show readers the inside scenes of the senator's office, the underground train that takes the senators from the Senate office building to the Capitol, the Capitol steps press conference, and the Capitol rotunda.

The last page of the book provides a sequence of events that show how a bill becomes a law. The seven simplified steps will be a starting point for more investigation into the discussion and work that is behind every bill that is passed (or rejected) in the legislative branch of the federal government.

Curriculum Link: Senator Edward M. Kennedy, Legislative Branch of the Government, Laws, Civil Rights

Background

In 2008, Senator Kennedy was diagnosed with brain cancer. Kennedy's book was written prior to Senator Kennedy's diagnosis of brain cancer so it represents his activities during his active workdays on the hill. Because of the cancer, Senator Kennedy's daily routine has changed considerably. He is largely absent from the Senate as he battles his disease, but he comes to the capitol for important votes.

After the assassinations of his brothers, President John F. Kennedy and presidential hopeful and former Attorney General Robert F. Kennedy, Ted Kennedy became a senator from Massachusetts and actively worked to continue some of his brothers' interests: civil rights, health care, and so forth. This book provides excellent information about how a bill becomes a law.

Extension Ideas

1. Investigate and discuss the role of the three branches of government: the executive, judicial, and legislative.
2. Investigate the procedure for getting a bill passed in your state and compare and contrast it with the procedure at the national level.
3. Brainstorm a list of bills your group thinks should be made to the state code. Are there any that are important enough that your group wants to campaign to have presented to the legislature for consideration?
4. Visit the White House's Web site at <http://whitehouse.gov> and locate the names and addresses of the senators who represent your state. Write them a letter thanking them for the support of a cause you endorse or soliciting their support for a cause.

Books to Explore

Burke, Richard E., William Hoffer, and Marilyn Hoffer. (2003) *The Senator: My Ten Years with Ted Kennedy*. St. Martin's Griffin.

Donovan, Sandy. (2003) *Making Laws: A Look at How a Bill Becomes a Law*. Lerner Publishing Group.

Feldman, Ruth Tenzer. (2003) *How Congress Works: A Look at the Legislative Branch*. Lerner Publishing Group.

26

Blackbeard's Last Fight
by Eric Kimmel

Idea Shelf

Off the southernmost coast of North Carolina and its string of barrier islands lies an island officially designated as Smith Island but commonly known as Bald Head Island. Local legend tells us that the normally lush green island's high knoll was worn down to dirt (bald) because pirates regularly sat up on it to watch for ships coming between the islands and mainland. When ships got toward the end of the channel, the pirates would attack. Pirate stories are prevalent in the history of many communities along the U.S. eastern coastline. Read Blackbeard's story and then set out to find other stories and tie them into geographical locations or events. One such connection is between pirates and Mardi Gras in New Orleans.

Kimmel, Eric. (2006) *Blackbeard's Last Fight*. Illustrated by Leonard Everett Fisher. Farrar, Straus and Giroux. ISBN-10: 0-374-30780-6; ISBN-13: 978-0-374-30780-6.

Bookshelf

Annotation

Blackbeard, thought to be Edward Teach, was a notorious pirate who terrorized North Carolina's Outer Banks (and much of the East Coast) in the early 1700s. When the governor of North Carolina gave the outlaw a full pardon, the governor of Virginia, Governor Alexander Spotswood, was not pleased. Governor Spotswood was concerned that the pardoned outlaw would not abandon his life of piracy and soon the entire eastern coastline of North America would be controlled by Blackbeard's pirates. Governor Spotswood wanted the Royal Navy to deal with Blackbeard, but when he met with Lieutenant Robert Maynard, the governor realized that the Royal Navy could not legally go after Blackbeard. The governor proposed that he hire his own ships and, of course, he would need an able officer to lead the crew—that officer would be Lieutenant Maynard. Two ships, the *Jane* and the *Ranger*, with full crews and Maynard in command, sailed to North Carolina's Ocracoke Inlet, where they encountered Blackbeard and his crew on the *Adventure*. After a night of waiting, Maynard moved his ships toward the *Adventure*, and a fierce battle ensued. In a dramatic end to the fighting, Blackbeard's crew boarded the *Jane's* deck, and after hand-to-hand combat, Blackbeard "receives his just desserts." Those familiar with the legend will know that Blackbeard's headless body floated around the *Jane* three times before sinking to the bottom of the ocean. Despite the fact that Blackbeard was decidedly an evil man, Maynard's expedition was entirely illegal. The story is fictionalized but Kimmel says that the facts of the battle are historically accurate.

Curriculum Link: Pirate, History of Communities, Legends and Maps

Background

Pirates played a big part in the history of the eastern shore and terrorized many who traveled along the coastline. Blackbeard was a notorious pirate along the Atlantic and Caribbean coasts from 1716 through 1718. There were many other pirates during the era of piracy.

Extension Ideas

1. Explore the use of pirates by George Washington to secure a victory during the American Revolution. Use Robert H. Patton's book *Patriot Pirates* to investigate the relationship between Washington and the pirates.
2. Explore the history of piracy. Many of the pirates that roamed the high seas (William Kidd, Edward "Blackbeard" Teach, Charles Vane, Sam "Black Bellamy" Bellamy, and two female pirates, Anne Bonny and Mary Read) did so off the coast of New England, most notably near the Carolinas and as far north as Nova Scotia and Canada, during the seventeenth and eighteenth centuries. Discover the legends surrounding their activities and their relationship to Mardi Gras in New Orleans.
3. Modern-day pirates are still operating in many parts of the world. Their activities are ruthless and terrorizing. Use your school or public library's subscription databases to locate articles about current-day pirates, and then compare and contrast their activities with the activities of the pirates from the "golden era of piracy" during the eighteenth century. One such article is by Stefan Lovgren, "Modern Pirates Terrorize Seas With Guns and Grenades" for *National Geographic News* (July 6, 2006). What bounty were (are) pirates seeking, what tactics do they use to plunder ships at sea, how did they treat the crew of the ships they stopped and boarded, and what did the government do to counteract the terror at sea?
4. Pirates are thought to have buried treasure all along the coasts where they plundered ships. While the information in James and Jeremy Owens's book *Lost Treasures of the Pirates of the Caribbean* is fictionalized, it is a lot of fun and provides an interactive map exercise and activity related to pirates that did populate the eastern coastline. Carry the pirate theme forward with Owens's book.
5. September 19 is International Talk Like a Pirate Day (a holiday invented in 1995 by John Baur and Mark Summers and later promoted by comedian Dave Barry).

Fans of the holiday are sure to love learning how pirates talk. Try it on September 19, or declare your own Talk Like a Pirate Day.

Books to Explore

Butterfield, Moira. (2005) *Pirates and Smugglers*. Kingfisher.

Choundas, George. (2007) *The Pirate Primer: Mastering the Language of Swashbucklers & Rogues*. Writers Digest Books.

Croce, Pat. (2006) *Pirate Soul: A Swashbuckling Journey Through the Golden Age of Pirates*. Running Press Books Publishers.

Howard, Barnaby. (2006) *The Best Book of Pirates*. Kingfisher.

Konstam, Angus. (2005) *The History of Pirates*. Mercury Books.

Lewis, J. Patrick. (2006) *Blackbeard: The Pirate King*. National Geographic.

Lubber, Captain William. (2006) *Pirateology: The Pirate Hunter's Companion*. Candlewick.

Matthews, John. (2006) *Pirates*. Atheneum.

Owen, James A., and Jeremy Owen. (2007) *Lost Treasures of the Pirates of the Caribbean*. With Lon Saline and Mary McCray. Simon & Schuster Books for Young Readers.

Patton, Robert H. (2008) *Patriot Pirates: The Privateer War for Freedom and Fortune in the American Revolution*. Pantheon.

Platt, Richard. (2004) *Pirate* (Eyewitness Books). DK Children.

27

Looking at Glass Through the Ages
by Bruce Koscielniak

What uses would your great-great-grandparents have made of glass? Your great-grandparents? How does this compare to the invention of plastic and its uses? This is a great book to build curiosity and thinking about inventions and when they came about. Make a list of ten items you use every day: toaster, mechanical pencil, and so forth. Then choose a time period or a person and investigate which of those items would have been available at that time. For example, could Abraham Lincoln have had a drink of water out of a glass made of glass? If not, what would he have used instead—a tin cup?

Idea Shelf

Koscielniak, Bruce. (2006) *Looking at Glass Through the Ages*. Illustrated by Bruce Koscielniak. Houghton Mifflin. ISBN-10: 0-618-50750-7; ISBN-13: 978-061850750-4.

Bookshelf

Annotation

The history and uses of glass are aptly shared in this lively volume of information about the evolution of the glass industry from 4,500 years ago. The discovery that silica sand and soda ash would produce beads (or gobs) of gemlike material was the first step in the development of glass production and use. Adding lime was found to add strength, and the addition of copper created beads of a blue-green color. Early glass containers were formed over a core of clay that was washed out after the glass was finished. Soon the Egyptians were using molds to create glass pieces in a more uniform and efficient manner. Tubes of various colored glasses were sliced off to create mosaic-like objects. In Syria around 30 BCE, artisans discovered that the molten glass could be blown into shapes. Luxury glass began to be made in green-tinted glass containers. Constantinople became the center for glass production and by 1250 was beginning to produce clear glass—using a highly secretive de-colorizer formula. The production of clear glass opened the possibilities for the development of eyeglasses and magnifying glasses. So the use of glass emerged from a practical application to an art form and in the process returned with renewed practical applications.

Curriculum Link: Glass Blowing, Artisans, Stained Glass, Metals

Background

Glass has been used for art purposes as well as for new practical uses. Etching of glass (engraving) and applying decorative enameling became popular with the Venetians. During the twelfth and thirteenth centuries, colored glass was produced for stained-glass windows.

For coloring:

cobalt = blue
iron = green
antimony = yellow
manganese = purple
gold = deep ruby reds

Mirrors were developed and convex mirrors became popular along with ornately decorated frames. When lead oxide was added to clear glass, the result was a brilliantly reflective lead crystal. Glassmakers discovered how to give a less expensive piece of glass a cut-glass appearance. Other techniques continued to be developed and products invented—glass tubes for laser light, florescent signs, and other specialty products. All from a process discovered 4,500 years ago.

Extension Ideas

1. In 1959, Sir Alastair Pilkington developed a process to produce flat glass (such as that used for window panes). The process is sometimes referred to as the "float glass process." Other processes include the "Pittsburgh process" and the "Libbey-Owens process." Investigate and explain one process in detail and tell how it differs from the other two processes mentioned above.
2. Discover what role George Ravenscroft (1618–1681) played in the development of glass.
3. Describe the process and reasons for producing plate glass.
4. Why is Friedrich Siemens and his invention of the tank furnace important to the development of glass production?
5. Investigate the invention by U.S. engineer Michael Owens (1859–1923) that helped to promote the production of glass. Explain how and why.

Books to Explore

Giblin, James Cross. (1988) *Let There Be Light: A Book About Windows.* Crowell.

28

A Place Where Sunflowers Grow
by Amy Lee-Tai

Use this book as an introduction to a focus on World War II, and specifically on how the war affected citizens on the home front, whether that be in the United States or in other nations around the world, particularly Germany, Japan, and other involved countries.

Idea Shelf

Lee-Tai, Amy. (2006) *A Place Where Sunflowers Grow*. Illustrated by Felicia Hoshino. Children's Book Press. ISBN: 0-89239-215-0.

Bookshelf

Annotation

Shortly after the bombing of Pearl Harbor, an event that began the United States involvement in World War II, American citizens of Japanese descent were taken from their homes and sent to camps in remote places. Many locations were sweltering and barren and subject to frequent dust storms. This story is based on actual events and tells of one girl, Mari, who misses her California home, with its flowers and friends. Given only a few days to leave their home, Mari's mother has brought a small handful of sunflower seeds and together the two of them plant the sunflower seeds in the ground outside their new home. By summer's end, the sunflowers have become a symbol of what was, and what may still be part of their future.

Mari's story is a fictionalized account—but according to the author, it is based loosely on the experiences of the author's mother and grandparents, who were part of the move from a comfortable California existence to a camp established in horse stables in Tanforan, California. The Tanforan stalls reeked of the manure from their former use. Eventually the family was relocated to an internment camp at Topaz, Utah, where the wind and dust blew against their tarpaper barrack. The author's grandmother, a respected Japanese American painter, had been forced to leave behind many paintings, but when they arrived at the internment camp, she and Lee-Tai's grandfather established art classes for young children. Here the children could express themselves with drawings of what made them happy. The past dominated their art as the present was often bleak. Their memories became the seeds that inspired fresh, beautiful paintings. The sunflower seeds and the sprouts that emerged became the seeds of hope for the future.

Amy Lee-Tai's story fictionalizes her ancestors' experiences while telling the story of Mari, the developing friendship between Mari and Aiko, and the story of a little-known part of history—the art classes in the Japanese internment camps of World War II. Hoshino's beautifully rendered, sunshine-filled illustrations are compositions that mimic the style and form of the artwork of Hisako Hibi, the author's grandmother. An added element of this book is the dual-language text that is in both Japanese and English.

Curriculum Link: Art—Japanese, World War II, Internment camps, Gardening

Background

Then-President Franklin D. Roosevelt signed an order on February 19, 1942, mandating the evacuation of more than 120,000 Japanese living in America. They were sent to one of ten internment camps in California, Idaho, Utah, Arizona, Wyoming, Colorado, and Arkansas. Two-thirds of those put under lock and key were American citizens. The official reason for the relocation was to appease the farmers who were competing with the Japanese labor and commerce, but it was fueled by the attack on Pearl Harbor, which heightened anti-Japanese sentiment. Two-and-a-half years after the camps were opened, they were closed in 1945, near the end of the war, It was more than two dozen years later that the U.S. government acknowledged the injustice of its actions and apologized to those who had been interned and began reparations—in the late 1960s, each living Japanese former detainee was given $20,000 as a cash stipend.

Extension Ideas

1. Learn about planting and growing sunflowers at the Burpee Company Web site, <http://www.burpee.com/sunflowers>.
2. Compare and contrast the situation surrounding the Japanese internment with the discrimination and profiling of the Muslim and Middle Eastern community in the aftermath of the 9/11 terror attacks and the destruction of the World Trade Center in New York City.
3. Read other stories of internment and discuss the conditions, map the campsites, and discuss how this series of events would be tolerated or not tolerated in today's United States. What do you think the reaction would be?

Books to Explore

Other books of internment (some picture books, some full-length):

Bunting, Eve. (1998) *So Far from the Sea*. Illustrated by Chris Soentpiet. Clarion. (picture book)

Deneberg, Barry. (1999) *The Journal of Ben Uchida, citizen #13559, Mirror Lake Internment Camp*. Scholastic. (novel)

Kadohata, Cynthia. (2006) *Weedflower*. Atheneum. (novel)

Mochizuki, Ken. (1993) *Baseball Saved Us*. Illustrated by Dom Lee. Lee & Low. (picture book)

Oppenheim, Joanne. (2006) *Dear Miss Breed: True Stories of the Japanese American Incarceration During World War II and a Librarian Who Made a Difference*. Scholastic Nonfiction.

Stanley, Jerry. (1994) *I am an American: A True Story of Japanese Internment*. Knopf. (Information book)

Tunnell, Michael O. (1996) *The Children of Topaz: The Story of a Japanese-American Internment Camp: Based on a Classroom Diary*. Holiday House. (novel)

Uchida, Yoshiko. (1996) *The Bracelet*. Illustrated by Joanna Yardley. Philomel. (early chapter book)

A postwar story that is particularly engaging is:

Judge, Lita. (2007) *One Thousand Tracings: Healing the Wounds of World War II*. Hyperion. Fourteen poems describe a philanthropic project begun after World War II, when the narrator's family sent a package to a needy German friend. That initial exchange brought shoes and clothes, coats, and canned food to European survivors. The tracings were tracings of feet so that correctly sized shoes could be sent.

On the WWW:

For a bibliography of *Historical Novels and Picture Books for World War II: Dr. Seuss and More*, focusing on experiences of young people in Europe and in the United States in the war and on the home front, see the bibliography available at <http://www.mcelmeel.com/curriculum/picturebooks_WWII.html>. The list includes titles that speak of many heroes of the war, including regular citizens young and old: Including Ira Hayes, a Native American (Pima) Marine who helped raise the flag at Iwo Jima, and the Navajo Code Talkers.

29

Henry's Freedom Box: A True Story from the Underground Railroad
by Ellen Levine

Idea Shelf

Slaves used desperate measures to obtain their freedom. Henry "Box" Brown is one of those ingenious slaves who found an unconventional method of obtaining liberty. Begin a focus on the quest for equal rights with this story and move to the struggle for freedom, voting, and full rights in our society.

Levine, Ellen. (2007) *Henry's Freedom Box: A True Story from the Underground Railroad.* Illustrated by Kadir Nelson. Scholastic Press. ISBN-13: 978-0-439-77733-9.

Bookshelf

Annotation

Henry Brown was a slave who plotted to gain his freedom by convincing a carpenter to nail him in a box. The box would then be mailed to northern abolitionists who would then free him. Ellen Levine's picture book is a fictionalized version of his escape north and provides additional details regarding Brown's family—a family sold from their home, a family he was not ever to see again, and about his ingenious escape to freedom.

The story is built on the facts gleaned from Brown's own narrative about his life and other source material. The facts are that Brown did not know when he was born. He did know that his mother had been sold away from him and sent to work in a tobacco factory. When he reached adulthood he met and married Nancy (with permission) and together they started a family. But his children also were born into slavery and all too soon his family was sold away from him, just as his mother had been. He then resolved to escape and made plans to be shipped north. His crate was sent first by horse-drawn cart to the train station, in Richmond, Virginia, where the box, with Brown sealed inside, traveled by train to a steamboat destined for Philadelphia. Upon arrival at the dock in Philadelphia, the crate was picked up by abolitionists, who took it to the home of one of the abolitionists. When the crate was pried open, Henry felt he had a birthday—the birthday of his freedom.

Curriculum Link: Underground Railroad, Slavery

Background

Researching the life of the real Henry Brown reveals that he was most likely born near Richmond, Virginia, in 1815 (some sources say 1816). His wife and three children were sold to a slave trader who took them deeper into the South. It was then that Brown vowed to escape north. With the help of friends, he was shipped to Philadelphia in a crate that was three feet long by two feet wide and two feet eight inches deep. Brown was five feet eight inches and 200 pounds. In the crate he took a minimal amount of food: a few biscuits and water. He also took a gimlet with which he could make air holes if the holes already made were covered during the trip. The crate took twenty-seven hours to move the 350 miles to freedom. Historians know that Brown spoke at a few anti-slavery lectures after arriving in the North but nothing more is known about him after 1864, except that after the Fugitive Slave Act was passed in 1850, Brown fled to Wales, the last place he was known to be. No one seems to know if he ever saw his family again.

Although he traveled unconventionally, Brown is considered to have escaped through the Underground Railroad as he too traveled on a secret route with the help of sympathetic abolitionists. Others who escaped on the Underground Railroad most often journeyed by foot through swamps and woodlands and across fields and rivers. The Ohio River was a popular crossing place, where those fleeing traveled across the river by boat and then made their way to a safe house and to freedom. Virginia Hamilton shared another version of the Henry Box Brown story in *Many Thousands Gone* as did Doreen Rappaport in *Escape from Slavery: Five Journeys to Freedom*.

One of the men in Philadelphia who received the carton containing Henry Box Brown was William Still. Still became known as the "father of the Underground Railroad."

Extension Ideas

1. Learn more about the Underground Railroad.
2. Investigate the life of Harriet Tubman. She was one of a network of slaves and free blacks that helped the Union's cause during the Civil War. Read Thomas B. Allen's *Harriet Tubman, Secret Agent: How Daring Slaves and Free Blacks Spied for the Union During the Civil War*.
3. Find out more about the role of the abolitionists in the quest for freedom. The following are names of abolitionists who were among the most well known. Discover how they helped the cause.

   a. William Still
   b. Gerrit Smith

  c. Salmon Chase
  d. David Ruggles
  e. Thomas Garrett
  f. William Purvis
  g. John Rankin
  h. William Wells Brown
  i. Frederick Douglass
  j. Henry David Thoreau
  k. Lucretia Mott
  l. Charles Langston
  m. Levi Coffin
  n. Susan B. Anthony
  o. Josiah Henson
  p. James Pennington

Books to Explore

Allen, Thomas B. (2006) *Harriet Tubman, Secret Agent: How Daring Slaves and Free Blacks Spied for the Union During the Civil War*. National Geographic Children's Books.

Espinosa, Rod, illustrator. (2007) *Underground Railroad*. Abdo & Daughters. (graphic narrative)

Hamilton, Virginia. (1993) *Many Thousand Gone: African Americans from Slavery to Freedom*. Illustrated by Leo Dillon and Diane Dillon. Scholastic Press.

Hopkinson, Deborah. (2003) *Sweet Clara and the Freedom Quilt*. Illustrated by James E. Ransome. Knopf.

Hopkinson, Deborah. (2005) *Under the Quilt of Night*. Illustrated by James E. Ransome. Aladdin.

Rappaport, Doreen. (1991; 1998) *Escape from Slavery: Five Journeys to Freedom*. HarperTrophy.

Weatherford, Carole Boston. (2006) *Moses: When Harriet Tubman Led Her People to Freedom*. Illustrated by Kadir Nelson. Hyperion.

Winter, Jeanette. (2008 reissue) *Follow the Drinking Gourd*. Knopf Books for Young Readers.

30

Willy and Max: A Holocaust Story
by Amy Littlesugar

Art treasures plundered during World War II are slowly being returned to their original owners or their families. Introduce the topic of ownership with this story. Then discuss the treasures as discussed here, or the stores, homes, and so forth confiscated or destroyed when Japanese citizens were interned in the United States (some say "held in detention camps"). Who owns an item if it was bought in good faith—even though it was actually stolen years before? This is a great debate topic.

Idea Shelf

Littlesugar, Amy. (2006) *Willy and Max: A Holocaust Story*. Illustrated by William Low. Penguin Young Readers Group. ISBN-10: 0399234837; ISBN-13: 978-0399234835.

Bookshelf

Annotation

Willy (a Christian boy) and Max (a Jewish boy) met when Max's father purchased a unique piece of art, *The Lady*, from Willy's father's antique store. The two boys became acquainted and promised one another to be friends forever. And they were until the Nazis invaded Belgium. At first they stayed, but when Max and his father had to flee, they returned the painting to Willy's father for safekeeping. The Nazis ransacked the antique shop and stole the painting. The boys never saw one another again.

Years later, a museum curator finds a picture of the two boys rolled up in a canvas painting that has been given to the museum. He is able to contact Willy, who is now living in the United States with his family—children and grandchildren. Willy tells the curator of the painting's true owner. The curator is able to contact Max's family, but Max is no longer living. The painting, however, succeeds in bringing Willy's family together with Max's, and another friendship is begun through the power of the painting. A note includes information about efforts to return to the rightful owners art pieces stolen by the Nazis.

Curriculum Link: World War II, Looted Treasures

Background

Art historians estimate that about one-fifth of the artworks in Europe were looted by the Nazis. Still more were removed by Allied troops for safekeeping, and some servicemen (including Americans) stole art left behind or that had been hidden for safekeeping. Many of these pieces can be found today in major museums and private collections. The original owners and their heirs now are beginning to reclaim their property. However, there are huge legal issues, as ownership must be proven. By now, many pieces of art have two "legitimate" owners. There was a prewar owner, and years after the war, others might have owned the artwork for decades with no knowledge that it had been stolen.

Extension Ideas

1. Locate current articles about the status of looted artwork by searching the Internet for "looted art" and "World War II." What efforts are being made to identify and return pieces of artwork to their rightful owners? What efforts do you think should be made? What are the problems and solutions to the problems caused by this looting?
2. Debate: All pieces of art that can be identified as looted items should be returned immediately to the original owners or their heirs without compensation to the current "owner."

Books to Explore

Alford, Kenneth D. (2003) *Nazi Plunder: Great Treasure Stories of World War II*. Da Capo Press.
Perry, Victor. (2000) *Stolen Art*. Gefen Publishing House.

31

Jackie's Bat
by Marybeth Lorbiecki

Discuss prejudicial behavior—the Ku Klux Klan practices prejudicial behavior in an overt and aggressive manner, but many others practice it in passive ways. Prejudice can be manifested toward anyone who is not like ourselves—race, religion, gender, country of origin, and so forth. After reading this book, make a list of behaviors that the young boy Joey engaged in that put him in the prejudicial behavior class. Then make a list of behaviors readers have observed others doing that displayed prejudicial behavior.

Idea Shelf

Lorbiecki, Marybeth. (2006) *Jackie's Bat.* Illustrated by Brian Pinkney. Simon & Schuster Books for Young Readers. ISBN-10: 0-689-84102-7; ISBN-13: 978-0-689-84102-6.

Bookshelf

Annotation

In this fictionalized story, readers are able to get a true sense of the type of prejudicial behavior that is directed toward Jackie Robinson during his first year in baseball's major leagues. It's the beginning of the 1947 baseball season and there's a new player in the locker room. It is the year Robinson becomes the first black player to play in the major leagues. It is also the first day for this year's batboy, Joey. The batboy's father has told him that "it ain't right, a white boy serving a black man." The first day, Jackie Robinson's "locker" is a nail on the wall and a folding chair. But the young batboy does what the manager tells him to. He hangs the uniforms in their correct lockers—and number 42 on the nail. He polishes all of the shoes—except number 42. Joey does what he is told but does nothing extra for the "colored" ballplayer. But over the course of the season, Robinson gives the other players and the batboy his respect. He works harder every day. On September 23, 1947, Robinson is declared Rookie of the Year and it's Jackie Robinson Day at Ebbets Field. And even Joey's father wears a button saying, "I'm for Jackie."

Curriculum Link: Jackie Robinson, Civil Rights, Negro Leagues

Background

Jackie Robinson became the first black player to play in the major leagues. While he was officially accepted as a legitimate player, he met many challenges in facing the fans and playing with and against other ballplayers. Other players followed in making inroads in the major leagues, including: Hank Greenburg as a first Jewish player, Roberto Clemente as a Hispanic player.

Extension Ideas

1. Discuss the presence of subtle prejudices in today's society.

   Civil rights legislation was finally passed in the 1960s. Great strides have been made since Robinson's entry into the world of baseball. But consider this story from a construction site in 2008: Two men, both sheet-metal construction workers, were working on a flood-damaged site where no electricity was available from normal sources. They need electricity for about five minutes to operate a specific tool. They had a generator, but it would take thirty minutes or so to drag the cords and so forth up to the area where they needed the power. One of the men approached another craft's journeyman crew, who had appropriate equipment nearby—equipment they weren't actually using at the time. He asked permission to use their equipment for the needed time, a request that is general practice among the crafts. He was refused. A few minutes later, the other man made the same request. He was given permission. The only discernible difference—the color of their skin.

   In another situation, a very overweight woman, a few days after weight reduction surgery, went to a hospital emergency room (five times) complaining of leg pain. Though she suffered from a blood clot and eventually died from it, her complaints were dismissed as her being "too lazy to exercise" after her surgery, psychotic behavior, and so forth. However, no tests were even given for clots, a somewhat normal test that most health care workers would consider, especially after surgery.

2. In small groups, discuss situations in which subtle discrimination has taken place. Take care not to malign people or businesses. Report the account factually and without using the names of people in the class/school or the names of local businesses. National political figures, for example, may be named if the accounts are well-substantiated. Emphasize the discussion of situations that are firsthand experiences—not rumors or urban legends and so forth.

Books to Explore:

Eig, Jonathan. (2007) *The Story of Jackie Robinson's First Season*. Simon & Schuster.

Maraniss, David. (2006) *Clemente: The Passion and Grace of Baseball's Last Hero*. Simon & Schuster.

McDonough, Yona Zeldis. (2006) *Hammerin' Hank: The Life of Hank Greenberg*. Illustrated by Malcah Zeldis. Walker & Company. (picture book)

Rampersad, Arnold. (1998) *Jackie Robinson: A Biography.* Ballantine.

Robinson, Sharon. (2006) *Promises to Keep: How Jackie Robinson Changed America.* Scholastic.

Simon, Scott. (2004) *Jackie Robinson and the Integration of Baseball.* John Wiley & Sons.

Winter, Jonah. (2005) *Roberto Clemente: Pride of the Pittsburgh Pirates.* Illustrated by Raul Colon. Atheneum/Anne Schwartz Books. (picture book)

32

Little Sap and Monsieur Rodin
by Michelle Lord

Idea Shelf

What a great way to introduce artist Auguste Rodin. Locate a few examples of his art on the WWW, create a bulletin board, and then introduce one dimension of his work by reading this book aloud.

Lord, Michelle. (2006) *Little Sap and Monsieur Rodin*. Illustrated by Felicia Hoshino. Lee & Low Books. ISBN-10: 1-58430-248-8; ISBN-13: 978-1-58430-248-3.

Bookshelf

Annotation

The story told by Lord is based on the facts, taken from historical records, of the actual encounter between the artist Auguste Rodin and Sap, one of the child dancers. Because of unrest in Cambodia and nearby regions, Cambodia sought protection from the French, and along with other countries in Southeast Asia, Cambodia became part of French Indochina. The Cambodian king did bring girls ages five or six into his royal palace in Phnom Penh to begin their dance training. His dance troupe entertained royalty and often traveled with the royal family around the world. Since the dance moves were based on many carvings on the temples created during the Khmer empire and its rule from the ninth through the fifteenth centuries, the dancers are often referenced as the Khmer dancers.

The facts of *Little Sap and Monsieur Rodin* are accurate but the actual details within the events are created in the mind of the author, and the color-washed images are fabricated by the illustrator. The illustrations and text juxtapose the peasant life of Little Sap with her life as part of the royal dance troupe. The thatched huts of the Cambodian countryside are accurately depicted. Little Sap's transition from her family's country home to her life in the royal palace as part of the troupe is shown in spot illustrations that help move the transition from page to page. Double-page spreads showing the royal palace dance practice, the trip to France, and the performances in Paris are shown in impressive detail. The setting for the sessions sketched by Auguste Rodin show a variance of location but with similar grace and fluency. The illustrations are outstanding in that they realistically interpret a time and place recorded in another way by an outstanding artist. The book is well-designed—the illustrations give readers a true sense of the historic place and time. The interplay between peasant life, life in the royal palace, and between Cambodia and France are outstanding and will give readers a true sense of both story and time.

Curriculum Link: Art—Auguste Rodin, Artist and Sculptor.

Background

In July 1906, the Cambodian king, King Sisowath, and Princess Soumphady took forty-two of their royal dancers to France to perform at an exhibition there. Renowned artist Auguste Rodin was enchanted by the dancers and produced some of his most famous sketches from his interaction with those dancers. He asked permission to sketch three of them, Sap, Soun, and Yem. The result was the famous *Danseuse Cambodgienne* sketches that were exhibited to wide acclaim in 1907. Rodin added brilliant color washes to the sketches—color that invoked his feeling of swaying flowers.

Auguste Rodin (November 12, 1840–November 17, 1917), known for his sculptures (particularly *The Thinker*), was also an oil painter and watercolorist. That body of work has been largely overlooked. He produced more than 7,000 drawings and prints. Rodin is said to have preferred amateur models and to have been fascinated by dance and spontaneous movement.

Extension Ideas

1. Investigate the artistic life of Rodin and create a time line noting the significant events in his life as an artist.
2. Prepare a visual presentation of Rodin's most famous works and include some representations of his famous sculptures and his watercolors known as *Danseuses Cambodgienne.*
3. Prepare a portrait gallery of Rodin and at least five of his artist contemporaries.

Books to Explore

Le Normand-Romain, Antoinette, and Christina Buley-Uribe. (2007) *Auguste Rodin: Drawings and Watercolors*. Thames & Hudson. This book explores the drawings made at the time Rodin was sculpting *The Gates of Hell* and his great watercolor nudes. Drawings are from the collection of the Musée Rodin, of which more than 350 are reproduced here. Le Normand-Romain is the curator of the museum. Buley-Uribe is also the coauthor of other books about Rodin.

Rilke, Rainer Maria. (2004) *Auguste Rodin* (Lives of the Artists series). Translated by Daniel Slager. Archipelago Books. The author, a renowned German poet and a contemporary of Rodin's, was hired by Rodin as his secretary. Rilke's essays about the work and development of Rodin as an artist are accompanied in this book by several reproductions of Rodin's little-known watercolors and drawings.

33

Of Numbers and Stars:
The Story of Hypatia
by Anne D. Love

Idea Shelf

Introduce a forward-thinking woman while emphasizing divergent thinking in the fields of mathematics and science. Let this book stimulate your students to create a list of theories that are plausible to their way of thinking, but perhaps in the realm of impossibilities to others. These theories may be reality at some time in the future.

Love, D. Anne. (2006) *Of Numbers and Stars: The Story of Hypatia.* Illustrated by Pam Paparone. Holiday House. ISBN-10: 08234-1621-6; ISBN-13: 978-0-8234-1621-9.

Bookshelf

Annotation

Greek women had few rights and even fewer opportunities to learn to read and write in the fourth century CE, when Hypatia was born into an extraordinary household. She grew to become a beloved scholar, philosopher, writer, and teacher. Her father had unique ideas about his daughter's education and role in society. Instead of learning how to manage a fine house, weaving, cooking, and sewing, Hypatia's father wanted her to learn to fish and to ride a horse. She often rode through the streets of Alexandria. She read all the great works of the poets and philosophers of the time. She became interested in nature and studied all the plants, trees, birds, and the patterns of the stars (constellations). Hypatia visited her father at the university and developed an interest in mathematical patterns. Her father recognized her interest and began to teach her arithmetic, and later geometry and astronomy. She became a noted astronomer, a respected mathematician, and a sought-after philosopher.

Curriculum Link: Hypatia, Inventions, Religion versus Science

Background

Much information swirls around the story of Hypatia's role in the world of science and mathematics. What seems to be constant in all accounts is her role as an influential female in the field of science and mathematics at a time when women were not generally respected or even allowed into the scholarly arena. She is credited with developing a procedure for charting celestial bodies and the invention of the hydrometer that is used to determine the relative density of liquids. Whether or not she had a real role in the invention of the astrolabe (which some say actually predates her development by more than a century) is in question.

She was openly a pagan but was reportedly respected by many Christians. In the end, however, her scientific theories angered some Christians as being counter to their religious dogma. Thus, one day in March 415 CE, during Lent, she was dragged from her carriage by an angry sect and killed in a most brutal and grisly manner.

As the years have passed, her legacy has been reexamined and her role in the development of many theories and inventions acknowledged or discounted. She is acknowledged as a scientist and mathematician as well as being considered a philosopher by historians who have examined primary sources providing evidence of her contribution to the world. Her father had tutored her in developing her physical health, her mental health and intellect, and her ability to use her words and voice to influence others. In summary, Hypatia was the first woman to make a substantial contribution to the development of mathematics and science.

Little actual documentation of Hypatia's work remains today. Her contributions were largely ignored for centuries. When her work was brought to the forefront, many scholars had different interpretations of how much Hypatia was responsible for and what were merely her collaborations with or responses to other scientists' work.

Extension Ideas

1. Investigate the significance of the development of the charting of the stars (constellations) and the hydrometer. Relate the importance to Hypatia's work.
2. Make a time line showing the time span of Hypatia's life as well as the lives of other noted mathematicians born in Egypt during the same century. (This might be an appropriate time to introduce the correct use of print/online encyclopedia resources.)

   Abu Kamil Shuja
   Ahmes
   Diophantus
   Euclid
   Heron
   Hypsicles
   Menelaus
   Pappus
   Ptolemy
   Serenus

Theon (Hypatia's father)

Yunus

3. Some historians say that one of Hypatia's students, Synesius of Cyrene (378–430), developed the astrolabe that helped sailors determine the latitude and true north by measuring the angle between the sun and the horizon. Cyrene is said to have based his device on Hypatia's advice. What is the history of the development of the astrolabe? How does Hypatia fit into that history, according to modern historians?

4. After investigating the origin of the astrolabe, debate whether Hypatia was responsible for the development of the astrolabe or whether Hypatia did little more than encourage the real developers of the astrolabe.

5. Compare Hypatia's influence on the body of knowledge with that of:

Confucius (551–479 BCE)

Aristotle (384–322 BCE)

Plato (427–347 BCE)

Marcus Aurelius Antonius (121–180 CE)

Buddha (563–483 BCE)

Socrates (469–399 BCE)

Investigate the contributions made by each of these philosophers and debate their relative importance to the collective body of knowledge contributed to ancient culture.

Books to Explore

Aristotle and Richard McKeon, ed. (2001) *The Basic Works of Aristotle*. Modern Library.

Augustus, Caesar Marcus Aurelius Antoninus. (2007) *The Meditations of Marcus Aurelius Antonius*. Forgotten Books.

Cathcart, Thomas, and Daniel Klein. (2007) *Plato and a Platypus Walk into a Bar: Understanding Philosophy Through Jokes*. Harry N. Abrams.

Cathcart, Thomas, and Daniel Klein. (2008) *Aristotle and an Aardvark Go to Washington: Understanding Political Doublespeak Through Philosophy and Jokes*. Harry N. Abrams.

Chopra, Deepak. (2007/2008). *Buddha: A Story of Enlightenment*. Harper One. (This is a fictional account of the life of Prince Siddhartha, who became the Buddha. Questions and answers about the tenets of Buddhism follow the narrative.)

Freedman, Russell. (2002) *Confucius: The Golden Rule*. Illustrated by Frederic Clement. Arthur A. Levine Books.

Gruzalski, Bart. (1999) *On the Buddha*. Wadsworth Publishing.

Hanh, Thich Nhat. (1999) *The Heart of Buddha's Teaching*. Broadway.

Inglis, John. (1999) *On Aquinas*. Wadsworth Publishing.

May, Hope. (1999) *On Socrates*. Wadsworth Publishing.

Peterman, John. (1999) *On Plato*. Wadsworth Publishing.

Plato, John M. Cooper, and D. S. Hutchinson. (1997) *Plato: Complete Works*. Hackett Publishing Company.

Thomson, Garrett. (1999) *On Aristotle*. Wadsworth Publishing.

34

Julia Morgan Built a Castle
by Celeste Davidson Mannis

Use this book as a segue into designing on paper and perhaps actually constructing a model building. A model built or drawn to scale via this activity could incorporate creativity as well as mathematical calculations.

Idea Shelf

Mannis, Celeste Davidson. (2006) *Julia Morgan Built a Castle*. Illustrated by Miles Hyman. Viking Juvenile. ISBN: 0-670-05964-1.

Bookshelf

Annotation

Julia Morgan (1872–1957) grew up in California with her eye on activities normally reserved for the male members of her family. She did not particularly enjoy playing with dolls or other traditionally female pastimes. She loved adventure, and during her youth observed the many buildings going up and wondered how they fit together. She met her cousin Pierre LeBrun, an architect in New York City. She thought he had the most exciting job in the world. Julia began to dream of being an architect, too. Morgan was the only woman in her engineering class. Her favorite teacher, Bernard Maybeck, played an important role in helping her figure things out. She applied to an architecture school in France. For two years, she waited to be accepted; she was admitted and spent four years there—she made milestones. She became the first licensed woman architect. When the earthquake of 1906 destroyed much of San Francisco, the buildings Morgan had designed were still standing. She had completed more than 450 projects by the time William Randolph Hearst approached her in 1919 to build him a summer home in the Santa Lucia Mountains, just above the village of San Simeon, California. The project went on for twenty-eight years before work was stopped in 1947.

An author's note provides additional details about Morgan's career and about the San Simeon Castle. End pages provide a look at architectural drawings.

Curriculum Link: Architects, Careers, William Randolph Hearst

Background

William Randolph Hearst (April 29, 1863–August 14, 1951) was a self-made millionaire, having made his fortune by operating his father's newspaper empire. (His father was given *The San Francisco Examiner* as payment for a gambling debt.) After graduating from Harvard, Hearst took over the newspaper and became an American newspaper magnate and leading newspaper publisher. He built an empire of thirty newspapers. He ran for political office in New York State but lost each time. His influence came through his newspaper empire. While Hearst became more conservative in his later life, his estate was anything but. His estate near San Simeon, on a hill overlooking the Pacific Ocean, was located halfway between Los Angeles and San Francisco. In 1957, a few years after his death, the Hearst Corporation donated the estate to the state of California. It is now a State Historical Monument and a National Historic Landmark and is open for public tours. The estate was officially named "La Cuesta Encantada" ("The Enchanted Hill"), but Hearst most often referred to it as "the ranch."

Hearst approached Julia Morgan when she was forty-seven years of age and an established San Francisco architect. In 1947, Hearst left the castle for the last time and work was stopped on San Simeon. Morgan was seventy-five years old. She retired in the early 1950s and lived a quiet life until her death in 1957, the year the estate was donated to the state.

Extension Ideas

1. The state of California maintains a Web site about the Hearst Castle, the Hearst San Simeon State Historical Monument at <http://www.hearstcastle.com/>. The site has information about the principals involved in building the Hearst Castle. Investigate their backgrounds and create a time line showing the intersections of their lives.
2. Even though Hearst was said to be conservative, he respected the work of Morgan—a pioneer as a woman in the field of architecture. What other projects and opinions did Hearst have about events of a national and political nature? In light of today's political environment, which would you consider to be conservative?

Books to Explore

About Julia Morgan/Randolph Hearst:

Boutelle, Sara Holmes. (1995) *Julia Morgan, Architect*. Abbeville Press.

Kastner, Victoria. (2000) *Hearst Castle: The Biography of a Country House*. Harry N. Abrams.

Proctor, Ben. (1998) *William Randolph Hearst: The Early Years, 1863–1910*. Oxford University Press.

Proctor, Ben. (2007) *William Randolph Hearst: The Later Years, 1911–1951*. Oxford University Press.

Wilson, Mark. (2007) *Julia Morgan: Architect of Beauty*. Gibbs Smith Publisher.

About building/architecture:

Ames, Lee J. (1991) *Draw 50 Buildings and Other Structures: The Step-by-Step Way to Draw Castles and Cathedrals, Skyscrapers and Bridges, and So Much More....* Broadway.

Arbogast, Joan Marie. (2004) *Buildings in Disguise: Architecture That Looks Like Animals, Food, and Other Things.* Boyds Mills Press.

Caney, Steven. (2006) *Steven Caney's Ultimate Building Book.* Running Press Kids.

Salvadori, Mario. (2000) *The Art of Construction: Projects and Principles for Beginning Engineers & Architects.* Chicago Review Press.

35

Jeannette Rankin: First Lady of Congress
by Trish Marx

Idea Shelf

Hillary Rodham Clinton made a million cracks in the glass ceiling when she ran a very vigorous campaign for the presidency of the United States. Her groundbreaking campaign, although unsuccessful in gaining the nomination, did open the doorway a little wider for women. Her campaign was followed by the nomination of Sarah Palin for vice president of the United States on the Republican ticket. Geraldine Ferraro, who was nominated as a vice presidential candidate on the 1984 Democratic ticket alongside Walter Mondale, preceded both Clinton and Palin. Jeannette Rankin, however, was first to crack through the glass ceiling when she became the first woman to be elected to the U.S. Congress, in 1916. Share some history and inspire students to break their own barriers by sharing Rankin's story. Ask students to choose someone they know who broke a barrier (no matter how small of a step it was) and to develop an oral, written, or visual presentation about that person.

Marx, Trish. (2006) *Jeannette Rankin: First Lady of Congress.* Illustrated by Dan Andreasen. Margaret K. McElderry Books. ISBN-10: 0-689-86290-3; ISBN-13: 978-0-689-86290-8.

Bookshelf

Annotation

Jeannette Rankin was born on June 11, 1880, in Montana. Her father had come from Canada and her mother from New Hampshire. John and Olive Rankin raised six children, Jeannette being the oldest. When she was just nine years old, Montana became a state. At the age of twelve, she sewed up a nasty gash on a horse on the family ranch. She was industrious and worked hard. She became the first Rankin child to attend the University of Montana—a school her father helped to open. She began a teaching career while her brother, Wellington, went off to Harvard in Boston, Massachusetts. When Jeannette and a college friend traveled to Massachusetts to visit, Wellington saw to it that they were able to experience the social life and shopping in the area. He even took them to Washington, D.C., where Jeannette met President Theodore Roosevelt. Rankin also wanted to see the slums, and from all of her experiences she came to know that she had to return to Montana and help *all* women have better lives. One way she could do that was to work for a law that would allow women to vote—and then they could vote for laws that would benefit women and children.

Soon she found her way back east, where she studied social work at the New York School of Philanthropy. Her work in the reformist movement caused her to be even more resolved to make a difference. She was almost thirty years old when she moved to Washington State and enrolled at the University of Washington in Seattle to study how to make and change laws. She helped the women of Washington State gain the right to vote—it was just the fifth state to pass suffrage laws. Upon returning to Montana, she began her work to get the vote for women in that state. She worked long and hard for suffrage. The bill introduced in 1910 was defeated but finally passed in 1914.

By 1915, Rankin was thinking about her future. She traveled by herself to New Zealand to think and reflect on her goals. When she returned, she had renewed her spirit by observing the strong women she met there.

Rankin's next step was to run for Congress—she did and was elected. It took days for all of the ballots to arrive in the capitol. After first being told she had lost, she found out on November 10, 1916, that she had been elected. She would be the first woman in the U.S. Congress. The next years were as eventful. She voted against U.S. involvement in World War I and lost her reelection bid. She settled near Athens, Georgia, and began to enjoy a simple life, reading by candles, sleeping on a sleeping porch, and mentoring young girls and boys.

By 1937, there was talk of another war, and Rankin (who would be fifty-nine years old in 1939) decided to run for Congress again. She was against war as much as ever. By now her brother was a wealthy rancher and he offered to give her advice and financial support if she moved back to Montana. In 1940, she was, once again, elected to Congress. Montanans were firmly behind her antiwar stance until the attack on Pearl Harbor, and then her antiwar stance was once again in disfavor. She was the only person to vote "no" to authorize entry into the war. That ended her career in Washington and she returned to Georgia. But Rankin continued to be active in her antiwar efforts. One of her last efforts was to lead a march against the Vietnam War—she was eighty-seven years old. She died in California on May 18, 1973, just weeks before her ninety-third birthday.

Curriculum Link: Legislative Branch, Women in Politics, Women's Suffrage

Background

Jeannette Rankin was the first woman to be elected to the U.S. Congress; since then, 250 more women have served in Congress (212 as representatives and thirty-one as senators; eight women have served in both chambers). Nancy Pelosi of California became the first woman to serve as Speaker of the House.

Extension Ideas

1. Locate the names of women who served in the U.S. Congress from a specific state. Creatively report to colleagues about the person you have identified; create posters, interviews, plays about her life, and so forth.
2. Create a list of ten facts about women in Congress.
3. Use the facts from the government's Women in Congress Web site at <http://womenincongress.house.gov/> to help analyze the trend in the number of women serving in the U.S. Congress over the years, and develop a presentation about these women: posters, a PowerPoint presentation, a "hall of fame," or other visual display.

Books to Explore

Palmer, Barbara. (2008) *Breaking the Political Glass Ceiling: Women and Congressional Elections.* Routledge.

Sanbonmatsu, Kira. (2006) *Where Women Run: Gender and Party in the American States.* University of Michigan Press.

36

Marvelous Mattie: How Margaret E. Knight Became an Inventor
by Emily Arnold McCully

Begin a focus on inventions and inventors with this account of a young inventor. Plan to make a flat-bottomed sack, a procedure developed by Margaret E. Knight. Share her idea and think about what else might be invented/developed.

Idea Shelf

Bookshelf

McCully, Emily Arnold. (2006) *Marvelous Mattie: How Margaret E. Knight Became an Inventor*. Illustrated by Emily Arnold McCully. Farrar, Straus and Giroux. ISBN-10: 0-374-34810-3; ISBN-13: 978-0-374-34810-6.

Annotation

This is a biography of Margaret E. Knight, who was born on February 14, 1838, in York, Maine, and died on October 12, 1914, in Framingham, Massachusetts. Her father died when she was ten and soon her mother moved Knight and her two brothers to Massachusetts, where her mother and brothers could find work in the mills. By the time Mattie was twelve, she was working in the mills, too. One day she witnessed an accident and that set her to thinking about a safeguard to prevent the loom from hurting (or killing) anyone when the yarn/thread broke. She designed a guard of sorts that would protect or stop the loom the minute the shuttle came loose. Knight was always interested in machines and often built things such as kites and sleds for her brothers. The safety stop action device for the loom was her first real invention.

As Knight grew older, she moved out on her own, and after several jobs, went to work in a paper-bag-making factory. The bags were the envelope type. She thought the bags would be more convenient if they had flat bottoms so she set out to create the design and make a machine to manufacture such bags. She kept detailed notes of every stage of the development. She had a machine shop build a prototype but Charles F. Annan stole the design and patented it one week before Knight arrived at the patent office. She had to hire an attorney, but her detailed drawings convinced the judge that she was indeed the inventor even though Annan asserted that, "Miss Knight could not possibly understand the mechanical complexities of the machine."

Knight won that litigation. At the end of the trial, a representative of a manufacturing firm offered her $50,000 for the invention. She declined and went into business for herself. The *Woman's Journal* published an article about her manufacturing enterprise in its December 2, 1872, issue.

Curriculum Link: Inventions, Women Inventors, Paper Bags, Child Labor

Background

After she moved with her mother to Massachusetts, Knight became part of the textile industry that used much child labor. At ten, she started working at Amoskeag Mills in Manchester, New Hampshire, and by age twelve, she had developed the safety stop mechanism for the loom at the mills. Perhaps her most used invention is the flat-bottomed paper bag—but few are aware of the inventor's name. The need for her first invention, the safeguard for the weaving loom, resulted from the unsafe conditions in the textile mills; many of the mills involved child labor (as evidenced by Knight's work there). Lewis Hine was an investigative photographer who was instrumental in bringing attention to the plight of the child laborers and helped prompt the establishment of the National Child Labor Committee.

Another topic inherent in this book is the fact that women could not, in the early years of U.S. history, register (patent) inventions in their own names. The earliest patent granted to a woman was awarded December 8, 1808, to Hazel Irwin of Boston, Massachusetts. Many inventions that we now know to have been invented by women were officially credited to their husbands or fathers, a fact that probably contributed to Charles F. Annan's belief that he could assert Knight's inability to understand her own invention and that he could convince a jury based on that assertion.

Extension Ideas

1. Prepare a presentation introducing Knight to others. Investigate more about her. What else did she invent? What inventions are still actively in use today?
   Ideas for types of presentations:

   - Written presentation
   - List "Ten Things to Know About Margaret E. Knight"
   - PowerPoint presentation
   - "Radio" interview with Knight regarding her inventions or perhaps her strategy for presenting her defense against Annan's assertion that he rightly owned the copyright to the paper-bag-folding machine
   - A play depicting a scene in her life
   - Lead a roundtable discussion about her work and life

2. What role did Lewis Hine play in the development of child-labor laws? Present to others your findings (use one of the presentation ideas from the above list or another type of presentation that might be appropriate).
3. Read a fictional account involving child labor and Lewis Hine, *Counting on Grace* by Elizabeth Winthrop (Wendy Lamb Books, 2006).
4. Investigate women inventors and prepare a presentation to introduce a collection of inventors to others or concentrate on one specific inventor and prepare a presentation similar to one of those suggested for Knight.
5. Develop a time line showing the evolution of the National Child Labor Committee and discuss its implication for factories, children, and the nation's economy in general.
6. Investigate the lives and work of these women inventors and prepare displays showing their inventions and how they affect the lives of people today.

- Randi Altschul
- Virgie Ammons
- Dr. Betsy Ancker-Johnson
- Mary Anderson
- Virginia Apgar
- Barbara Askins
- Patricia Bath
- Miriam E. Benjamin
- Patricia Billings
- Katherine Blodgett
- Bessie Blount
- Sarah Boone
- Rachel Fuller Brown
- Ursula Burns
- Alexa Canady
- Jewel Plummer Cobb
- Josephine Garis Cochran
- Martha J. Coston
- Dianne Croteau
- Marie Curie
- Marion Donovan
- Ellen F. Eglin
- Gertrude Belle Elion
- Angela D. Ferguson
- Edith Flanigan
- Helen Free
- Sally Fox
- Frances Gabe
- Lillian Gilbreth
- Sarah E. Goode
- Bette Nesmith Graham
- Temple Grandin
- Evelyn Boyd Granville
- Dannellia Gladden Green
- Kathryn "KK" Gregory
- Bessie Blount Griffin

- Ruth Handler
- Betty Wright Harris
- Elizabeth Lee Hazen
- Beulah Henry
- Dorothy Crowfoot Hodgkin
- Krisztina Holly
- Erna Schneider Hoover
- Grace Hopper
- Aprille Joy Ericsson Jackson
- Shirley Ann Jackson
- Mary Phelps Jacob
- Mae Jemison
- Amanda Theodosia Jones
- Marjorie Stewart Joyner
- Anna Keichline
- Mary Kenner
- Mary Kies
- Reatha Clark King
- Gabriele Knecht
- Margaret Knight
- Stephanie Louise Kwolek
- Hedy Lamarr
- Ada Lovelace
- Annie Turnbo Malone
- Sybilla Masters
- Ann Moore
- Krysta Morlan
- Bessie Nesmith
- Lyda Newman
- Julie Newmar
- Ellen Ochoa
- Alice H. Parker
- Betty Rozier
- Patsy Sherman
- Mildred Austin Smith
- Giuliana Tesoro
- Valerie Thomas
- Ann Tsukamoto
- Harriet Tubman
- Lisa Vallino
- Madame C. J. Walker
- Ruth Wakefield
- Mary Walton
- Carol Wior
- Jane Cooke Wright
- Rosalyn Sussman Yalow
- Roger Arliner Young
- Chavonda J. Jacobs Young
- Rachel Zimmerman

Books to Explore

Bartoletti, Susan Campbell. (1999) *Kids On Strike!* Houghton Mifflin.

Brill, Marlene Targ. (2001) *Margaret Knight, Girl Inventor*. Millbrook.

Casey, Susan. (1997) *Women Invent! Two Centuries of Discoveries That Have Shaped Our World*. Chicago Review Press.

Freedman, Russell. (1994) *Kids at Work: Lewis Hine and the Crusade Against Child Labor*. Clarion.

Lasky, Kathryn. (2003) *Vision of Beauty: The Story of Sarah Breedlove Walker*. Illustrated by Nneka Bennett. Candlewick.

McCully, Emily Arnold. (1996) *The Bobbin Girl*. Dial.

Mofford, Juliet H. (1997) *Child Labor in America* (Perspectives on History Series). Photographs by Lewis Hine. Discovery Enterprise.

Stille, Darlene R. (1995) *Extraordinary Women Scientists*. Children's Press.

Sullivan, Otha Richard. (2001) *Black Stars: African American Women Scientists and Inventors*. Wiley.

Thimmesch, Catherine. (2000) *Girls Think of Everything: Stories of Ingenious Inventions by Women*. Illustrated by Melissa Sweet. Houghton Mifflin.

Thimmesh, Catherine. (2002) *The Sky's the Limit: Stories of Discovery by Women and Girls*. Illustrated by Melissa Sweet. Houghton Mifflin.

Tucker, Tom. (1998) *Brainstorm! The Stories of Twenty American Kid Inventors*. Farrar, Straus and Giroux.

37

Christmas in the Trenches
by John McCutcheon

Idea Shelf

The "peace truce" at Christmastime during World War I really did happen, and this book helps us know about the event and provides a peek into the nature of war in the early 1900s. Students who have had parents, aunts, uncles, brothers, or cousins involved in the Iraq and Afghanistan wars may have some thoughts on how the war environment has changed drastically. Today, there would be no trenches, but there are air strikes called in by Global Positioning System locations. Technology has changed how wars are fought. Trenches have been replaced by computerized maps and strategic maneuvers calculated by statistics fed into a database.

McCutcheon, John. (2006) *Christmas in the Trenches*. Illustrated by Henri Sorensen. Peachtree Publishers. ISBN-10: 1561453749; ISBN-13: 978-1561453740.

Bookshelf

Annotation

In 1984, singer and songwriter John McCutcheon first heard the story of the Christmas Truce in the trenches during World War I. The story McCutcheon heard actually began in 1914 during World War I. Over the years, the story has been passed from soldier to soldier and from family to friend. Since the truce actually occurred in several locations along the trenches, there were variations on the same theme. McCutcheon found a song in the story—a narrative song that was not meant to be historical but rather to be representative of the truce. McCutcheon's song—now the text for his book—is pure fiction but conveys the spirit of the events that occurred in many places across the trenches.

Curriculum Link: World War I (1914–1919)

Background

During World War I, German soldiers positioned themselves in trenches across from trenches where French and English soldiers were positioned. Guns were aimed at the opposing trenches and battles ensued. But on Christmas Eve 1914, the melodious strands of well-known Christmas songs came from German trenches. Soon singing emanated from both trenches. Eventually the men emerged to the banks above the trenches, and for a short time, in many locations along the trenches, the men warmed themselves in a universal friendship brought about by the season. The following day, the moment was set aside and fighting resumed—at least until Christmas Eve 1915, when a few repeat incidents occurred. This is a well-documented event that has found little publicity over the years. Various soldiers returned with similar stories of truces that occurred in different locations along the 1,548 miles of trenches dug during the war. While this seems like an unusual event in today's times, when going to war means total war, temporary truces were not uncommon in earlier wars. Soldiers often washed their clothes and filled their canteens side by side in a river. Even during the U.S. Civil War, after the huge loss of life at Cold Harbor, Virginia, both Union and Confederate soldiers declared a truce in order to bury their dead—they traded souvenirs as well.

Extension Ideas

1. Learn more about the World War I truce episodes by searching on the WWW using these terms "world war I Christmas truce" (key into the search engine without the quotes). Any site with information will need to be evaluated for credibility. This would be an excellent opportunity to engage students in activities to assess the credibility of informational sites.
2. Compare the circumstances surrounding the World War I Christmas Truce with the events that take place in Trinka Hakes Noble's *The Last Brother*, a story from the Civil War.

Books to Explore

Granfield, Linda. (1995; 2005) *In Flanders Field: The Story of the Poem by John McCrae*. Fitzhenry & Whiteside Ltd.

Granfield, Linda. (2002) *Where Poppies Grow: A World War I Companion*. Fitzhenry & Whiteside Ltd.

Noble, Trinka Hakes. (2006) *The Last Brother*. Illustrated by Robert Papp. Sleeping Bear Press.

Weintraub, Stanley. (2002) *Silent Night: The Story of the World War I Christmas Truce*. Plume.

Wunderli, Stephen. (2003) *Silent Night, Holy Night: The Story of the Christmas Truce*. Illustrated by Robert T. Barrett with a CD narrated by Walter Cronkite accompanied by the Mormon Tabernacle Choir. Shadow Mountain.

38

Hammerin' Hank: The Life of Hank Greenberg
by Yona Zeldis McDonough

Idea Shelf

Jackie Robinson broke the color barrier in baseball. Hank Greenberg broke the barrier for Jewish players. Introduce this courageous man to students and ask them to identify other people (either in public or in their personal lives) who are courageous and have made inroads for those who follow them. This is a great discussion topic.

Bookshelf

McDonough, Yona Zeldis. (2006) *Hammerin' Hank: The Life of Hank Greenberg*. Illustrated by Malcah Zeldis. Walker Books for Young Readers. ISBN-13: 978-0-8027-8997-6 (hardcover); ISBN-10: 0-8027-8997-8 (hardcover); ISBN-13: 978-0-8027-8998-3 (reinf.); ISBN-10: 0-8027-8998-6 (reinf.)

Annotation

Not the first Jewish player in the major leagues but certainly one of the most notable, Hank Greenberg was booed and faced much prejudicial behavior. An encounter with Jackie Robinson, the first black baseball player in the major leagues, showed a level of empathy and friendship between the two of them.

Henry Benjamin Greenberg grew up in New York, first in Greenwich Village and later in the Bronx. After school he played ball for hours and came home at dark. His parents did not approve of his interest in making a career of baseball but he was determined. After three years in the minor leagues, he was called up to the Detroit Tigers' major league team. The year was 1933.

In 1938, Greenberg edged close to the home-run record of Babe Ruth—he hit fifty-eight in the season and had five games left to beat the record, sixty home runs in a season. But opposing pitchers did not give him the opportunity to hit two more home runs;

each chose to walk him. There were other records, though. In 1941, Pearl Harbor was bombed, and Greenberg was the first major league player to enlist. He returned to the major leagues when the war was over in 1945. His first year back was astounding. The Tigers won the World Series that year. A salary dispute with the Tigers took him to the Pirates for the 1947 season. Eventually, Greenberg retired from active play and became involved in management, and then he retired from baseball entirely, carving out a career on Wall Street. He became the first Jewish co-owner of a major league team and the first Jewish player inducted into the Baseball Hall of Fame. He died in his sleep in 1986 at the age of seventy-four.

The final pages of this book present statistics, a chronology, and a time line of Greenberg's life as well as a glossary of terms and a bibliography of resources.

Curriculum Link: Biography, Baseball, Overcoming Adversities, Jewish history

Background

Greenberg became the first notable Jewish major league ballplayer, the first Jewish co-owner of a Major League Baseball team, the Jewish player inducted into the Baseball Hall of Fame, and first major league ballplayer to enlist in World War II.

Extension Ideas

1. Compare the career of Greenberg with that of Jackie Robinson. Create a time line of each of their careers, marking significant events in each man's career.
2. Compare and contrast incidents in their lives—how were each treated in the major leagues? How did Robinson and Greenberg face adversity?
3. Research and make a list of other firsts in Major League Baseball. Who was the first to pitch a no-hitter? Who was the first player–manager? And so forth.

Books to Explore

Greenberg, Hank, and Ira Berkow. (2001) *Hank Greenberg: The Story of My Life*. Benchmark Press.

39

Gone Wild: An Endangered Animal Alphabet
by David McLimans

Idea Shelf

What's happening with endangered animals in your area? What is being done to rescue endangered animals? Share this book and then investigate endangered animals in your community, state, and region. Present the information to fellow students.

Bookshelf

McLimans, David. (2006) *Gone Wild: An Endangered Animal Alphabet.* Walker & Company. ISBN-10: 0-8027-9563-3 (hardcover); ISBN-13: 978-0-8027-9563-2 (hardcover); ISBN-10: 0-8027-9564-1; ISBN-13: 978-0-8027-9564-9.

Annotation

Many of the animals on the planet are endangered, some critically, and some less so, and some are vulnerable or threatened. The endangered animals selected for inclusion in this book were chosen because they presented the illustrator with illustrative possibilities.

A = Chinese alligator
B = Madagascar tree boa
C = naked characin
D = blue duck
E = St. Helena earwig
F = Andean flamingo
G = swan goose
H = Bushman hare
I = crested ibis
J = Florida scrub-jay
K = Keys short-winged conehead katydid

L = snow leopard
M = prairie sphinx moth
N = black-spotted newt
O = spotted owl
P = piping plover
Q = spotted-tail quoll
R = black rhinoceros
S = Oriental white stork
T = Andean yapir
U = bald-headed uakari
V = Baluchistan vole
W = Ethiopian wolf
X = cape-clawed frog
Y = wild yak
Z = Grevy's zebra

The main section of the book presents each of these animals with an illustration of the animal in the shape of the alphabetical letter and boxed statistics: class, habitat, range, threats, and status.

The final pages list each of the animals again in a red silhouette against black. The text that accompanies the silhouette describes the animal and its habitat and expands on the reasons the animal is vulnerable or endangered. A list of ten agencies/organizations (and their Web sites) that work with conservation is appended along with a list of seven books for further reading.

Curriculum Link: Endangered Animals, Illuminated Letters

Background

When McLimans portrayed each animal, he used a graphic black and white embellished letter to represent each. In medieval days, monks created illuminated letters to draw attention to various letters in manuscripts. The illumination always was embellished with gold that shone light through the colored paint that was part of the decoration. McLimans's work is not technically an illuminated letter, but his black and white creations are embellishments that have common elements.

Extension Ideas

1. Investigate the origin and style of illuminated letters from medieval days to the present. Try making some decorated letters as an art project. Use your initials to create a piece of artwork.
2. Investigate information about any of the endangered animals featured in McLimans' book or in *Panda Bear, Panda Bear, What Do You See?* by Bill Martin Jr. and Eric Carle (Henry Holt, 2003).

- water buffalo
- spider monkey
- macaroni penguin
- whooping crane
- bald eagle
- sea lion
- panda bear
- red wolf
- black panther
- green sea turtle

3. Investigate additional threatened or endangered animals and create a poster about an animal in a style similar to McLimans' work in *Gone Wild*.

- black-footed ferret
- African elephant
- Asian elephant
- Florida panther
- American alligator
- Chinese alligator
- Tibetan antelope
- giant sable antelope
- giant armadillo
- bandicoot (several species)
- bats (several species)
- American black bear
- Mexican grizzly bear
- Mongolian beaver
- Jamaican boa (and other species)
- Mexican bobcat
- cheetah
- chimpanzee
- chinchilla
- whooping crane
- mountain yellow-legged frog

Books to Explore

Donald, Rhonda Lucas. (2002) *Endangered Animals*. Scholastic.

Hoose, Phillip. (2004) *The Race to Save the Lord God Bird*. Farrar, Straus and Giroux.

Martin, Bill Jr. (2003) *Panda Bear, Panda Bear, What Do You See?* Henry Holt.

Montgomery, Sy. (2006) *Quest for the Tree Kangaroo: An Expedition to the Cloud Forest of New Guinea*. Illustrated by Nic Bishop. Houghton Mifflin.

40

Into the West: From Reconstruction to the Final Days of the American Frontier
by James McPherson

This book has several sections that can be shared with various units dealing with the years following the Civil War. Read the "Reconstruction Begins: 1863–1864," discussing the western movement, and read "The American Frontier: 1865." Much little-known information about Native Americans can be found in "The First Settlers: The Native Americans." Share these chapters, one by one—it's too much for one sitting. And then engage in some great discussions.

Idea Shelf

McPherson, James M. (2006) *Into the West: From Reconstruction to the Final Days of the American Frontier.* Atheneum Books for Young Readers/Simon & Schuster. ISBN-10: 0-689-86543-0; ISBN-13: 978-0-689-86543-5.

Bookshelf

Annotation

This ninety-page picture book filled with photographs provides a brief overview/introduction to several topics pertaining to the events that followed the Civil War through the end of the nineteenth century. Each topic is introduced with a single-page essay and illustrated with full-page period illustration or photo. A Quick Facts sidebar deals with each topic. Topics include:

The Civil War
Reconstruction Begins: 1863–1864

Topics to investigate:

- Wade-Davis Bill
- Pocket veto

The Homestead Act
The American Frontier: 1865
  Topics to investigate:

- Statehood of California, Oregon, Nevada, and Kansas
- Discovery of gold in California and Nevada

The First Settlers: The Native Americans
  Topics to investigate:

- Cherokee chief Stand Watie, a Confederate brigadier general who was the last Confederate commander to surrender (June 23, 1865)
- Citizenship of Native Americans (status and rights)
- Mode of transportation, including triangular-shaped carts, "travois"

Assassination of President Abraham Lincoln
  Topics to investigate:

- John Wilkes Booth (April 14, 1865)
- Dr. Samuel Mudd (origin of phrase "your name is mud")
- Abolitionist John Brown

Andrew Johnson and Presidential Reconstruction
  Topics to investigate:

- Role of Thaddeus Stevens, a Republican representative from Pennsylvania

Contrabands and Freedmen
  Topics to investigate:

- Term "contraband" as applied to slaves as seized property and contraband gained from the war—African Americans who escaped to the North (and to freedom)
- Freedman's Bureau (and its role in helping both black and white southerners)

Carpetbaggers and Scalawags
  Topics to investigate:

- Define "carpetbaggers" (northerners who stayed or traveled to the South to become part of the southern government's inner structure); "scalawags" (southerners who were believed to have joined the North when they took a job in the new state's administration/government)

The Transcontinental Railroad
  Topics to investigate:

- Chinese immigration in America
- Central Pacific Railroad (blasted its way east from California)
- Union Pacific Railroad (moved west across the prairie from Nebraska)
- Promontory Point, Nevada, May 10, 1869, the site of the last mile of railroad track
- Cause of buffalo extinction

The Civil War Amendments
Topics to investigate:

- The Thirteenth Amendment, which had to be ratified by states that wished to rejoin the Union (abolished slavery)
- The Fifteenth Amendment (authorized the vote for free men but did not include women; that was to come in 1920 with the Nineteenth Amendment)
- Susan B. Anthony (tested the Fifteenth Amendment in November 1872)

Land and Social Reform in the South
Topics to investigate:

- Sharecroppers
- Confiscated land and the role of Freedman's Bureau

Sodbusters and Barbed Wire
Topics to investigate:

- 1874 plague of grasshoppers across the prairie
- Fences on the prairie
- Invention of barbed wire (by Illinois farmer Joseph F. Glidden) and its impact on frontier life

Congressional Reconstruction
Topics to investigate:

- The sixteeen African Americans elected to Congress during this time

The Impeachment of Andrew Johnson
President Ulysses S. Grant
Topics to investigate:

- Relationship to writer/publisher Samuel Clemens (Mark Twain)
- Military career

Corruption, Scandal, and the Civil Servant
Topics to investigate:

- Mark Twain (Samuel Clemens) and Charles Dudley Warner—role in writing about business/political scandals
- Credit Mobile scandal
- Bribes (including President Ulysses S. Grant's first-term and second-term vice presidents Schuyler Colfax Jr. and Henry Wilson)

Immigrants
Topics to investigate:

- General trends of immigration: Danes in Montana, Germans in North Dakota, Czechs in Iowa, Polish in Illinois, Chinese in California, etc.

Roughing It: Women on the Frontier
  Topics to investigate:

- Establishing schools on the frontier
- Montgomery Ward (business and mail-order sales)

Wyoming Territory and Women's Suffrage
  Topics to investigate:

- Wyoming statehood
- Nineteenth Amendment
- History of women's suffrage
- Seneca Falls, New York, and its role in women's rights
- Esther Morris (a leader for women's suffrage in Wyoming)

The Civil Rights Act of 1875
  Topics to investigate:

- Readmission of seceded states (all had been readmitted by 1868 except Texas, which wasn't readmitted until 1870)
- Blanche Bruce and Hiram Revels, two African American representatives from Mississippi
- Revels' relationship to Confederate president Jefferson Davis
- Senator Charles Sumner and his role in denouncing discrimination

Prejudice, Racism, and the Ku Klux Klan
  Topics to investigate:

- Ku Klux Klan Act of 1871
- Nathan Bedford Forrest
- President Ulysses S. Grant

The End of Reconstruction: 1877
  Topics to investigate:

- Civil service system
- President Rutherford B. Hayes
- Freedman's Bank and Freedman's Aid Society

The Cowboy
  Topics to investigate:

- Origin of the present meaning of the word "cowboy"
- Era of the cowboy (1865–1885)
- Theodore Roosevelt's career as a cowboy

The Cattle Drives
  Topics to investigate:

- Branding cattle
- Creating unique brands
- Inventions that changed the way cowboys worked (such as refrigeration)

Map for Highways for the Herds
    Topics to investigate:

- Distance traveled

Broken Treaties and Reservations
    Topics to investigate:

- Native American concepts of land ownership
- Treaties signed 1853–1857 (both with Native Americans and with groups such as the Texans
- General Allotment Act of 1887 or Dawes Severalty Act (sponsored by Senator Henry L. Dawes)
- Chief Sitting Bull (Sioux)
- Crazy Horse (Sioux)
- Chief Satanta (Kiowa tribe)
- Chief Red Cloud (Sioux)

The Outlaws
    Topics to investigate:

- Dalton Brothers (Bob, Emmett, and Grattan)
- Pearl Hart (who was known in 1899 as the last stagecoach bandit in the West)
- Billy the Kid
- Belle Starr
- Jesse James
- Frank James
- Quantrill Raiders
- Younger Brothers (Cole, Jim, Bob, and John)
- Butch Cassidy (Robert LeRoy Parker) and the Sundance Kid (Harry Alonzo Longabaugh)

The Wild West in Popular Culture
    Topics to investigate:

- Ned Buntline, "king of the dime novelists"
- Buntline Special
- Buffalo Bill (Medal of Honor winner; real name William Cody)
- Wild Bill Hickok (James Butler Hickok)
- Annie Oakley (Little Sure Shot)

The Lawmen
    Topics to investigate:

- Frederick Douglass
- Judge Roy Bean
- Wyatt Earp (and brothers Virgil and Morgan)
- John Henry "Doc" Holliday
- Calamity Jane
- Pat Garrett
- Bass Reeves

The Indian Wars in the Northern Plains
  Topics to investigate:

- Chief Joseph of the Nez Perce
- Coleville Reservation in Washington State (where Chief Joseph was sent)
- Indian Territory (where the members of the Nez Perce were forced to go)

Sitting Bull, Crazy Horse, and the Sioux
  Topics to investigate:

- Sitting Bull
- Crazy Horse
- Lakota Sioux

The Battle of the Little Bighorn
  Topics to investigate:

- George Armstrong Custer
- Thomas Custer
- Crazy Horse

The Buffalo Soldiers
  Topics to investigate:

- Henry O. Flipper (the first African American to graduate from West Point)
- First Sergeant Moses William
- Ninth and Tenth calvary regiments

Frontier Arts and Letters
  Topics to investigate:

- Samuel Clemens (Mark Twain)
- Albert Bierstadt (western landscapes—paintings)
- Thomas Moran
- National Park Service
- Willa Cather
- Frederick Remington
- Laura Ingalls Wilder
- Owen Wister
- O. E. Rölvaag
- Orion Clemens (brother of Samuel Clemens and secretary to the territorial governor of Nevada)

Indian Wars in the Southwest
  Topics to investigate:

- Lieutenant General Philip Sheridan
- Tosawi, Comanche chief
- Bureau of Indian Affairs
- Fort Wingate

- Navaho (1863 events)
- Colonel Kit Carson
- Bosque Redondo
- Treaty of 1868

Geronimo and the Apache
    Topics to investigate:

- General George Crook
- Apache Chief Geronimo
- Carlisle Indian School, Pennsylvania
- Kiowa and Comanche offer of part of their reservation to the Apache
- Apache removal to Marion, Florida (and its ramifications)
- Vincent Colyer (Vincent the Good; a member of an Indian reform group)

The Ghost Dance
    Topics to investigate:

- Ghost Dance (history of)
- Sun Dance (history of)
- Sitting Bull's death (circumstances)
- Wounded Knee (history of massacre by cavalry)

The Last Days of the Frontier: 1890
    Topics to investigate:

- Role of the Census Bureau in declaring the frontier closed
- Establishment of the national census

The final pages of the book provide a glossary of terms, a bibliography, a list of Web sites for further research and investigation, and a full index.

Curriculum Link: Post-Civil War Era, Westward Movement

Background

With the signing of the Emancipation Proclamation and the discovery of gold in the West, the United States was going through many changes, politically, culturally, and economically. McPherson touches on just a few of the topics that are affected.

Extension Ideas

1. Use individual pages of this book as a read-aloud selection to build a background of knowledge for your students.
2. Encourage additional investigation of specific topics by identifying subtopics that might yield interesting questions to research.

3. Develop appropriate research technique instructional sessions to help students locate information necessary for finding the information they are interested in discovering. Recognize that each introductory page will not necessarily yield questions left unanswered and of interest, but many of them will. Capitalize on the interest generated.

Books to Explore

Each topic in the annotation will have a different set of books, periodical articles, and encyclopedia articles that will provide information on the topic. Use the topics to investigate suggestions as starting points to delve further into the topic introduced by the pages in McPherson's book. Explore your school and public libraries and the Internet (instruction regarding the credibility of Web sites would be useful lessons in conjunction with this search for more information).

41

Tuttle's Red Barn: The Story of America's Oldest Family Farm
by Rich Michelson

Read this book and then set out to investigate some landmarks in your community. What is the history? Standardize the writing presentation and then combine the chapters about each landmark into a book of community history. Make multiple copies and sell them at your school's next book fair.

Idea Shelf

Michelson, Rich. (2007) *Tuttle's Red Barn: The Story of America's Oldest Family Farm*. Illustrated by Mary Azarian. Putnam Juvenile. ISBN-10: 0399243542; ISBN-13: 978-0399243547.

Bookshelf

Annotation

John Tuttle left his home country, England, in 1632 and sailed across the Atlantic to settle in what was to become Dover, New Hampshire. His homestead was established on seven acres of land that have remained as the family farm for 375 years.

As the farm passed from generation to generation, the individuals participated in and observed the expansion of New England, fought in the American Revolution, became part of the Underground Railroad, sold maple syrup to Abraham Lincoln, and brought the first Model T to their community. Along the way, they added acreage (now more than forty acres) and transformed their farm's old red barn into a vibrant country store (1957) where they sell fresh produce, baked goods, and cheeses. In 1987, the family built a new building to showcase their expanded offerings. This book aptly provides a panorama of America's history through the story of this single farm and the Tuttle family.

Curriculum Link: Family History, New Hampshire,
Tourist Information, Genealogy

Background

For up-to-date information on the farm as it is today, visit Tuttle's Red Barn's Web site
at <http://www.tuttlesredbarn.net/>.

Extension Ideas

1. Create a historical time line from 1630 to the present day. On the top of the line put
   in the Tuttle family events and below the line put in significant events from the history of the United States: who is president, major political events (wars, Declaration
   of Independence, etc.), inventions, and births and deaths of famous people in U.S.
   history.
2. Write a history of a popular location in your community. Interview people who
   have been associated with that location over as many years as possible. Then
   research in local history sources to find out as much information as possible. Check
   the local history section of your public library and the local newspaper archives.
3. Create a similar history for a location within your state. Create brochures and other
   public-relations items to promote that particular location.

Books to Explore

The Tuttles and the Red Barn are included in brief entries in the following books focusing on
   New Hampshire sites:
Scheller, Kay, and Bill Scheller. (2001) *Best New Hampshire Drives: 14 Tours in the Granite
   State*. Rev. ed. Jasper Heights Press.
Weeks, Silas B. (2002) *New England Quaker Meetinghouses, Past and Present*. Friends United
   Press.

42

Yankee Doodle America: The Spirit of 1776 from A to Z
by Wendell Minor

Pick twenty-six days and read one chapter a day—learn more about U.S history. Students will have their knowledge of history enhanced, and when these topics are encountered in formal class studies, they will have some schema regarding the person or event. Eventually, the ABC arrangement might become a model for investigative pieces that students write. Have each pupil choose a letter of the alphabet and write about a person or event in your community or during a historic period.

Idea Shelf

Minor, Wendell. (2006) *Yankee Doodle America: The Spirit of 1776 from A to Z*. Putnam Juvenile. ISBN: 0-399-24003-9

Bookshelf

Annotation

Minor identifies twenty-six significant people/places associated with the American Revolution (1765–1783). Each event is afforded an illustration and a short paragraph detailing its significance to the revolution. The items are:

A = Acts (Stamp Act)
B = Boston Massacre
C = Common Sense
D = Declaration (Declaration of Independence)
E = East India Company
F = Franklin (Benjamin)
G = George III (King, of England)
H = Henry (Patrick)
I = Independence

J = Jefferson (Thomas)
K = Knox (Henry)
L = Liberty
M = Militia
N = Native American
O = Old North Church
P = Pitcher (Molly)
Q = Quakers
R = Revere (Paul)
S = Stars and Stripes
T = Trenton
U = United (United States of America)
V = Valley Forge
W = Washington (George)
X = X Regiment (British Tenth)
Y = Yorktown
Z = Zane (Ebenezer; daughter Elizabeth)

Curriculum Link: History, United States

Background

This alphabetical organization uses twenty-six names/events in American history to organize chapters that bring readers twenty-six snippets of American history.

Extension Ideas

1. Read other history books, organized with an alphabetical listing. Then use this book and the others as models. Use the alphabet as an organizational device to make a list of important people/events in any era of history, the world, or any country. Annotate your list.

Books to Explore

Cheney, Lynn. (2002) *America: A Patriotic Primer*. Illustrated by Robin Preiss Glasser. Simon & Schuster Children's Books.

Chin-Lee, Cynthia. (2005) *Amelia to Zora: Twenty-Six Women Who Changed the World*. Illustrated by Megan Halsey and Sam Addy. Charlesbridge.

Chin-Lee, Cynthia. (2006) *Akira to Zoltán: Twenty-Six Men Who Changed the World*. Illustrated by Megan Halsey and Sam Addy. Charlesbridge.

43

Quest for the Tree Kangaroo: An Expedition to the Cloud Forest of New Guinea
by Sy Montgomery

This book is a great way to introduce another part of the world—New Guinea—and to highlight the work that goes on to save animals and the environment. It might even spark some career choices. Use this book as an introduction to a group reading of *The Race to Save the Lord God Bird* by Phillip Hoose.

Idea Shelf

Montgomery, Sy. (2006) *Quest for the Tree Kangaroo: An Expedition to the Cloud Forest of New Guinea.* Illustrated by Nic Bishop. Houghton Mifflin Books for Children. ISBN-10: 0-618-49641-6; ISBN-13: 978-0-618-49641-6.

Bookshelf

Annotation

A full summary of the scientific expedition to locate and help save from extinction, the rarest of the rare—the tree kangaroo. Ten kinds of tree kangaroos exist in the world today; the Matschie's tree kangaroo is among those living in the exotic cloud forests of New Guinea. New Guinea is the second-largest island on Earth (second only to Greenland) and has a variety of environments—jungles, mountains, volcanoes—and a large variety of strange and interesting animals. The tree kangaroo is the subject of this exhibition led by scientist Lisa Dabeck. She and her research team—a team that came to include the book's author and photographer—are intent on saving the tree kangaroo. The photographs are amazing and capture the atmosphere of this incredible ecosystem.

Maps in the book clearly show the geographical location. Discussions about conservation help readers know what they can do to contribute to saving animals and the environment that nurtures those animals. The details of the job each member of the research team does will all help inspire young scientists who might aspire to work in some capacity with nature, animals, or scientific exploration.

Curriculum Link: Endangered Animals, Scientific Exploration, Tree Kangaroo, New Guinea

Background

Sy Montgomery is a widely known writer in the area of nature and conservation. She has encountered an angry silverback gorilla in Zaire, a vampire bat in Costa Rica, snakes in Manitoba, and tarantulas in French Guiana. She accompanies scientific teams on expeditions and observes the process of uncovering endangered or threatened species.

For this book, Montgomery accompanied fellow scientist Lisa Dabeck, and photographer Nic Bishop to the cloud forest of New Guinea, where they attached little radios to as many of the tree kangaroos as they could. The radios allowed the team of scientists to follow the animals while monitoring their behavior, and collecting data for their research.

Extension Ideas

1. Choose an endangered animal and provide statistics about how many of the species still exist and locate information about what factors are causing that particular species to be threatened or endangered.
2. Create a world map showing natural habitat locations for at least twenty-five endangered animals. If none still exist in that habitat, create some type of code to indicate that. Some endangered animals exist only in captive situations.
3. Research programs and efforts to rescue a specific endangered animal from extinction. Create an informational pamphlet explaining the program and goals and expectations.

Books to Explore

Donald, Rhonda Lucas. (2002) *Endangered Animals*. Scholastic.
Hoose, Phillip. (2004) *The Race to Save the Lord God Bird*. Farrar, Straus and Giroux.
McLimans, David. (2006) *Gone Wild: An Endangered Animal Alphabet*. Walker & Company.

44

Quiet Hero: The Ira Hayes Story
by S. D. Nelson

Drug addiction and alcoholism are diseases that millions of people struggle with year in and year out. Many survive and share their stories of success in overcoming with others. But in some ways that does young students a disservice as many wonderful people struggle and do not survive; this is one of those stories, a story that *must* be shared with students so they get a full picture of the problems of addiction to drugs or alcohol.

Idea Shelf

Nelson, S. D. (2006) *Quiet Hero: The Ira Hayes Story.* Lee & Low Books. ISBN-10: 1-58430-263-1; ISBN-13: 978-1-58430-263-6.

Bookshelf

Annotation

Ira Hayes, a Pima Indian, was one of the soldiers who raised the U.S. flag on Iwo Jima. He was a U.S. Marine fighting in World War II when he was immortalized in Joe Rosenthal's famous photograph. Hayes was thrust into the public's eye when his identity was revealed and the government called him back from the front lines to promote war bonds with the other two survivors, Rene Gagnon and John Bradley. Hayes was never comfortable with the spotlight and that, along with the sudden loss of his purpose (being part of the Marines fighting for freedom) and his loneliness caused him to struggle with alcoholism. The disease finally took his life. He died on January 24, 1955, at the age of thirty-two.

An author's note provides additional details and dates surrounding Ira Hayes, his formative years, and his life as a U.S. Marine.

Curriculum Link: Native American Heroes, Alcoholism

Background

According to the U.S. government statistics from the National Center for Health Statistics, 61 percent of adults drank alcohol during the statistical year 2005. Thirty-three percent drank five or more drinks at least one day during the year. Even more telling is that, not counting accidents or homicides, 21,634 deaths were caused by alcohol. Alcoholic liver disease took the lives of 12,928 people. Alcoholism statistics reported by the National Center for Health indicate 13.8 million Americans, more than 7 percent of the population ages eighteen and older, have problems with drinking. Other organizations report statistics that has professionals estimating that 40 percent of the population will have an addiction problem at some point in their life (alcohol, drugs, gambling, etc) and that an addict's disease will directly impact the lives of four to five others.

Extension Ideas

1. Investigate the effect of alcoholism and drugs on the U.S. culture. Who has been affected by alcoholism/drugs? Family? On the national level? And so forth.
2. Research: What are the effects of fetal alcoholism?
3. Conduct a survey to determine the effect of alcohol on your community. Develop your questions, prepare the survey, distribute the survey, and then compile the results.
4. Many cultural contributions by Native Americans have gone undocumented because records and accounts were not considered important enough to keep in relation to them. It was not until 1832 that census takers even counted Native Americans individually. Many states did not issue Native Americans birth certificates and in fact, as recently as 1945, birth certificates were assumed not to be available and "new," post-birth certificates were issued. Some cases resulted in duplicate birth certificates issued in two different counties.

Books to Explore

Black, Claudia A. (2002) *It Will Never Happen to Me: Growing Up with Addiction as Youngsters, Adolescents, Adults.* Hazelden.

Dolmetsch, Paul. (1986) *Teens Talk About Alcohol and Alcoholism.* Doubleday.

Hornik-Beer, Edith. (2001) *For Teenagers Living With a Parent Who Abuses Alcohol/Drugs.* Backinprint.com.

45

How We Are Smart
by W. Nikola-Lisa

A great introduction to the way we learn and think. Once our strengths are iden-tified, students can begin to develop their other types of "smartness"—an effort that will enhance their overall success in learning.

Idea Shelf

Nikola-Lisa, W. (2006) *How We Are Smart*. Illustrated by Sean Qualls. Lee & Low Books. ISBN-10: 1-58430-254-2; ISBN-13: 978-1-58430-254-4.

Bookshelf

Annotation

To realize how learning takes place, especially how our own learning takes place, puts us in a position of power. To assist learners to identify how they learn, Nikola-Lisa has profiled several achievers with a biographical narrative, included an informational poem about each person's "smartness," and has included a quote exemplifying the subject's approach to learning.

Profiled subjects include:

- Luis Alvarez—as a physicist, he helped develop the atomic bomb, radar landing systems, and the detection of subatomic particles
- Maria Tallchief—America's first prima ballerina
- Thurgood Marshall—First African American Supreme Court justice
- Annie Jump Cannon—Classified more than 350,000 stars and helped to develop and refine Harvard's star classification system.
- Tito Puente (Ernest Anthony "Tito" Puente Jr.)—musician, composer, and band-leader. Preformed more than 10,000 concerts, completed 2,000 arrangements, wrote 400 songs, and made 120 albums, and won six Grammy Awards
- Patsy Takemoto Mink—First minority woman in the U.S. Congress; she fought for civil rights for all

- Matthew Henson—Became, along with Robert Peary on April 6, 1909, one of the first explorers to reach the North Pole
- Georgia O'Keefe—One of the most important twentieth-century American artists, known for her large-scale paintings
- Alexander Posey—Considered one of the most important Native American writers of his time
- Marian Anderson—Invited by First Lady Eleanor Roosevelt to sing on the steps of the Lincoln Memorial and was the first African American to sing at the Metropolitan Opera in New York City
- I. M. Pei—Ieoh Ming Pei. A Chinese-born architect who designed many projects, including the East Wing of the National Gallery of Art in Washington, D.C., and the Glass Pyramid visitor entrance to the Louvre Museum in Paris, the World Trade Center in Miami, the John F. Kennedy Library in Boston, and the Miho Museum in Shiga, Japan.
- Ynes Mexia—Became a student of botany at the age of fifty-five and eventually traveled around the world, collecting species from Brazil to Alaska. She discovered many plant species (estimates range as high as 500) and collected close to 145,000 species, including those she discovered.

Curriculum Link: Language Arts—Research, Brain Research

Background

Howard Gardner developed and popularized the theory of multiple intelligences in 1983. Each of the people featured in this book are associated with one of his multiple intelligences. Learn more about the subjects who have achieved and about the intelligences proposed by Dr. Gardner.

Dr. Gardner proposed these intelligences:

- Linguistic intelligence ("word smart")
- Logical-mathematical intelligence ("number/reasoning smart")
- Spatial intelligence ("picture smart")
- Bodily-kinesthetic intelligence ("body smart")
- Musical intelligence ("music smart")
- Interpersonal intelligence ("people smart")
- Intrapersonal intelligence ("self smart")
- Naturalist intelligence ("nature smart")

The theory was of high interest when it was interpreted further by Thomas Armstrong, who suggested that learners might access new information through these modalities:

- Words (linguistic intelligence)
- Numbers or logic (logical-mathematical intelligence)
- Pictures (spatial intelligence)
- Music (musical intelligence)

- Self-reflection (intrapersonal intelligence)
- A physical experience (bodily-kinesthetic intelligence)
- A social experience (interpersonal intelligence)
- An experience in the natural world (naturalist intelligence)

Extension Ideas

1. In this collection, for example, Georgia O'Keefe is described as having spatial intelligence ("picture smart"), Maria Tallchief as having bodily-kinesthetic intelligence ("body smart"), and Luis Alvarez as having logical-mathematical intelligence ("number/reasoning smart"). Discuss the type of "smart" each of the other subjects are and identify characteristics that are indicative of a particular type of intelligence.
2. List your own learning characteristics and discuss the intelligences that are your strengths.
3. If one is not "picture smart," what actions might be taken to strengthen one's abilities in that area? Discuss the other types of intelligences—what can be done to strengthen a particular intelligence?

Books to Explore

Armstrong, Thomas, and Jennifer Brannen. (2002) *You're Smarter Than You Think: A Kid's Guide to Multiple Intelligences.* Free Spirit Press.

Gardner, Howard. (1993) *Multiple Intelligences: The Theory in Practice.* Basic Books.

46

Galileo's Journal: 1609–1610
by Jeanne K. Pettenati

Idea Shelf

Learning about inventors and inventions can be motivated with this account of Galileo's life during a nine-month period. If he discovered these things in nine months, what did he do with the rest of his life? This book offers a great opportunity for discovery.

Pettenati, Jeanne K. (2006) *Galileo's Journal: 1609–1610*. Illustrated by Paolo Rui. Charlesbridge. ISBN-10: 1-57091-879-1; ISBN-13: 978-1-57091-879-7.

Bookshelf

Annotation

Pettenati used dates and information from Galileo's own writing to create an account of his discoveries during a nine-month period from July 1609 to March 1610. During that time, Galileo learned of a new invention—"a tube for seeing things far away." He set out to make one. The "spyglass" was at first rather modest, allowing him to see animals in his garden, but as he refined the idea and used more powerful concave and convex lenses, he created a tube so powerful that he was able to observe the moon and Pluto. The device was later called a telescope. Galileo's observations of Pluto through its lenses helped him make a most startling discovery. At first, in January 1610, he thought the objects to either side of Pluto were stars, but after making careful observations and taking detailed notes, he concluded that Pluto has four moons that revolve around it. Galileo published his findings in a book titled *The Starry Messenger*. Many of the quotes in Pettenati's book come from that publication. The four largest moons of Pluto are now referred to as "Galilean moons."

An author's note explains that Galileo went on to develop other ideas about the universe and eventually was exiled back to his home in Florence by religious leaders in Rome. Galileo was accused of teaching a forbidden view of the universe. He was forbidden to teach at the university or to tutor individual students. The last nine years of his life was spent in Florence, where he continued his experiments and observations—and continued to meet many visitors. He died in 1642.

Curriculum Links: Invention of the Telescope, Kuiper Belt, Oort Cloud

Background

Galileo was a celebrated Italian scientist, and Pettenati has focused on his most notable discoveries. At the end of his life, Galileo was blind due to cataracts and glaucoma. He died in Arcetri the same year Isaac Newton was born.

The Kuiper Belt is part of outer space along the ecliptic outside the orbit of Neptune. It is often called our solar system's final frontier. As of now, no spacecraft has ventured into the Kuiper Belt. But by 2015, NASA plans to send a mission to Pluto that will be able to penetrate into the Kuiper Belt. The Oort Cloud includes objects that were formed closer to the sun than the Kuiper Belt objects. Both are the source of many comets and space objects.

Extension Ideas

1. Currently the status of Pluto as a planet is in question. Information about the controversy can be found at Science News @ NASA. "Much Ado About Pluto." NASA <http://science.nasa.gov/newhome/headlines/ast17feb99_1.htm> (this Web site includes additional links leading to more information).
2. Explore the invention of the telescope, including the involvement of Hans Lippershey (c. 1570–c. 1619) of Holland.
3. Use Maxine Kumin's book, *The Microscope*, as a model for a bio-poem. Write a poem about Galileo.
4. Galileo was just one among many noted inventors of the time. Make a list of other seventeenth-century inventors and create a portrait gallery of famous scientists. Create a plaque, to be posted along with the subject's portrait, detailing the inventor's accomplishments.

Books to Explore

Bendick, Jeanne. (1999) *Along Came Galileo.* Beautiful Feet Books.
Kumin, Maxine (1984) *The Microscope.* Illustrated by Arnold Lobel. HarperCollins.
Reeves, Eileen. (2008) *Galileo's Glassworks: The Telescope and the Mirror.* Harvard University Press.
Sis, Peter. (1996) *Starry Messenger.* Farrar, Straus and Giroux.

47

Antonyms, Synonyms & Homonyms
by Kim Rayevsky

Idea Shelf

Get out those grammar books and introduce your standard lesson with this look at antonyms, synonyms, and homonyms. Identify other word pairs and create original illustrations to depict the concept of pairs of words.

Rayevsky, Kim. (2006) *Antonyms, Synonyms & Homonyms.* Illustrated by Robert Rayeusky. Holiday House. ISBN-10: 0-8234-1889-8; ISBN-13: 978-0-8234-1889-3.

Bookshelf

Annotation

Zany illustrations create visual images to illuminate the concepts of:

Antonyms (opposite meanings)

- left-right
- farther from-closer to
- cowardly-courageous
- inside-outside
- clean-dirty
- nice-naughty
- messy-neat
- up-down

Synonyms (different words with same meanings)

- limousine, automobile, car, vehicle, wheels
- argue, fight
- baby, infant

- music, tune
- wet, drenched

Homonyms (same sound and sometimes the same spelling, but different meanings)

- see-sea
- plane-plain
- hear-here
- where's-wears
- tow-toe
- missed-missed
- whole-hole

Curriculum Link: Language Arts—Antonyms, Synonyms, and Homonyms; Word Choice

Background

An antonym is defined as a word that means the opposite of another word. A synonym is defined as a word having the same or nearly the same meaning as another. The definition for homonym is a little more complicated: technically, while a homonym is commonly defined as a word the same as another in sound and spelling (sometimes both), but different in meaning, a homonym is a word that is sometimes used as a synonym for homophone and homograph. A distinction between the three terms does exist. Homophones are words that sound alike, whether or not they are spelled differently, such as *pear* (a fruit), *pare* (to cut), and *pair* (two items that are alike) or spelled the same as *bear* (to support) and *bear* (an animal). Homographs are words that are spelled the same but may or may not be pronounced the same. *Spruce* is the name of a tree but *spruce* also means to make things neat—as in spruce up the place. *Spruce* is a word that is spelled the same and pronounced the same, but with two unrelated meanings—making *spruce* and *spruce* homographs. But to stand in a *row* (roh) or to be part of a *row* (rou)—a fight or disturbance—illustrates homographs where two words spelled alike are pronounced differently and have two different meanings. To know how to pronounce *row* one must have the word in context to know which word is intended.

Technically, a homonym is both a homophone and a homograph as a homonym is alike in spelling and in pronunciation but has different meanings—*bear* (the animal) and *bear* (to support).

Homonym seems to have emerged as a term used for any of these situations when a word is used in a nontechnical context.

Extension Ideas

1. Use the double-page spreads showcasing the selection of words as a model and then create additional pages with other word examples for each section of the book.

2. Write sentences using several related homonyms, antonyms, or synonyms in the same sentence. Example: "I sighted a Web site that I could use in my paper so I cited it on my note cards." Or: "The wind blew down the factory built with blue stones—the factory that manufactured bleu cheese dressing."

3. Illustrate on a large poster a sentence created in Number 2.

4. Create a classroom book of the sentences and illustrations.

5. As a class, generate an ongoing list of homonyms, antonyms, and synonyms as they are used in conversations/discussions within the classroom. Keep the list on a large scroll-like piece of butcher paper on the wall.

6. Generate a list of homonyms that have merged as synonyms. For example, homonym has become a synonym for homographs and homophones, although technically they are different terms. A similar instance has occurred with the term "chrysalis," which is technically the pupa of a butterfly, and "cocoon," which is the pupa of a moth. However, in recent years, the terms have become synonymous with this definition: chrysalis—a pupa, especially of a moth or butterfly, enclosed in a firm case or cocoon. Identify other terms that have emerged with synonymous meanings over time.

Books to Explore

Cleary, Brian P. (2004) *Pitch and Throw, Grasp and Know: What Is a Synonym?* (Words Are Categorical). Illustrated by Brian Gable. CarolRhoda Books.

Cleary, Brian P. (2006) *Stop and Go, Yes and No: What Is an Antonym?* (Words are Categorical). Illustrated by Brian Gable. Millbrook Press.

Dahl, Michael. (2007) *If You Were a Synonym* (Word Fun). Illustrated by Sara Gray. Picture Window Books.

Loewen, Nancy. (2007) *If You Were an Antonym* (Word Fun). Illustrated by Sara Gray. Picture Window Books.

Loewen, Nancy. (2007) *If You Were a Homonym or a Homophone* (Word Fun). Illustrated by Sara Gray. Picture Window Books.

48

A Pair of Polar Bears
by Joanne Ryder

Use this book as a model for writing about polar bears and other animals and their habitats.

Idea Shelf

Ryder, Joanne. (2006) *A Pair of Polar Bears: Twin Cubs Find a Home at the San Diego Zoo*. Illustrated with photographs from the San Diego Zoo. Simon & Schuster Children's Publishing. ISBN-10: 0-689-85871-X; ISBN-13: 978-0-689-85871-0.

Bookshelf

Annotation

When two small orphan polar bears are found in the northernmost reaches of the Alaska wilderness, they are rescued and transported hundreds of miles south to the San Diego (California) Zoo. At first they are kept in the San Diego hospital, where they are quarantined for thirty days. During their stay, they are introduced to some of the objects and routines they will soon encounter in the Polar Bear Plunge exhibit at the zoo. The cubs learn to play with objects, explore, figure out how to do things on their own, and learn to swim. The polar bear's Latin name is *Ursus maritimus*, which means "sea bear." In the wild they may have roamed all winter hunting for seals, but at the zoo they are introduced to bits of their new habitat a little at a time. The brother and sister are given names that reflect their Inuit homeland—*Kalluk* (Ka-look) is the name of the male cub. In Inuit, the word means "thunder." Kalluk's sister is named *Tatquiq* (Tot-keek), a name meaning "moon."

Curriculum Link: Endangered Animals, Zoo Animals, Alaskan Animals

Background

Points for discussion: What is the natural habitat of polar bears, how many are there, and how can you find more information about the statement "each bear's fur looks white." (But it really isn't. Each hair is a clear hollow tube. Sunlight bouncing off a bear's fur makes it look white.)

Extension Ideas

1. Investigate the natural habitat of polar bears, map it, describe it, and show the animals' habitat range.
2. List ten things you know about polar bears.
3. Connect to activities suggested for: McLimans, David. (2006) *Gone Wild: An Endangered Animal Alphabet*. Walker & Company. (See chapter 39.)

Books to Explore

Kazlowski, Steven. (2008) *The Last Polar Bear: Facing the Truth of a Warming World*. Mountaineers Books. (adult)

McLimans, David. (2006) *Gone Wild: An Endangered Animal Alphabet*. Walker & Company.

Rosing, Norbert. (2006) *The World of the Polar Bear*. Firefly Books.

49

This Is the Dream
by Diane Z. Shore and Jessica Alexander

Add this book to those you just must read in conjunction with any discussion of the civil rights' struggle.

Idea Shelf

Bookshelf

Shore, Diane Z., and Jessica Alexander. (2006) *This Is the Dream*. Illustrated by James Ransome. Amistad/HarperCollins. ISBN-10: 0-06-055519-X (trade binding); ISBN-13: 978-0-06-055519-1 (trade binding); ISBN-10: 0-06-055520-3 (library binding); ISBN-13: 978-0-06-055520-7 (library binding).

Annotation

With bold paintings and collages created from portraits, paintings, and photographs, James Ransome graphically depicts the emotion and impact of the lyrical text chronicling the civil rights movement of the 1960s. Water fountains labeled "white" and "colored" begins the section depicting the segregation that is commonplace in the South. Buses, restaurants, libraries, and schools are all divided by color and the "separate but equal" dictates of the government. But then comes the day when "colored" students integrate a Montgomery, Alabama, school—three students are shown entering with soldiers and a crowd waving Confederate flags. The location is not mentioned in the text, but the setting and time line is clear. School integration is followed by depiction of the bus boycott, lunch counter sit-ins, and civil rights marches. A double-page collage with a background of a photograph on a mass march with superimposed "posters" of Ella Baker, Walter White, Thurgood Marshall, and Dr. Martin Luther King Jr. and the phrase "Justice for All" directly below the posters and above the text explains that these leaders and their powerful voices helped the nation move toward freedom and justice for all. The following pages show a different society: water fountains are shared by blacks and whites, where the rule is "take turns and share"; on buses, each passenger chooses his/her own seat; restaurants and libraries and schools are open to all—those who "answered the call … dreaming of freedom and justice for all."

Curriculum Link: Art—Romare Bearden, Art—Robert Rauschenberg, Martin Luther King Jr., Civil Rights, Thurgood Marshall, Ella Baker, Walter White

Background

Martin Luther King Jr. is associated with the civil rights movement of the 1960s but there were other leaders as well. Ransome's graphic depictions are the bold interpretation of courageous actions taken during those days.

Extension Ideas

1. Make a list of the contemporaries of Dr. Martin Luther King Jr. and investigate additional information about their role in the civil rights movement.
2. Read Deborah Wiles's picture book, *Freedom Summer*, and discuss other events that were occurring during this period of time. A lot of businesses and public facilities were closed in 1964 when people decided they would rather close their public pools, ice cream parlors, and so forth, rather than let non-whites enjoy those areas as whites always had.
3. Coretta Scott King, along with her husband Martin Luther King Jr., saw the vision for civil rights. Read about her life and work and discuss the impact that she had on the civil rights movement.
4. James Ransome's collages were influenced by the work of two of his favorite artists, Romare Bearden and Robert Rauschenberg. Investigate the work of those two artists and then discuss how you think Ransome's work reflects the influence he acknowledges came from their art.

Books to Explore

Greenberg, Jan. (2003) *Romare Bearden: Collage of Memories*. Harry N. Abrams.

Jakoubek, Robert. (2008) *Martin Luther King, Jr.* (Black Americans of Achievement). Checkmark Books.

Kotz, Mary Lynn. (2004) *Rauschenberg: Art and Life*. Harry N. Abrams.

Shange, Ntozake. (2009) *Coretta Scott*. Illustrated by Kadir Nelson. Amistad.

Wiles, Deborah. (2002) *Freedom Summer*. Illustrated by Jerome Lagarrigue. Simon & Schuster.

50

MOM and DAD Are Palindromes:
A Dilemma for Words ...
and Backwards
by Mark Shulman

This book offers a little fun with wordplay; read it and then identify other palindromes over a period of days. Hang a large piece of poster board and encourage students to add their own palindromes (graffiti style) onto it.

Idea Shelf

Shulman, Mark. (2006) *MOM and DAD Are Palindromes: A Dilemma for Words ... and Backwards.* Illustrated by Adam McCauley. Chronicle Books. ISBN-10: 0-8118-4328-9; ISBN-13: 978-0-8118-4328-7.

Bookshelf

Annotation

More than 101 palindromes hid among the words and phrases—words and phrases that read the same forward and backward. The narrator Bob provides a nonsensical text that includes many palindromes: Bob, did, miss sim, redder, kayak, race car, otto, pup, put up, eye, o no, and more. Bob realizes that some of the palindromes are not palindromes when their full name is used, that is, dad = father, mom = mother, Anna = Annabelle, and of course his own Bob = Robert. He vows to always use his full name: Robert Trebor. Clever and observant readers will realize the subtle humor.

Curriculum Link: Language Arts—Palindromes; Word Choice

Background

A palindrome is a word or phrase that reads the same whether it is written from the front or from the back. Those who are adept at creating palindromes can create entire sentences that read the same from the front or the back.

Most sources credit Sotades (living during the third century BCE in Greek-ruled Egypt) for inventing palindromes. For a time they were called "Sotadic verses." Sotades met his demise when after insulting King Ptolemy in one of his verses; the king had him wrapped in lead (or put in a lead box) and thrown into the sea. Since Sotades was also known for his lascivious verses, the term "Sotadic," in the beginning, referred to both his somewhat lewd verse and those with reversible sequence of letters. The term "palindrome" is thought to have evolved in 1629 from the Greek "palindromos," a word derived from *palin,* "again and back" and *dromos,* "a running."

Extension Ideas

1. Create additional palindromes, words, phrases, and entire sentences.
2. Write phases or sentences that are palindromes and then illustrate the phrase or sentence.
3. Make a class list of students who have names that are palindromes.

Books to Explore

Agee, John. (1992) *Go Hang a Salami! I'm a Lasagna Hog!: and Other Palindromes.* Farrar, Straus and Giroux.

Agee, John. (1994) *So Many Dynamos! and Other Palindromes.* Farrar, Straus and Giroux.

Agee, John. (1999) *Sit on a Potato Pan, Otis! More Palindromes.* Farrar, Straus and Giroux.

Agee, John. (2002) *Palindromania.* Farrar, Straus and Giroux.

Donner, Michael. (1996) *I Love Me, Vol. I. Wordrow's Palindrome Encyclopedia.* Algonquin.

Hansen, Craig. (1995) *Ana Nab a Banana: A Book of Palindromes.* Plume.

Miller, Allan. (1997) *Mad Amadeus Sued a Madam.* Illustrated by Lee Lorenz. David R. Godine.

Russell, Mark J. (2007) *No Garden One Dragon: Palindromes in Verse.* iUniverse, Inc.

Saltveit, Mark. (2001) *A Man, A Plan ... 2002; The Year in Palindromes.* The Palindromist Press.

Terban, Marvin. (1985) *Too Hot to Hoot: Funny Palindrome Riddles.* Illustrated by Giulio Maestro. Clarion.

Books (novels) with characters with palindrome names:

Sachar, Louis. (1998) *Holes.* Random House. (Stanley Yelnats)

Skolsky, Mindy Warshaw. (2000) *Welcome to the Grand View, Hannah! (aka Hannah is a Palindrome).* Illustrated by Patrick Faricy. HarperCollins. (Hannah; Otto)

51

Tour America: A Journey Through Poems and Art
by Diane Siebert

Get out a map and pinpoint each of the places that were part of the Tour America journey.

Idea Shelf

Siebert, Diane. (2006) *Tour America: A Journey Through Poems and Art.* Illustrated by Stephen Johnson. Chronicle Books. ISBN-10: 0-8118-5056-0; ISBN-13: 978-0-8118-5056-8.

Bookshelf

Annotation

Tour America: A Journey Through Poems and Art takes readers from New Hampshire to San Francisco, showing us landmarks, impressive scenery, and unusual sights and scenes. Diane Siebert is an accomplished poet whose lyrical and descriptive verses are the perfect accompaniment for the brilliant artwork of Stephen Johnson. Along this tour, readers will be introduced to the many gargoyles on buildings in New York City, natural locations (such as Niagara Falls and the Badlands), and other man-made attractions (such as Chicago's EL and the Golden Gate Bridge).

The opening pages of the book feature a map showing the location of the twenty-six sites (representing twenty-two states) featured on the next pages. Each double-page spread has a poem about the site/location; smaller maps showing the relative location within the United States; a partial postmark from the location; and a boxed, fact-filled paragraph and an artful illustration created by Johnson.

The first attraction featured is Lucy the Elephant in Margate, New Jersey. The elephant is actually a building six stories tall. Originally built in 1881, the elephant was a gimmick to attract land buyers to the area. Later she was used as a home and still later as a bar. Eventually, though, she fell into disrepair and had to be refurbished. Today the elephant is a historic landmark. More information about Lucy the Elephant can be located at the attraction's official Web site at <http://www.lucytheelephant.com>. Additional sites are abundant and can be located by typing "Lucy Elephant Margate" into your favorite Internet search engine.

From Lucy we move on to the gargoyles, the man-made attractions, and other sights and scenes across America.

Curriculum Link: Architecture, Gargoyles, Geography, United States

Background

Every community has attractions sometimes hidden away and sometimes in plain view. Siebert has highlighted attractions she found on a ten-year journey across the United States that she and her husband took on motorcycles. She looked at the buildings, man-made attractions, and those formed naturally in nature. She wrote in her journal and took pictures.

Extension Ideas

1. Choose an interesting attraction in the local community. Take a photograph of the attraction and write a short paragraph or poem. Then create a double-page spread (modeled after the features in *Tour America*) for that attraction. Post it in a gallery celebrating *your* community. Include a box of facts and a narrative about the site you are featuring.
2. Write a newspaper article about the place/attraction featured in #1.
3. Create an advertisement for the place/attraction featured in #1.
4. Plan a five-state journey on a motorcycle. Create a map showing your trip. Write a journal chronicling your travels through those states and sharing information about what you saw on your trip. Who did you meet? What did you see? What weather did you encounter? And so forth.
5. Lucy the Elephant is the oldest example of zoomorphic architecture left in the United States. *Buildings in Disguise: Architecture That Looks Like Animals, Food, and Other Things* contains more information about zoomorphic and mimetic architecture (architecture that imitates something) and includes a dog and a duck, giant baskets, hotdogs, and numerous other mimetic structures. Read Joan Marie Arbogast's *Buildings in Disguise* and create an architectural drawing or scale model of a building you design.
6. Spectacular structures such as the Golden Gate Bridge are featured in *Tour America* as well as statues in Minnesota, the Gateway Arch in St. Louis, Missouri, and the Washington Monument. George Sullivan shares photographs of more interesting buildings in his book *Built to Last: Building America's Amazing Bridges, Dams, Tunnels, and Skyscrapers*. *The Wonderful Towers of Watts* by Patricia Zelver features the Towers of Watts—an elaborate set of towers. The towers were built by Simon "Old Sam" Rodia, a self-styled artist who created unique constructions in inner-city Los Angeles. Find examples of spectacular structures in your state.

Photograph or locate pictures of those structures and write a narrative about them. Put both together on a poster and then feature the posters in a gallery about your state.

7. Gargoyles originated in Europe and they once had a purpose; however, present-day gargoyles are more decorative than functional. New York City is thought to have the most gargoyles of any city in the United States. Even Midwestern towns (such as Cedar Rapids, Iowa) have gargoyles on some buildings built in the first half of the twentieth century.

Books to Explore

Arbogast, Joan Marie. (2004) *Buildings in Disguise: Architecture That Looks Like Animals, Food, and Other Things.* Boyds Mills Press.

Crist, Darlene Trew. (2001) *American Gargoyles: Spirits in Stone.* Illustrated by Robert Llewellyn. Clarkson Potter.

Davis, Kenneth. (2004) *Don't Know Much About the 50 States.* Illustrated by Renee Andriani. HarperCollins.

Gutman, Bill. (2002) *The Look-It-Up Book of the 50 States.* Illustrated by Anne Wertheim. Random House Books for Young Readers.

Hopkins, Lee Bennett. (2000) *My America: A Poetry Atlas of the United States.* Illustrated by Stephen Alcorn. Simon & Schuster's Children's Publishing.

Keller, Laurie. (1998) *The Scrambled States of America* by Laurie Keller. Henry Holt. DVD available from Scholastic Video Collection (2004).

Leedy, Loreen. (1999) *Celebrate the 50 States.* Holiday House.

Sullivan, George. (2005) *Built to Last: Building America's Amazing Bridges, Dams, Tunnels, and Skyscrapers.* Scholastic.

Zelver, Patricia. (1994; 2005) *The Wonderful Towers of Watts.* Illustrated by Frané Lessac. Boyds Mills Press.

52

John, Paul, George & Ben
by Lane Smith

Idea Shelf

While focusing on the Revolutionary War, introduce the five patriots and then read aloud this humorous book and identify the truth and the exaggerations in this book. The "facts" that are not true have some basis in history—identify the basis if you can.

Smith, Lane. (2006) *John, Paul, George & Ben*. Hyperion Books for Children. ISBN-10: 0786848936; ISBN-13: 978-0786848935.

Bookshelf

Annotation

Revolutionary War heroes John Hancock, Paul Revere, George Washington, Ben Franklin, and Thomas Jefferson are depicted during their childhoods. The four "lads" and independent Tom (always off doing his own thing) are the subject of this book. While much of the humor involves historical fact, this book also includes some historical falsehoods. Readers will need some background on the actual events in order to fully absorb the humor in each of Lane Smith's episodes featuring these lads: John Hancock is best known for his bold signature on the Declaration of Independence. Paul Revere was actually a silversmith whose shop sold silver pieces (not underwear). George Washington did not chop down his father's cherry tree. Ben Franklin was well-known for his inventions and writings, particularly *Poor Richard's Almanac*, which included a large number of wise sayings such as "A stitch in time saves nine." Thomas Jefferson lived out his life in a home he built (Monticello) and is credited with authoring the Declaration of Independence. An author's note at the end sets "the record straight with ye olde True and False section."

Curriculum Link: Declaration of Independence, Monticello, Paul Revere's Ride, George Washington, Thomas Jefferson, Benjamin Franklin, Paul Revere, John Hancock, Revolutionary War

Background

The five Revolutionary War figures are among those most often regarded as the major heroes in the founding of the United States. Smith includes several clever illustrations in his depictions. The portraits at the beginning of the book show the men as children, while the final portraits show them as adults—more the way we are familiar with seeing them. He gives a visual nod to the British legends the Beatles and their album *Abbey Road*.

Extension Ideas

1. Extensively read and study the lives of these five figures. Compare and contrast the information gleaned from Smith's book with the information gained from other, more scholarly sources.
2. Discuss how Smith took the facts and molded them into a humorous look at the childhoods of these four men. Write five facts about a well-known public servant, locally or nationally. Use those facts to write a historical but humorous tale about that person's childhood. Draw a caricature of that event.

Books to Explore

About John Hancock:

Fritz, Jean. (1997) *Will You Sign Here, John Hancock?* Illustrated by Trina Schart Hyman. Putnam Juvenile.

Ransom, Candice. (2004) *John Hancock.* Illustrated by Tim Parlin. Lerner Publications.

About Paul Revere:

Forbes, Esther Hoskins. (1990) *America's Paul Revere.* Illustrated by Lynn Ward. Sandpiper.

Fritz, Jean. (1996) *And Then What Happened, Paul Revere?* Illustrated by Margot Tomes. Putnam Juvenile.

Winter, Jonah. (2003) *Paul Revere and the Bell Ringers.* Illustrated by Bert Dodson. Aladdin.

About George Washington:

Adler, David A. (2005) *George Washington: A Holiday House Reader.* Illustrated by John C. Wallner. Holiday House.

Giblin, James Cross. (1992) *George Washington: A Picture Book Biography.* Illustrated by Michael Dooling. Scholastic.

About Benjamin Franklin:

Fleming, Candace. (2003) *Ben Franklin's Almanac: Being a True Account of the Good Gentleman's Life.* Atheneum/Anne Schwartz.

Fradin, Dennis Brindell. (2002) *Who Was Ben Franklin?* Illustrated by John O'Brien and Nancy Harrison. Grosset & Dunlap.

Fritz, Jean. (1976) *What's the Big Idea, Ben Franklin?* Illustrated by Margot Tomes. Putnam Juvenile.

About Thomas Jefferson:

Doeden, Matt. (2006) *Thomas Jefferson: Great American.* Capstone Press.

Giblin, James Cross. (1994) *Thomas Jefferson: A Picture Book Biography.* Illustrated by Michael Dooling. Scholastic.

53

Bessie Smith and the Night Riders
by Sue Stauffacher

Any discussion of the Ku Klux Klan or civil rights (particularly during the 1950s) could be introduced with a reading of *Bessie Smith and the Night Riders*.

Idea Shelf

Stauffacher, Sue. (2006) *Bessie Smith and the Night Riders*. Illustrated by John Holyfield. Putnam Juvenile. ISBN: 0-399-24237-6.

Bookshelf

Annotation

Bessie Smith comes to town in her specially outfitted train car, "Bessie Smith and her Harlem Frolics." It seems that everyone in town is out to greet her and her entourage—and most of them will be in the tent that night to hear the musical performance. Everyone, that is, except for Emmarene Johnson, a little girl who admires Bessie Smith but does not have the money for a ticket. However, once the ticket-taker leaves his station, Emmarene creeps forward and pulls back a corner of the tent and sneaks a look at the performance. While she is crouched outside, she sees the "Night Riders"—the Ku Klux Klan—approach the tent on horseback with torches flaming. Emmarene quickly slips into the tent and warns Bessie Smith, who immediately steps outside and confronts the horsemen. She cusses and then flaps her arms like a Phoenix and sings in such a fashion that the hooded men retreat and leave, the torches accidentally catching a few of their robes on fire.

Curriculum Link: Civil Rights, Ku Klux Klan

Background

This fictionalized story incorporates the character of Emmarene into the tale and adds some dramatics to the real event. But the incident did occur in July 1927, near Concord,

North Carolina. Bessie Smith and the Harlem Frolics had set up their tent to give a show to the people of Concord. The heat that night was stifling, and one of the musicians stepped outside the tent to get some fresh air. He saw about a dozen Klansmen pulling up the tent stakes (which would have collapsed the tent and killed people inside). The musician, unseen, ran back onto the stage and told Bessie (who had just completed a song). She commanded that the prop boys follow her and together they went outside and found the Klansmen. The prop boys quickly ran off—but six-foot-tall Bessie pulled herself up and is said to have cursed and shouted at the men. The men turned and ran. She later is said to have called the prop boys, "sissies." She may have saved hundreds of lives that night.

Extension Ideas

1. Investigate the origin of and tactics used by the Ku Klux Klan to intimidate blacks and other minorities, keep them from exercising their right to vote, and prevent them from participating in society freely.
2. Who is Bessie Smith? Read about her and create a time line showing the major events occurring in the United States during her life. What other historical figures would she have known and have interacted with during her career?

Books to Explore

Feinstein, Elaine. (1986) *Bessie Smith*. Viking Adult.

Martinez, J. Michael. (2007) *Carpetbaggers, Cavalry, and the Ku Klux Klan: Exposing the Invisible Empire During Reconstruction*. Rowman & Littlefield Publishers.

Moore, Carman. (1969) *Somebody's Angel Child: The Story of Bessie Smith*. T. Y. Crowell.

54

Wings of Light: The Migration of the Yellow Butterfly
by Stephen Swinburne

Use a map to follow the route of the yellow butterfly and then study the routes typically taken by other migrating animals.

Idea Shelf

Swinburne, Stephen R. (2006) *Wings of Light: The Migration of the Yellow Butterfly*. Illustrated by Bruce Hiscock. Boyds Mills Press. ISBN: 1-59078-082-5.

Bookshelf

Annotation

Watercolor illustrations depict the migration of the cloudless sulphur butterfly (*Phoebis sennae*) from the rain forests of the Yucatan Peninsula, to the southern states, and up into the Central and New England states. Cloudless sulphurs weigh less than half a gram and yet are able to migrate more than 2,000 miles. Wind and predators take a toll on many of the insects that also must find food and shelter along their journey. While other migration patterns are not detailed in the book, an author's note mentions other butterflies that do migrate: painted ladies, red admirals, buckeyes, and the monarch, which is the only butterfly with a birdlike migration (south in the fall and north in the spring). Hummingbirds, sea turtles, and whales are among some other animals that migrate.

Curriculum Link: Migration; Butterflies, Animals, and Birds That Migrate

Background

Monarch butterflies have had their migration patterns studied and documented extensively. Much information is available in books and on the Internet. Their migration patterns might be the subject of further study.

Extension Ideas

1. Involve students in Annenberg Media's Journey North project. Its Web site invites classes to participate in tracking birds and animals (and butterflies) that migrate. See <http://www.learner.org/jnorth/>.
2. Investigate the migration patterns of other animals that migrate.

Books to Explore

Elphick, Jonathan, ed. (2007) *Atlas of Bird Migration: Tracing the Great Journeys of the World's Birds*. Firefly Books.

Rylant, Cynthia. (2006) *The Journey: Stories of Migration*. Illustrated by Lambert Davis. The Blue Sky Press.

55

George Crum and the Saratoga Chip
by Gaylia Taylor

Snack on potato chips and introduce George Crum as the Native American/ African American inventor who made the first chips in upstate New York.

Idea Shelf

Taylor, Gaylia. (2006) *George Crum and the Saratoga Chip.* Illustrated by Frank Morrison. Lee & Low Books. ISBN-10: 1-58430-255-0; ISBN-13: 978-1-58430-255-1.

Bookshelf

Annotation

George Speck, known as George Crum, was the son of an African American father (a horse jockey) and a Native American mother. Crum and his sister Kate grew up in the Adirondack Mountains, and once he was grown, he hunted and fished for a living. One day in the outdoors, a Frenchman showed Crum how to cook fresh fish and game. He came to like cooking and eventually became the chef at the Moon Lodge in Sarasota Springs, New York. It is at Moon Lodge that a hard-to-please customer sent Crum's potatoes back to the kitchen, saying they were not crisp enough. That is when George sliced some potatoes ultra thin, fried them an extra long time in hot fat, and served them. The response was unexpected—and soon Crum's Saratoga Chips were attracting many patrons to the Moon Lodge. After a few years, Crum opened his own restaurant, Crum's Place.

Curriculum Link: African Americans, George Crum, Inventors, Native Americans

Background

George Crum's father was Abraham Speck (an African American jockey), but during his career as a horse jockey, he used the name "Crum." Eventually Abraham came north to

Saratoga Springs, New York, and married Catherine, a woman from the Huron tribe. George was born and although his legal name was George Speck, he used the name George Crum (as his father had done). He lived a pretty colorful life. For a period of time he was an Indian trader, but by 1853, he was employed at a plush lodge in Saratoga Springs. That is where the episode in Penelope Stowell's book, *The Greatest Potatoes*, takes place. In 1860, he opened his own restaurant—and some say the reason he could do so is he had the cheap labor of his multiple wives (some say five). Some writers refer to George Speck "Crum" as African American while others choose to focus on his Native American heritage.

His restaurant survived for thirty years, until 1890. Crum died in 1914 at the age of ninety-two.

Extension Ideas

1. Compare the tale of Crum's invention of the potato chip as told by Taylor to the version put forth by Stowell.
2. Crum's Saratoga Chip led to a whole new food product and has ended up as the Frito-Lay Company. Research the involvement of Crum's chip to the product today—an industry that employs 65,000 people. These are people/events that had a part in the development.
   a. In 1895, William Tappendon of Cleveland, Ohio, was one of the first to sell potato chips in grocery stores.
   b. The potato peeler was invented in the 1920s.
   c. Bill and Sallie Utz started Hanover Home Brand Potato Chips in Hanover, Pennsylvania, in 1921.
   d. Laura Scudder's 1926 invention of the wax paper bag made packaging chips economical and convenient for selling.
   e. In 1932, Herman Lay founded Lay's in Nashville, Tennessee.
3. The potato chip turned 155 years old in 2008; investigate the history of other favorite snacks. When were they invented? How do those snacks fare in terms of sales and popularity as compared to the potato chip?
4. Some say that George's sister Kate Speck Wick might have been the inventor and that George didn't even serve the chips at his own restaurant. If that is so, how might this "fact" fit with the status of women at the time? Early in the history of the United States, women could not patent their own inventions; many items invented by women (or African Americans) were patented in the names of a husband, father, or white master/boss. Potato chips, however, were never patented.

Books to Explore

Fox, William S., and Mae G. Banner. "Social and Economic Contexts of Folklore Variants: The Case of Potato Chip Legends." *Western Folklore* 42 (1983 May): 114–126.
Stowell, Penelope. (2005) *The Greatest Potatoes*. Illustrated by Sharon Watts. Jump At the Sun.

56

Perfect Timing: How Isaac Murphy Became One of the World's Greatest Jockeys
by Patsi B. Trollinger

Introduce Isaac Murphy as a black athlete who set the mark for many other athletes (white, black, and otherwise). Jackie Robinson made a mark in baseball, Arthur Ashe in tennis, Wilma Rudolph in track, and Isaac Murphy in horse racing. Use this book as a springboard to discuss contributions to the sports culture or as a discussion starter for civil rights.

Idea Shelf

Trollinger, Patsi B. (2006) *Perfect Timing: How Isaac Murphy Became One of the World's Greatest Jockeys.* Illustrated by Jerome LaGarrigue. Viking Juvenile. ISBN: 0-670-06083-6.

Bookshelf

Annotation

His grandparents had been slaves, but Isaac Murphy was still unable to go to school. The year was 1873 and there were few schools for black children in those days. Twelve-year-old Isaac helped his mother every day in her laundry business and although slight in size, he was used to doing heavy work. So the day he delivered laundry to the Owings household, Mr. Owings asked him if he wanted to learn to ride thoroughbreds. Murphy was in the perfect place at the perfect time. After several years at school, he rode his first horse—and lost. But it wasn't long before he mastered the timing and became a much sought-after jockey. He was known for his perfect timing—he knew just when to spur his horse to put on speed and when to hold back. As he grew older, he matured and gained weight during the off-season and found that each spring he had to crash diet to get down to the 110-pound weight necessary to ride a thoroughbred. One spring, dieting made him weak, and he was not able to fight off the pneumonia that followed. He died at the age of thirty-five on February 12, 1896.

Curriculum Link: Civil Rights, History—African Americans, Horse Racing

Background

The author's note details the significance of Murphy's timing in relation to his career. If he had been born twenty years earlier, he would have been a slave rider. Twenty years later and the racial climate would have prevented him from riding as white jockeys would not ride with blacks.

Murphy was the only American jockey to have won the Kentucky Derby, the Kentucky Oaks, and the Clark Stakes. Three of his derby wins were unequaled for thirty-nine years. He was the first jockey to be voted into the Jockey Hall of Fame (1955) at the National Museum of Racing in Saratoga Springs, New York.

Black jockeys dominated American racing before the Civil War. Fourteen of the fifteen jockeys at the May 17, 1875, inaugural Derby were black.

By 1922, most black jockeys had disappeared from racing. Nowadays, racial equality has brought back blacks—along with Hispanics, Asians, and women jockeys. Isaac Murphy was the first jockey to be named to the National Museum of Racing Hall of Fame. Readers can learn about other jockeys by visiting the Web site for the hall of fame at http://www.racingmuseum.org/hall/.

Extension Ideas

1. Create a time line showing the leading jockey from the early 1850s to the present time. Investigate each jockey's heritage and status in the horse-racing world. How does that information fit with the information that indicates the disappearance of black jockeys by 1922? What is the current status of black jockeys and other minorities?
2. Explain all the ways timing fits into Murphy's life.
3. What other black athletes were active and leaders in their sport during the same period of time as Murphy? Or who followed him on the racetrack?
4. The jockeys Isaac Murphy, Ron Turcotte, Eddie Delhoussaye, and Jimmy Winkfield all have one thing in common. Research to find out what achievement or attribute the four share.

   (Answer: these four are the only jockeys, white or black, to win back-to-back Kentucky Derbies. Isaac Murphy (1890 and 1891), Ron Turcotte (1972 and 1973), Eddie Delhoussaye (1982 and 1983), and Jimmy Winkfield (1901 and 1902).
5. Investigate other black or minority athletes and discuss how their achievements have impacted our culture. Arthur Ashe is one of those athletes.

Books to Explore

Ashe, Arthur. (1988) *A Hard Road to Glory: #3*. Warner Books.
Ashe, Arthur. (2000) *A Hard Road to Glory: A History of the African American Athlete: Baseball*. Amistad.

57

Probuditi!
by Chris Van Allsburg

Introduce the element of irony in writing with this book. Then springboard into the four most commonly used elements in writing: allusion, metaphor, symbolism, and irony. Read other books and identify when these elements are being used.

Idea Shelf

Van Allsburg, Chris. (2006) *Probuditi!* Houghton Mifflin Books for Children. ISBN-10: 0-618-75502-0; ISBN-13: 978-0-618-75502-8.

Bookshelf

Annotation

Calvin delights in teasing his younger sister, Trudy, and his birthday is no exception. He begins the day by putting a spider in her bed. After his mother discovers this, she lectures him about his behavior but then gives him his birthday present—two tickets to a matinee showing of Lomax the Magnificent, a magician and hypnotist. Calvin's mother suggests that perhaps he would like to take his sister to the performance, but the tickets are his so Calvin decides to take his friend Rodney. But that does not end the fun. When the boys come home from the show, they decide to use some of their inspiration to hypnotize Trudy. And of course, they do try. But Trudy is very perceptive and she finds a way to show that she is not as gullible as they might think. Although the boys think they have hypnotized Trudy, she is clearly aware of what is going on. In the end, she turns the tables on them and shows that she is really the one who has tricked them. This book has a surprise ending in the manner of O. Henry.

Curriculum Link: Language Arts: O. Henry, Irony, Twist Endings

Background

O. Henry (1862–1910) is the pseudonym of American writer William Sydney Porter, who wrote hundreds of short stories. He is known for his clever use of twist endings, as well as for his subtle sense of humor and his superb characterization. His twist endings are the result of irony or coincidental circumstances. Among his most well-known short stories are "The Gift of the Magi," "The Ransom of Red Chief," "The Cop and the Anthem," and "After Twenty Years."

O. Henry uses the literary technique of *irony* to create his twist endings and entertainment value of his short stories.

Writers use several literary tools to create their stories. Allusion, metaphor, symbolism, and irony are commonly used. Irony is perhaps the most common technique used by satirists. The meaning of irony is often misunderstood. Irony is an underlying meaning of a statement or when a situation is in contrast with what is apparent. There are many types of irony; the type associated with the twist ending is *situational irony*.

Synonyms for irony include caustic remark, sarcasm, and satire. The other techniques include (with definitions):

- Allusion = An allusion is a reference, within a literary work, to another work of fiction, a film, a piece of art, or even a real event.
- Metaphor = A metaphor is a figure of speech in which an implicit comparison is made between two dissimilar things that actually have something important in common.
- Symbolism = Symbolism involves representing things or events by means of symbols or of attributing symbolic meanings or significance to objects, events, or relationships.
- Irony = Irony is the use of words to express something different from and often opposite to their literal meaning.

Extension Ideas

1. Discuss the irony in *Probuditi!*. Is there a true ironic ending?
2. Read as many O. Henry short stories as may be available and identify the ironic situations in each.
3. Listen (and read) the lyrics to Alanis Morissette and Glen Ballard's song, "Ironic." Discuss how each situation mentioned could be a situation that is truly ironic if given an added twist.

Books to Explore

Henry, O. (2006) *The Gift of the Magi*. Illustrated by Lisbeth Zwerger. Simon & Schuster. (picture book)

Henry, O. (2003) *The Gift of the Magi and Other Stories*. Scholastic Paperbacks.
Henry, O. (2007) *41 Stories*. Signet Classics.
Hollander, John, ed. (2005) *Stories for Young People: O. Henry* (Stories for Young People). Illustrated by Miles Hyman. Sterling.

Music

Morissette, Alanis and Glen Ballard. (1995) "Ironic" (song). A single produced by Maverick/Reprise, it first appeared as one of the twelve tracks on the album *Jagged Little Pill*, which included "Ironic" in addition to "You Oughta Know (Acoustic/Live from the Grammy Awards)," "Mary Jane [Live]," and "All I Really Want [Live]."
Comment: Many critics have argued that there is no irony in Morissette's song lyrics; rather, that the incidents are merely coincidental or examples of cosmic irony (not true irony) at best. Irish comedian Ed Bryne analyses the lack of irony in the lyrics by pointing out that there is nothing ironic about being stuck in a traffic jam and being late for something unless you are a town planner on the way to giving a presentation about solving traffic congestion in the very area where you are stuck in the traffic jam. Having rain on your wedding day is not ironic unless your spouse-to-be is a meteorologist and was responsible for setting the date. And a no-smoking sign on a smoke break is just inept administration at your job; however, a no-smoking sign in a cigarette factory is ironic. That being said, writing lyrics for a song titled "Ironic" that contains no irony may be the most ironic connection of all. (See Extension Idea #3 above.)

58

Lucy Maud Montgomery: The Author of *Anne of Green Gables*
by Alexandra Wallner

Idea Shelf

Many readers are first introduced to the Anne of Green Gables books when the story is featured on public television. The series Anne of Green Gables, The Collection (Five-Disc Box Set) is available from a number of sources. This biography not only introduces life during the World War I era in Canada, but also reveals the inspiration the author uses to create a piece of literature from her own life. The lives of other writers will make interesting reading and a chance to compare and contrast the authors' real lives with incidents in their books.

Wallner, Alexandra. (2006) *Lucy Maud Montgomery: The Author of Anne of Green Gables.* Holiday House. ISBN: 0-8234-1549-X.

Bookshelf

Annotation

Alexandra Wallner summarizes the life of Lucy Maud Montgomery through sequential events in her life. Montgomery was born on Prince Edward Island in 1874. Her mother died when Montgomery was just two years of age. A few years later, seeking a better life in western Canada, Montgomery's father left her with her maternal grandparents in Cavendish. She was well cared for but lonely so she sought companionship in her writing and reading. She attended school and helped her grandparents. When she was thirteen, her father asked her to live with him (and his new wife) in western Canada, but after a year she returned to her grandparents' home in Cavendish. She finished school, earned a teacher's certificate, taught, and spent a year at the university. When her grandfather died unexpectedly, she returned home to care for her grandmother—she took care of her for the next thirteen years. It was during this time that Montgomery sent off the manuscript for *Anne of Green Gables*—a story loosely based on her own situation. It was published in 1908. She became secretly engaged to Reverend Ewan Macdonald and after her grandmother's death in 1911, the couple married. The Macdonalds moved to Ontario; Montgomery did not ever return to Prince Edward Island to live. The family lived in several locations, and after their two sons Chester (b. 1912) and Ewan (b. 1915) were grown, Ewan Macdonald retired. In 1935, the couple moved to Toronto, where Montgomery died in 1942. Ewan died a year later, in 1943. Both are buried in Cavendish near the house where Montgomery had lived with her grandparents.

Curriculum Link: Language Arts, Biography, Lucy Maud Montgomery, *Anne of Green Gables*

Background

Wallner uses many phrases that demand readers to make inferences. For example, she says, "Ewan's spirits were low and he needed care." Other sources speak of Ewan suffering often from "melancholy"—acknowledged today as depression.

   Wallner also makes an omission that might have been a conscious decision to eliminate the need for further explanation. She says, "They had two sons: in 1912, Chester, and in 1915, Ewan." But in other accounts of Montgomery's life, readers will find that in 1914, the couple had another son. That son, Hugh, was stillborn.

Extension Ideas

1. Read aloud this book as an introduction to *Anne of Green Gables*. Afterward, discuss what elements of Montgomery's life are mirrored in her novel.
2. Read aloud this book as an introduction to the genre of biography. Use it to introduce longer biographies of other writers, particularly Montgomery.
3. Make a time line of Montgomery's life. Note significant events in her life along the bottom of the time line and note major events in society in general along the top of the time line.
4. Ask a student or group of students to identify a biography of a writer that they wish to read, then:
   a. Identify, locate, and read a number of the author's books/stories.
   b. Read a biography of the writer.
   c. Discuss/examine the biography to identify connections of the author's life to the author's work.
   d. Write a brief essay supporting your inferences about the connections from the author's life to the events, characters, and outcomes in the author's writing.
5. Ask a student or group of students to identify a biography of a writer that they wish to read, then:
   a. Identify, locate, and read a number of the author's books/stories.
   b. Read a biography of the writer.
   c. Assemble groups of readers, each of whom have read a different biography, and ask each reader to share information about their writer and his/her story.

About the Biographies of Writers

The biographies/autobiographies cited in the Books to Explore section represent conventional sequential biographies as well as others written in unique ways; some are written with unique insight into a time in our world that will help us understand specific periods of history and diverse cultures. Isaac Bashevis Singer (who grew up near Warsaw, Poland) tells of turbulent war-filled years; Anita Lobel tells of five years of hiding from the Nazis and her life on the run; and Joseph Bruchac's life with his Abenaki grandparents in upstate New York provides a glimpse into a culture not often represented in books. Gary Paulsen shares snippets of his life as he recounts periods of his life through the relationships he had with dogs. Each of the authors has a story to tell—a story that led them onto the writer's path. Sometimes the path is dark and filled with loneliness or sadness—or even terror. Other paths are idyllic. But all are eventful and give the teen reader an insight into the lives of beloved authors of books they have read or are reading.

d. Ask each group of readers to identify common characteristics that each writer possesses—characteristics that perhaps contributed to their success as a writer.

e. After each characteristic has been identified, make a list of each author discussed and cite incidents from that writer's biography that exemplifies how that characteristic connected with the writer's life.

f. Each group should devise a way that they can share the characteristics and the way that characteristic played into the lives of the writers.

Books to Explore

About Lucy Maud Montgomery:

Heilbron, Alexandra. (2001) *Remembering Lucy Maud Montgomery*. Dundurn Press.

McCabe, Kevin. (1999) *Lucy Maud Montgomery Album*. Fitzhenry & Whiteside Limited.

Sauerwein, Stan. (2004) *Lucy Maud Montgomery: The Secret Life of a Great Canadian Writer* (An Amazing Stories Book). Altitude Publishing Canada Ltd.

About Other Popular Writers:

Classics:

Carpenter, Humphrey, and J. R. R. Tolkien. (1977) *Tolkien: A Biography*. HarperCollins.

Davis, Philip. (2007) *Bernard Malamud: A Writer's Life*. Oxford University Press.

Miller, Calvin Craig. (2002) *Spirit Like a Storm: The Story of Mary Shelley*. 2nd edition. Morgan Reynolds Publishing.

Schoell, William. (2004) *Mystery and Terror: The Story of Edgar Allan Poe* (Writers of Imagination). Morgan Reynolds Publishing.

Singer, Isaac Bashevis. (1986) *A Day of Pleasure: Stories of a Boy Growing Up in Warsaw.* Farrar, Straus and Giroux.

Children's Writers:

Byars, Betsy. (1992) *The Moon and I.* Julian Messner.

Cleary, Beverly. (1988) *A Girl from Yamhill.* HarperCollins/HarperTeen.

Cleary, Beverly. (1995) *My Own Two Feet: A Memoir.* HarperCollins/HarperTeen. (sequel to *A Girl from Yamhill*)

Cohen, Charles D. (2004) *The Seuss, the Whole Seuss and Nothing But the Seuss: A Visual Biography of Theodor Seuss Geisel.* Random House.

Lobel, Anita. (2000) *No Pretty Pictures: A Child of War.* HarperTrophy.

Young-Adult Writers:

Bruchac, Joseph. (1997/2001) *Bowman's Store: A Journey to Myself.* Lee & Low Books.

Fleischman, Sid. (1996) *The Abracadabra Kid: A Writer's Life.* Greenwillow.

Hopkins, Lee Bennett. (1999) *Been to Yesterdays: Poems of a Life.* Boyds Mills Press.

Lowery, Lois. (1998) *Looking Back: A Book of Memories.* Houghton Mifflin/Walter Lorraine Books.

Naylor, Phyllis Reynolds. (2001) *How I Came to Be a Writer.* Rev. ed. Aladdin.

Paulsen, Gary. (1998) *My Life in Dog Years.* Delacorte Books for Young Readers.

Spinelli, Jerry. (1998) *Knots in My Yo-Yo String.* Alfred A. Knopf.

Yep, Laurence. (1999) *The Lost Garden.* Peter Smith Publisher, Inc.

59

Dear Mr. Rosenwald
by Carole Boston Weatherford

Idea Shelf

Put these three names in front of your students:

- Andrew Carnegie
- John D. Rockefeller
- Julius Rosenwald

And then ask: Which of these philanthropists established 14,000 libraries at the turn of the century?

After reading Weatherford's book, discuss who Rosenwald was and use the book to begin a research project into the work of Carnegie, Rockefeller, and Rosenwald. The comparison of their work and their foundations will highlight the different philosophies held by those who engage in philanthropy.

Weatherford, Carole Boston. (2006) *Dear Mr. Rosenwald*. Illustrated by R. Gregory Christie. Scholastic Press. ISBN-10: 0439495229; ISBN-13: 978-0439495226.

Bookshelf

Annotation

In the early 1920s, Julius Rosenwald, the president of Sears, Roebuck, was inspired by Booker T. Washington to give millions to build schools for African American children in the rural South, on the condition that the local community raised money, too. This picture book tells the story from the viewpoint of Ovella, ten, part of a sharecropper family, who attends a rough one-room schoolhouse when she is not picking cotton ("Instead of learning long division/I'll be working in the fields"). Weatherford's short lines in clear free verse and Christie's exuberant gouache and colored-pencil illustrations show Ovella as part of a vibrant family and community, hard at work, passing the plate in church, and, finally, thrilled to be welcoming the teacher to the exciting new school ("no more eight grades in one room"). The story ends with the child's dream: "One day, I'll be a teacher."

Curriculum Link: Industrial Revolution Era; Philanthropy, Perpetual

Background

Julius Rosenwald lived during the same era as Andrew Carnegie and John D. Rockefeller. Their names are more recognizable because they believed in establishing foundations that were intended to be perpetual in nature. Rosenwald believed that each generation should be responsible for philanthropy within their generation and then the following generation would be able to take care of their generation. A few years after Rosenwald's death, his foundation ended.

Question to ask: Which of these philanthropists established 14,000 libraries at the turn of the century?

- Andrew Carnegie
- John D. Rockefeller
- Julius Rosenwald

You might have said Andrew Carnegie and you would have been correct if we were talking about "building" the libraries and if the number of libraries had been 1,689. But the answer to this carefully worded question is Julius Rosenwald who, with his wife Augusta, created a foundation that helped establish, in existing southern schools, more than 14,000 libraries with the donation of carefully selected resource materials. These "libraries" went into the 4,977 new schools built by the foundation and in other rural schools in fifteen southern states. Rosenwald, who made his fortune with Sears, Roebuck, was a man inspired by the work of Booker T. Washington and is one of many historical leaders who have positively contributed to the United States.

Dear Mr. Rosenwald focuses on Rosenwald's philanthropy and the building of one Rosenwald school. Southern black children often attended school in dilapidated buildings—shacks, corncribs, and any other available location. Ovella was one of those students, and when the professor from the normal school (a school created to train high school graduates to be teachers) came to tell about the Rosenwald grant and challenge to the community, her school was excited. Together they raised a share of the money and worked hard to get the school built. One of the fundraisers was a "box party." A box party as it is described in *Dear Mr. Rosenwald* was a party where the members of the community boxed up gifts, often homemade items such as pies, hand carvings, and so forth. During a social gathering, the unopened boxes were auctioned off. Potential buyers gathered their clues as to what was in the box by the smells of the contents, the weight, and sometimes even a guess based on knowledge about the person who donated the box.

Later, when the school was built, it was furnished with "hand-me-down" desks and books from the white school. But it was, for the black students, a brand-new school.

Extension Ideas

1. Investigate the philanthropic activities of Carnegie, Rockefeller, and Rosenwald. Divide into teams and debate the question of which of these men (and their wives) was the most influential philanthropist to this time. Focus on the long-reaching effect of their particular philanthropic activities.
2. Investigate and map all of the Rosenwald schools that are still standing.
3. How many Carnegie libraries were built in your state? How many are still being used as libraries? What other alternative uses are being made of the Carnegie libraries if they are no longer being used as libraries?
4. Hold a box party to raise money for your school library.

Books to Explore

Ascoli, Peter Max. (2006) *Julius Rosenwald: The Man Who Built Sears, Roebuck and Advanced the Cause of Black Education in the American South* (Philanthropic and Nonprofit Studies). Indiana University Press.

Chernow, Ron. (2004) *Titan: The Life of John D. Rockefeller*. Vintage.

Hoffschwelle, Mary S. (2006) *The Rosenwald Schools of the American South* (New Perspectives on the History of the South). University Press of Florida.

Kent, Zachary. (1999) *Andrew Carnegie: Steel King and Friend to Libraries*. (Historical American Biographies). Enslow Publishers.

Laughlin, Rosemary. (2004) *John D. Rockefeller: Oil Baron and Philanthropist*. (American Business Leaders). Morgan Reynolds Publishing.

Simon, Charnan. (1998) *Andrew Carnegie: Builder of Libraries* (Community Builders). Children's Press (CT)

60

The 39 Apartments of Ludwig van Beethoven
by Jonah Winter

With today's musicians often being eccentric characters, this book is just the one to introduce this classical musician in the same vein—he was very eccentric. His thirty-nine apartments were just one of the ways Ludwig van Beethoven showed his eccentricity.

Idea Shelf

Bookshelf

Winter, Jonah. (2006) *The 39 Apartments of Ludwig van Beethoven.* Illustrated by Barry Blitt. Schwartz & Wade Books. ISBN-10: 0-375-83602-0 (trade); ISBN-10: 0-375-93602-5 (library binding); ISBN-13: 978-0-375-83602-2 (trade); ISBN-13: 978-0-375-93602-9 (library binding).

Annotation

From the reproduction of musical scores, in Beethoven's own hand, on the end pages, to the lively illustrations on the interior pages, this book provides part of the energy and vibrancy of the music of Ludwig van Beethoven. Beethoven (1770–1827) did live in Vienna, Austria and did, in fact, live in thirty-nine apartments during his adult life. He also owned several legless pianos. What we don't know is why he moved so often, how he managed to move his pianos from apartment to apartment, and the nuisance his loud music caused for his many neighbors. Beethoven composed what many consider his greatest work, the *Ninth Symphony*, after he became completely deaf.

Curriculum Link: Classical Music, Ludwig van Beethoven, Music, Parody

Background

Beethoven was born on December 17, 1770, at Bonn. His father tutored him in music, and by the time Ludwig was seven and a half years of age, he had begun to perform. His talent thrust him into the world of music when at age twelve, his first work, *9 Variations in C Minor for Piano* on a march by Ernst Christoph Dressler, was published. At age fourteen, he was appointed organist of the court of Maximilian Franz, Elector of Cologne. He felt a responsibility to his younger brothers after the death of his father and, later, his mother. When one of his young brothers died, he became a co-guardian of a nephew. He lived an eccentric and sometimes strange life in Vienna. Supported as an independent musician by friends, he found himself free to compose what he wanted, when he wanted. Sadly, he gradually lost his hearing, but continued composing. Studies in 2005 seemed to confirm what has been long suspected—Beethoven's years of poor health, strange behavior, and ultimate death in 1827 was caused by lead poisoning. He died in 1827 at the age of fifty-six.

Extension Ideas

1. This book highlights some of the eccentric behaviors of the great composer Beethoven—both the author and the illustrator (through his illustrations) have created a parody of this man. Discuss what a parody is and then identify the ways (in words and pictures) that the author and artist create the parody.
2. Writing: Choose another musician or person of interest and create a fictionalized biographical account based on one or two unusual (or prominent) characteristics of the person you have selected.
3. Investigate the symptoms of lead poisoning and research the medical practices of the era in which Beethoven lived—how would he have been subjected to lead poisoning?
4. Create a time line of Beethoven's life. Include the dates of his most famous compositions.

Books to Explore

Breuning, Gerhard von. (1995) *Memories of Beethoven: From the House of the Black-Robed Spaniards*. Cambridge University Press.

Kerst, Friedrich. (1964) *Beethoven: The Man and the Artist, as Revealed in His Own Words*. Dover Publications.

Krull, Kathleen. (1993) *Lives of the Musicians: Good Times, Bad Times* (and What the Neighbors Thought). Illustrated by Kathryn Hewitt. Harcourt.

Lockwood, Lewis. (2005) *Beethoven: The Music and the Life*. W. W. Norton & Company.

Mai, François Martin. (2007) *Diagnosing Genius: The Life and Death of Beethoven*. McGill-Queen's University Press.

61

Mama: A True Story in Which a Baby Hippo Loses His Mama During a Tsunami, but Finds a New Home and a New Mama
by Jeanette Winters

This book is the ultimate title for sharing the economy of words to convey an idea. Read this book, use the pictures, and discuss what readers think was really going on. Then read other accounts to verify their inferences.

Idea Shelf

Bookshelf

Winters, Jeanette. (2006) *Mama: A True Story in Which a Baby Hippo Loses His Mama During a Tsunami, but Finds a New Home and a New Mama.* Illustrated by Jeanette Winters. Harcourt Children's Books. ISBN-10: 0-15-205495-2; ISBN-13: 978-0152-05495-3.

Annotation

The illustrations and two simple words ("mama" and "baby") repeated over and over depict the plight of a baby hippo who was separated from his mother when a tsunami caused a group of hippos to be swept out to sea from Kenya's Sabaki River. After a night in the ocean, the young hippo was found near Malini. While he weighed more than 650 pounds, he was less than a year old and was motherless. Kenyan officials transported the young hippo fifty miles away to Haller Park in Mombasa. The young hippo, now named Owen, was put into an enclosure with several other animals. Still looking for his mother, Owen found a 130-year-old tortoise named Mzee ("old man" in Swahili). While the main story itself is a minimal textbook whose tale is told mainly through illustrations, the details of the story are contained in an author's note.

Curriculum Link: Animal Refuge Centers, Natural Disasters, Tsunami

Background

During a 2004 tsunami off the coast of Africa, a mother hippo was apparently lost at sea. When her baby hippo washed up on the shore, she was rescued and taken to an animal sanctuary, Haller Park, in Mombasa. The baby hippo was adopted by Mzee, a century-old tortoise. Her tale was popularized when the story and accompanying pictures were put on the Internet and nonfiction books were written about the unlikely pair.

Extension Ideas

1. Explore and locate information (on the Internet) about the current situation involving Mzee and Owen. Are they both still living in the park? How much does Owen weigh now? Are Mzee and Owen still friends?
2. Investigate natural disasters (specifically tsunamis) and the ramifications from those events. What changes as a result of the disaster? How did life in the geographical area change? How did the disaster affect the people involved?

Books to Explore

Hatkoff, Isabella, Craig Hatkoff, and Dr. Paula Kahumbu. (2006) *Owen and Mzee: The True Story of a Remarkable Friendship*. Scholastic.

Hatkoff, Isabella, Craig Hatkoff, and Dr. Paula Kahumbu. (2007) *Owen and Mzee: The Language of Friendship*. Scholastic.

Krauss, Erich. (2005) *Wave of Destruction: The Stories of Four Families and History's Deadliest Tsunami*. Rodale Books.

Langley, Andrew. (2006) *Hurricanes, Tsunamis, and Other Natural Disasters* (Kingfisher Knowledge) Kingfisher.

62

Brothers
by Yin

Begin a focus on the railroad and its impact on the movement west. This is also a good book to investigate the treatment of Chinese and immigration rules.

Idea Shelf

Yin. *Brothers*. (2006) Illustrated by Chris Soentpiet. Philomel Books. ISBN-10: 0399234063; ISBN-13: 978-0399234064.

Bookshelf

Annotation

The Irish and the Chinese met in the middle of Utah as they built the Transcontinental Railroad. In this tale, "based on actual historical events," the Irish and the Chinese meet in San Francisco. Ming, who appears to be eleven or twelve years of age, has arrived from China to be with his older brothers Wong and Shek. But Wong has gone off to work on the railroads and Shek must go to work on a vegetable farm for a few days each week. Ming must take care of the store and the few Chinese customers that come in. Not many Chinese have money, and the store's customers are very few. Ming disobeys his older brother's admonishment and one day when he is bored he slips past Stockton Street, out of Chinatown, where he discovers children and a school. While Ming watches the children, a young boy of a similar age approaches Ming. Their meeting is tentative at first but over days and weeks develops into a real friendship. Patrick teaches Ming to speak English and together they enjoy idyllic days at the store. Patrick takes Ming home to meet his family and the O'Farrell's welcome Ming warmly, telling him stories and inviting him to eat with them. As the friendship between Ming and Patrick and his family grows, the store begins to fail. Fewer and fewer customers are coming in. But spurred on by a chance comment by Shek, Patrick and Ming decide to invite the English-speaking members of San Francisco into the store. The two boys create a large banner for the outside—a banner that says "General Store—We Speak English." Patrick is there to help when the first English-speaking customer stops in a day or so later, and

Ming uses his new language skills to greet and wait on others as the number of customers grows. The friendship between Ming and the entire O'Farrell family is solidified when Mr. O'Farrell comes to the store with several of his co-workers. And just as in history, Shek's store begins to attract more and more customers from outside the boundaries of Chinatown. The detail in Soentpiet's magnificently executed watercolors gives the reader much to explore. The book follows the American experience of Shek and Wong, whom we first meet in *Coolies,* a book by the same collaborators. *Coolies* tells the story of Shek and Wong's work on the railroad and their eventual return to San Francisco and the opening of the general store—the same general store that is part of the *Brothers* story.

Curriculum Link: Transcontinental Railroad, Abraham Lincoln, Immigration

Background

Abraham Lincoln signed the authorization for the nation's first transcontinental railroad on May 20, 1862. That fact helps us date the era of this book. The railroad was completed on May 10, 1869. During 2009 many events honored Abraham Lincoln and his legacy with a yearlong bicentennial celebration.

Family interviews can play a part in using this book as the author of *Brothers* is Chinese. Her parents were immigrants from Hong Kong, and many of the Transcontinental Railroad workers came from the family's ancestral village in Toishan-Canton, China. When Yin was writing about the railroad and Chinatown, she interviewed her grandmother and checked her memories against other primary sources in locations such as the Consolidated Paper Families: Identity, Immigration Administration, and Chinese Exclusion. An author's note in *Brothers* builds the historical context for the story and lists several resource references concerning the immigration of the Chinese and the Irish to America. A school plays a significant role in *Brothers* so resources about the history of schools in America are included as well.

Extension Ideas

1. During the time that the story retold in *Brothers* was taking place, the Civil War was raging in the eastern and southern states. Read accounts of the Civil War and compare and contrast the life of a boy in San Francisco to the responsibilities of a boy in the Civil War. Read the chapter "Children at War" in Martin W. Sandler's *Lincoln Through the Lens: How Photography Revealed and Shaped an Extraordinary Life* (Walker Books for Young Readers, 2008).
2. Investigate trends in immigration during the 1860s. Many Chinese were immigrating. During the 1860s, 10,000 Chinese were said to been involved building the western leg of the Central Pacific Railroad. The average pay for the Chinese was thirty-five dollars a month. On average, each worker could net eighteen dollars or so per month, but the work was dangerous and hard.
3. Investigate the prejudices of the times. For example: Nine-tenths of the railroad workers were Chinese. But in the photographs taken when the golden stake was

driven at the Promontory Point where the east and the west met, not one Chinese worker was included.

4. What is the Chinese Exclusion Act of 1882? Why was the act established?
5. Many Chinese arrived in America and were processed through Angel Island, which became the western Ellis Island. Many immigrants suspected of being "Paper Sons" were detained at Angel Island. Investigate the history of Angel Island.

Books to Explore

Brimmer, Larry Dane. (2001) *Angel Island* (Cornerstones of Freedom). Children's Press/ Scholastic.

Currier, Katrina Saltonstall. (2005) *Kai's Journey to Gold Mountain: An Angel Island Story*. Illustrated by Gabhor Utomo. Angel Island Association.

Lai, Him Mark, et al. (1999) *Island: Poetry and History of Chinese Immigrants on Angel Island, 1910–1940*. University of Washington Press. (Note: Selections from this 174-page book will be appropriate as read-alouds.)

Lee, Milly. (2006) *Landed*. Illustrated by Yangsook Choi. Farrar, Straus and Giroux.

Paulson, Timothy J. (2004) *Irish Immigrants* (Immigration to the United States). Facts on File.

Sandler, Martin W. (2008) *Lincoln Through the Lens: How Photography Revealed and Shaped an Extraordinary Life*. Walker Books for Young Readers.

Teitelbaum, Michael. (2004) *Chinese Immigrants* (Immigration to the United States). Facts on File.

63

R is for Rhyme: A Poetry Alphabet
by Judy Young

Idea Shelf

Use these twenty-six poems to highlight an element of poetry over a period of twenty-six days. This will be a simple exercise for building poetry schema.

Young, Judy. (2006) *R is for Rhyme: A Poetry Alphabet*. Illustrated by Victor Juhasz. Sleeping Bear Press. ISBN: 1-58536-240-9.

Bookshelf

Annotation

This book offers a wonderful alphabet defining twenty-six poetic terms. Large double-page spreads illustrate each letter of the alphabet and its accompanying verse provides examples. For example "A is for Acrostic" is accompanied by a short acrostic verse. A sidebar on the page discusses and explains what an acrostic is, and the picture illustrates the sample poem. Each of the following entries deals with a different poetry concept. The glossary at the end of the book defines additional terms, such as alliteration and poetic license.

Curriculum Link: Language Arts—Poetry; Acrostic, Ballad, Cinquain, Doublet, End Rhyme, Free Verse, Ghazal, Haiku, Iambic, Jingle, Kyrielle, Limerick, Metaphor, Narrative, Onomatopoeia, Picture Poem, Concrete Poetry, Quatrain, Rap, Sonnet, Tanka, Ubi Sunt, Villanelle, Weak Rhyme, Xanadu, You Voice, First Person, Zany Words

Background

Poetry comes in many forms. Those who restrict poetry to a basic structure that they are comfortable with do a disservice to others who might wish to create a poem in quite a different form—and those who restrict the form a writer's poetic expression takes, do not truly understand the genre. In the Books to Explore section that follows, we have included other books that will assist in developing an understanding of various poetic forms.

Before you begin to explore poetry forms with young readers and writers, please take a moment to search out *Anastasia Krupnik* by Lois Lowry (Houghton Mifflin, 1979) and read pages 8–13. I think you will find that you will not want to emulate the rigidity of Mrs. Westvessel.

Extension Ideas

Each of the double-page spreads in this book can be read aloud and utilized as a springboard to another discussion of a poetic form. Use the book as a basis for an extended emphasis on the poetic form.

Each of the topics associated with individual letters of the alphabet inspire additional language experiences. The following are brief notes about each term and expression.

1. Acrostic: poetic example in the book, "Drawing"

   a. The section will stimulate thinking about synonyms. A good chance to introduce the use of a thesaurus to explore synonyms.
   b. Want to try your hand at writing an acrostic? Use a name (perhaps write a group/class poem using your name as the basis) and create a descriptive acrostic based on the person's personality.
   SUZI
   Sensitive and shy
   Unusually creative
   Zany and very funny
   Interesting and animated

2. Ballad: poetic example in the book, "Ballad of the Butterfly and Rose"

   a. Discusses stanzas and meter (patterns of unstressed and stressed syllables) and extend the lesson with other examples.
   b. Explore the poetry of two well-known poets who became well known for their ballads.

      i. Stephen Vincent Benét (1898–1943) was a popular and highly acclaimed poet who became well known, particularly for his "John Brown's Body" (1928), an epic narrative poem about the U.S. Civil War. Benét was awarded two Pulitzer prizes for his poetry. A book that contains several narrative poems/ballads of historical figures is *Book of Americans* by Rosemary Benét and Stephen Vincent Benét (Henry Holt & Company, 1987).
      ii. Robert W. Service (1874–1958) wrote the well-known "Cremation of Sam McGee" that is included in *Best Tales of the Yukon Including the Classic "Shooting of Dan McGrew" and "The Cremation of Sam McGee"* (Running Press Books, 2002). Service is known for chronicling the Klondike gold rush (early 1900s) and the frozen Yukon Territory. He was a bank teller and lived between 1909 and 1912 in a log cabin on 8th Avenue in Dawson City, Yukon. After his poetry made him prosperous, he traveled to Europe, married a French

woman, and wrote about many other subjects. He died in France and is buried in the local cemetery in Lancieux, France.

3. Cinquain: "My Shadow"

Cinquain

For more information about the cinquain form and its many variations, visit ‹http://www.cinquain.org›, a site devoted to the legacy of Adelaide Crapsey.

Toleos, Aaron. (2005–2006) "A scholarly exploration of the American cinquain as popularlized by Adelaide Crapsey." This is available at ‹http://www.cinquain.org›.

   a. A cinquain is any poem or stanza that has five lines.
   b. Adelaide Crapsey (1878–1914) developed a "Crapsey Cinquain" that has a syllable count of 2-4-6-8-2. She did not invent the cinquain but rather used the five-line poem and, inspired by the Japanese haiku and tanka, developed what she believed to be "the shortest and simplest possible in English verse."

4. Doublet: "Rain to Snow?" (Note: The doublet was invented by Lewis Carroll in 1879.)
5. End Rhyme: "How Would You Act?" (Note: Discusses rhyming patterns.)
6. Free verse: "White Rabbits with Red Wings" (Notes: Modern free verse began with Walt Whitman's *Leaves of Grass*, and explanation mentions the work of Carl Sandburg, Langston Hughes, E. E. Cummings, and William Carlos Williams.)
7. Ghazal: "My Baby Brother" (Notes: This ancient Persian poetry form from 1000 BCE is used widely in Iran, Iraq, and India. Mentions English work of Jim Harrison and Andrienne Rich. Five to twelve couplets [two-line stanzas].)
8. Haiku first line: "pearly triangles" (Notes: Haiku is a poem of three lines of five-seven-five syllable count per line; generally focuses on nature. Also mentions senryu [SEN-ree-you], which has same syllable count but focuses more on humans or man-made products. Haiku writers: Matsuo Basho, Kobayashi Issa.)
9. Iambic: "Two Chains" (Notes: The most common meter in English poetry. The meter is made up of "iambs" two syllables long; the first syllable is unstressed.)
10. Jingle: "The Sweet Tooth Candy Shop" (Notes: A jingle is a simple catchy poem about a light or humorous topic,)
11. Kyrielle: "Oh, Don't You Wish" (Notes: This is an old French poetry form in which each syllable has four lines and each line has eight syllables; the last line of the first stanza is also the last line of another stanza.)
12. Limerick: "The Ballerina" (Notes: A limerick is a five-line poem using rhyme and humor with a rhyme pattern—aabba. Discusses thesaurus and synonyms. Does not mention the master of limericks, Edward Lear.)
13. Metaphor: "Bluebird" (Notes: A metaphor "is" something else; a related poetic tool is a simile that says, "something is LIKE something else."
14. Narrative: "Reading Homer" (Notes: A narrative poem tells a story. Examples are *The Odyssey* by Homer, *John Brown's Body* by Stephen Vincent Benét, and "A Girl's Garden" and "Stopping by the Woods on a Snowy Day" by Robert Frost.)
15. Onomatopoeia: "The Ears of the Elephant" (Notes: a poetic device that uses onomatopoeia words. Two types: euphonic words (sounds soft and smooth), cacophonous words (hard, hoarse, and rough.)
16. Picture Poem: "The Kite" (Notes: A picture poem is arranged in a configuration to make a shape. Some other names for picture poems are shape poems, concrete

poems, and calligrams. George Herbert wrote shaped poems in the 1600s but Guillaume Apollinaire is often referred to as the inventor of shape poems [1900s].)

17. Quatrain: "My Quilt" (Notes: A quatrain is a poem written with four-line stanzas.) Other length stanzas have other names:

    monostich
    couplet
    tercet
    cinquain
    sestet
    septet
    octave

18. Rap: "Cowboy Rap" (Notes: Rap is a style of vocal music traced to jazz poetry chanted and performed aloud; cowboy poetry emphasizes the history and folklore of cowboys. 1886, Lysius Gough became the first Texas cowboy to publish a book of poetry. Early cowboy poems were in the style of a ballad; now they are written in many styles.)

19. Sonnet: "Yellow Dog" (Notes: Fourteen lines, iambic pentameter [five sets of unstressed/stressed syllables or five feet (sets) of paired syllables]. Rhyming patterns vary: Shakespearean English sonnet has a rhyme pattern of abab ccdcd efef gg. "Yellow Dog" is a Shakespearean rhyming pattern. A Petrarchan (Francesco Petrarch) sonnet has a rhyming pattern of abba abba cdc dcd.)

20. Tanka first line: "waxy hexagons" (Notes: Tanka is a Japanese poetry form written in syllabic lines of five-seven-five-seven-seven. Form preserved by Masaoka Shiki and Yossano Akiko in modern literature.)

21. Ubi Sunt: "Extinction" (Notes: This form calls out lists of people, ancient muses, etc., and asks "where are" these people; modern ubi sunt poetry often uses names of sports heroes, events in nature, etc. Pete Seeger used ubi sunt for his folk song "Where Have All the Flowers Gone?")

22. Villanelle: "The Rule" (Notes: The word means "country house," so these poems are generally about everyday things and events. Nineteen lines, six stanzas. First five stanzas have three lines. Dylan Thomas' "Do Not Go Gentle into That Good Night" is a villanelle; E. A. Robinson and W. H. Auden also wrote villanelles.

23. Weak Rhyme: "My Song" (Notes: Words that almost rhyme are weak rhymes; they are also called slant, off, near, or half rhymes. Example: easy/crazy; sing/nothing; end/again. Visual rhymes are those that look as if they should rhyme but do not. Example: good/food. They are sometimes referred to as eye rhymes.)

24. Xanadu (ZAN-a-doo): "Xanadu" (Notes: This describes an imaginary place more beautiful and wonderous than anything in reality. Examples: "Kubla Khan" by Samuel Taylor—Kubla Khan visited Xanadu—and William Butler Yeats' "The Lake Isle of Innisfree." "Xanadu" wonders how to get to exotic places that other authors have written about—the land of Oz, Jack's beanstalk world, Narnia, Wendy/Peter Pan, and [Alice in] Wonderland.)

25. You Voice: "Hanging On" (Notes: This kind of poem uses "you" to make you feel like you are reading about yourself—second person. First person uses "I" and "we"; third person uses "he," "she," "they," and "it." The poem here includes a metaphor.)

26. Zany Words: "Skimble-scamble" (Notes: skimble-scamble = nonsense; wallaroo = kind of kangaroo; skedaddle = to leave quickly; glockenspiel = musical instrument; lickety-split = quickly; quidnunc = noisy person; plus many made-up words.)

Books to Explore

Examples of these types of poems can be found in collections and anthologies. If we have been able to identify specific books to correspond with the idea presented by the alphabetical entry, we have cited it below. If not, we have left space so those books you are able to indentify may be written directly in this book for your reference later.

1. Acrostic:
   (See the last sonnet in *A Wreath for Emmett Till*.)

2. Ballad:
   Benét, Rosemary, and Stephen Vincent Benét. (1987) *Book of Americans*. Henry Holt & Company.
   Service, Robert W. (2002) *Best Tales of the Yukon: Including the Classic "Shooting of Dan McGrew" and "The Cremation of Sam McGee."* Running Press Books.

3. Cinquain:
   Crapsey, Adelaide, and Susan Sutton Smith. (1977) *Complete Poems and Collected Letters of Adelaide Crapsey*. State University of New York Press.

4. Doublet:

5. Ending Rhyme:

6. Free Verse:
   cummings, e. e. (1994) *E. E. Cummings: Complete Poems (1904–1962)*. Liveright Publishing.
   Roessel, David. (2006) *Poetry for Young People: Langston Hughes*. Illustrated by Benny Andrews. Sterling.
   Sandburg, Carl. (2003) *The Complete Poems of Carl Sandburg*. Harcourt.
   Whitman, Walt. (2007) *Leaves of Grass*. Book Jungle. (Many other editions have become available since its first publication in 1855.)
   Williams, William Carlos. (2004) *William Carlos Williams: Selected Poems*. Library of America.

7. Ghazal:
   Harrison, Jim. (1996) *After Ikkyu and Other Poems*. Shambbala.

8. Haiku:
   Gollub, Matthew. (1998) *Cool Melons—Turn to Frogs: The Life and Poems of Issa. Story and Haiku Translations*. Illustrated by Kazuko G. Stone. Lee & Low Books.
   Mamatas, Nick. (2006) *Cthulhu Senryu*. Prime Books.

9. Iambic:

10. Jingle:

11. Kyrielle:

12. Limerick:
    Lear, Edward, and Holbrook Jackson, comp. (1951) *The Complete Nonsense of Edward Lear*. Dover Publications.
    Lear, Edward, and Vivian Noakes, ed. (2002) *Edward Lear: The Complete Verse and Other Nonsense*. Penguin.

13. Metaphor:

14. Narrative:
    Benét, Rosemary, and Stephen Vincent Benét. (1987) *Book of Americans*. Henry Holt & Company.
    Frost, Robert. (2001) *Stopping by Woods on a Snowy Evening*. Illustrated by Susan Jeffers. Dutton Juvenile.

15. Onomatopoeia:

16. Picture Poem (Concrete):
    Grandits, John. (2004) *Technically, It's Not My Fault: Concrete Poems*. Clarion.
    Grandits, John. (2007) *Blue Lipstick: Concrete Poems*. Clarion.

17. Quatrain:

18. Cowboy Rap:
    Cannon, Hal. (1975) *New Cowboy Poetry*. Gibbs Smith Publisher.
    Cannon, Hal. (1990) *Cowboy Poetry*. Gibbs Smith Publisher.
    Stanley, David, and Elaine Thatcher. (1999) *Cowboy Poets & Cowboy Poetry*. University of Illinois Press.

19. Sonnet:
    Nelson, Marilyn. (2005) *A Wreath for Emmett Till*. Illustrated by Phillippe Lardy. Houghton Mifflin.

20. Tanka:
    Shiki, Masaoka. (1998) *Songs from a Bamboo Village: Selected Tanka from Takenosato Uta*. Tuttle Publishing.
    Shiki, Masaoka. (2006) *Cien Jaikus*. Hyperion.

21. Ubi Sunt:
    Seeger, Pete. (1997) *Where Have All the Flowers Gone?: A Singer's Stories, Songs, Seeds, Robberies*. Sing Out Publications.

22. Villanelle:
    Auden, W. H. (1991) *Collected Poems*: Auden. Vintage.

23. Weak rhyme:

24. Xanadu:

25. You voice:

26. Zany words:

Picture This!

A Quick List of Picture Books for Your Classroom/Library

There are literally hundreds of picture books that could be parlayed into use in any classroom depending on their content, goals, and objectives. These are just a few of my favorites—favorites that may need to be found in libraries if they are no longer available for purchase. I've included a very brief annotation with some of these titles but not with others when I felt the title or keywords were explanation enough. Browse through these titles or use the Index of the Quick List to find specific books to incorporate into your classroom and literacy activities. Locate the book and make notes alongside the entry so that you have everything at your fingertips. Create your lesson folder and give it a number. Record that folder number here or use the number we have assigned. In any case, filing your lesson folders by number can make the process of locating material faster and all the discussion questions, annotations, charts, or notes about how you used the book will be at hand.

The Bookshelf

1. Adler, David A. (1990) *A Picture Book of Helen Keller*. Illustrated by John Wallner and Alexandra Wallner. Holiday House. (Social Studies and Character Education: Overcoming Adversities, Perseverance)

2. Adler, David A. (1993) *A Picture Book of Anne Frank*. Illustrated by Karen Ritz. Holiday House. (Social Studies: World War II) Pair with other books dealing with World War II.

3. Adler, David. (1997) *Hiding from the Nazis*. Illustrated by Karen Ritz. Holiday House. (Social Studies: World War II; Holocaust) Pair with *The Hiding Place* by Corrie Ten Bloom (Bantam, 1984).

4. Adler, David. (1999) *How Tall, How Short, How Faraway*. Illustrated by Nancy Tobin. Holiday House. (Mathematics: Measurement) Details several measuring systems such as the Egyptian system, the inch-pound system, and the metric system.

5. Ahlberg, Janet, and Allan Ahlberg. (1996) *The Jolly Postman*. Little, Brown. (Language Arts: Writing—Letter Writing) Launch a letter-writing unit.

6. Aliki. (1983) *Medieval Feast*. HarperCollins. (Social Studies: Middle Ages)

7. Aliki. (1999). *William Shakespeare & the Globe*. HarperCollins. (Literature: Shakespeare) Begin any study of Shakespeare with this biography.

8. Amis, Nancy. (2003) *The Orphans of Normandy: A True Story of World War II Told Through Drawings by Children*. Atheneum

Books for Young Readers. (Social Studies: World War II) Relates how 100 young schoolgirls, many of them orphans, and their teachers managed to escape the chaos of the Allied invasion of Normandy on June 6, 1944, by taking shelter in an iron mine for thirty-eight days and, after being forced out by the Germans, walked for twenty-nine days to reach safety behind Allied lines.

9. Ancona, George. (2003) *Murals: Walls That Sing*. Cavendish. (Art: Photo Essay, Murals)

10. Anderson, Joan. (1988) *A Williamsburg Household*. Illustrated by George Ancona. Clarion Books. (Social Studies: American History 1770–1776; Williamsburg, Daily Life, Black Family) Fiction but photos and information about clothing worn and housing provided by the Colonial Williamsburg Historic Association.

11. Angeletti, Roberta. (2000) *The Minotaur of Knossos*. Oxford University Press (Social Studies: Ancient Crete; Greek mythology, 2000 BCE, Minotaur)

12. Appelt, Kathi. (2005). *Miss Lady Bird's Wildflowers: How a First Lady Changed America*. Illustrated by Joy Fisher Hein. Harper-Collins. (Science: Environment—First Lady) Lady Bird Johnson, as the wife of President Lyndon Johnson developed a highway beautification program and promoted beautifying the nation's highways. Use this book as a call to action. What can *you* do to promote beautification of the community where you live?

13. Armstrong, Jennifer. (2003). *Audubon: Painter of Birds in the Wild Frontier*. Illustrated by Joseph A. Smith. Harry N. Abrams. (Art: John James Audubon, Nineteenth-Century Painter and Naturalist; Watercolors; Birds)

14. Arnold, Caroline. (2005). *The Skeletal System*. Lerner Publications Co. (Science: Biology) Brief introduction of the body and its bones.

15. Balgassi, Haemi. (1996) *Peacebound Trains*. Illustrated by Chris K. Soentpiet. Clarion Books. (Social Studies: Korean War, Seoul, Escape)

16. Barasch, Lynne. (2004). *Knockin' on Wood: Starring Peg Leg Bates*. Lee & Low Books. (Character Education: Perseverance) Presents a picture book biography of Clayton "Peg Leg" Bates, an African American who lost his leg in a factory accident at the age of twelve and went on to become a world-famous tap dancer.

17. Bartoletti, Susan Campbell. (2004) *The Flag Maker*. Illustrated by Claire A. Nivola. Houghton Mifflin. (Social Studies: American History—1812, Battle of Baltimore, Fort McHenry)

18. Bates, Katherine L. (1993) *America the Beautiful*. Illustrated by Neil Waldman. Atheneum. (Art/Music) Presents the 1893 poem written by Katharine Lee Bates illustrated with fourteen acrylic paintings by Waldman. Compare them to the images inspired by the song in other editions, including *America the Beautiful*, with illustrations by Wendell Minor (Putnam Juvenile, 2003).

19. Battle-Lavert. Gwendolyn. (2003) *Papa's Mark*. Illustrated by Colin Bootman. Holiday House. (Social Studies: African Americans, Voting Rights)

20. Bedard, Michael. (1992). *Emily*. Illustrated by Barbara Cooney. Doubleday Books for Young Readers. (Literature) Introduction to the reclusive poet, Emily Dickinson.

21. Behnke, Alison. (2005) *Chinese in America*. Lerner Publications Co. (Social Studies: Immigration) Examines the history of Chinese immigration to the United States, discussing why they came, what they did when they got here, where they settled, and the customs they brought with them.

22. Berry, S. L. (2004). *William Carlos Williams. Voices in Poetry.* Creative Education. (Literature) Introduction to the life and poetry of William Carlos Williams.

23. Birch, David. (1988) *The King's Chessboard.* Dial Books. (Mathematics: Geometric Progression) This book is set in India.

24. Bjork, Christina, and Lena Anderson. (1987) *Linnea in Monet's Garden.* Farrar, Straus and Giroux. (Art) Claude Monet's life and art.

25. Blake, Robert J. (1997) *Akiak: A Tale of the Iditarod.* Philomel Books. (Social Studies: Alaska)

26. Borden, Louise. (2000) *Sleds on Boston Common: A Story from the American Revolution.* Simon & Schuster. Illustrated by Robert Andrew Parker. (Social Studies: American History—American Revolution; Causes of War)

27. Borden, Louise. (2004) *The Greatest Skating Race: A World War II Story from the Netherlands.* Illustrated by Niki Daly. Margaret K. McElderry Books. (Social Studies: World War II—Netherlands) A tale, based on actual events, of a young boy who takes two younger children to safety by skating past the Nazi's. Pair with *Snow Treasure* by Maria McSwigan (Puffin pb, 2006)—an imaginary event but a plausible tale.

28. Borden, Louise. (2005). *The Journey That Saved Curious George: The True Wartime Escape of Margret and H.A. Rey.* Houghton Mifflin. (Social Studies: World War II, the Holocaust) Tells the story of the Reys and their flight from the Nazis when the Nazis invaded Paris during World War II.

29. Borden, Louise. (2006). *Across the Blue Pacific: A World War II Story.* Illustrated by Robert Andrew Parker. Houghton Mifflin.

(Social Studies: World War II/Language Arts—Writing) A soldier is the subject of a letter-writing campaign by some fourthgraders when he goes away to war in 1943.

30. Bosak, Susan V. (2004). *Dream: A Tale of Wonder, Wisdom & Wishes*. Illustrated by Leo Dillon, Diane Dillon, Robert R. Ingpen, Raul Colon, and others. TCP Press. (Language Arts) An inspirational piece (free verse) that will inspire discussions and writing about setting goals or having dreams and achieving them.

31. Bower, Tamara. (2005) *How The Amazon Queen Fought the Prince of Egypt*. Atheneum Books (Social Studies: Ancient Egypt) Serpot leads her Amazon warriors in battle against Prince Pedikhons of Egypt. Includes notes about Assyrian and Egyptian culture and hieroglyphics.

32. Branley, Franklyn. (1988) *Journey into a Black Hole*. Illustrated by Marc Simont. HarperCollins. (Science: Black Holes)

33. Bridges, Ruby. (1999). *Through My Eyes*. Scholastic. (Social Studies: School Integration) Ruby Bridges recounts the story of her involvement, as a six-year-old, in the integration of her school in New Orleans in 1960.

34. Brimner, Larry Dane. (2004) *Subway: The Story of Tunnels, Tubes, and Tracks*. Illustrated by Neil Waldman. Boyds Mills Press. (Social Studies: History of Subways in London, Paris, and New York.) Great introduction to architecture and transportation.

35. Bruchac, Joseph. (1998) *Many Nations: A Native American Alphabet*. Troll Communications. (Social Studies: Native Americans)

36. Bruchac, Marge. (2005) *Malian's Song*. Illustrated by William Maughan. Vermont Folklife Center. (Social Studies: Native

American History) The true story of the deliberate attack by British Major Robert Rogers on the St. Francis Abenaki community near Montreal in 1759. The oral story passed down through the generations is recounted in Abenaki and English text. In addition to the historic significance of this title, consider using it as a model for oral history projects in your community.

37. Brumbeau, Jeff, and Gail de Marcken. (2005) *The Quiltmaker's Journey*. Orchard Books. (Social Studies) A quiltmaker who grew up wealthy changes her view of life after seeing the poverty outside her own community. Research information about real-life people who have left their riches behind to help others.

38. Brumbeau, Jeff, and Gail de Marcken. (2001) *The Quiltmaker's Gift*. Orchard Books. (Art) A literary folktale featuring more than 250 quilt patterns, a greedy king, and a generous quiltmaker. Replicate the quilt squares.

39. Bryant, Jennifer. (2005) *Music for the End of Time*. Illustrated by Beth Peck. Eerdmans Books for Young Readers. (Social Studies: World War II, French Composer—Olivier Messiaen, German Prison Camp, *Quartet for the End of Time*) True story of French composer Oliver Messiaen, who was permitted to write and perform his music while a prisoner.

40. Bunting, Eve. (1996) *The Blue and the Gray*. Scholastic Press. (Social Studies: Civil War)

41. Bunting, Eve. (1998) *So Far from the Sea*. Clarion Books. (Social Studies: World War II—Japanese Internment)

42. Burns, Marilyn. (1994; 2008) *The Greedy Triangle*. Scholastic. (Mathematics: Geometry)

43. Byrd, Robert (2003) *Leonardo, Beautiful Dreamer*. Dutton Children's Books. (Art and Social Studies) A biography of da

Vinci, artist, inventor, scientist, and creator of "Mona Lisa"; he also conducted studies in the area of human anatomy and flight.

44. Capatii, Berenice, translator. (2004) *Klimt and His Cat.* Eerdmans Books for Young Readers. (Art: Gustav Klimt, 1880s, Paintings, Austrian Artist)

45. Celenza, Anna Harwell. (2003) *Pictures at an Exhibition.* Illustrated by Joann Kitchel. Charlesbridge. (Music: Modest Mussorgsky, Classical Music, Art, Piano Suite, *Pictures at an Exhibition*) Use to introduce the historical fiction mystery *Pictures at an Exhibition* by Sara Houghteling (Alfred A. Knopf, 2009).

46. Celenza, Anna Harwell. (2005) *Bach's Goldberg Variations.* Illustrated by Joann Kitchel. Charlesbridge. (Music: 1773, Johann Gottlieb Goldberg, Johann Sebastian Bach, *Goldberg Variations*)

47. Celenza, Anna Harwell. (2005) *The Farewell Symphony.* Illustrated by Joann Kitchel. Charlesbridge. (Music: 1770, Symphony No. 45)

48. Cheripko, Jan. (2004) *Caesar Rodney's Ride: The Story of an American Patriot.* Illustrated by Gary Lippincott. Boyds Mills Press. (Social Studies: Declaration of Independence.) Rodney, one of Delaware's representatives to the Second Continental Congress, suffered from asthma and a cancer that was slowly destroying his face, but knowing that his vote was crucial, he made the necessary ride to sign the Declaration of Independence.

49. Cherry, Lynne. (1990) *The Great Kapok Tree.* Harcourt Brace. (Science: Environment; Rain Forest)

50. Chin-Lee, Cynthia, and Terri de la Pena. (1999) *A is for the Americas.* Orchard Books. (Social Studies: Central Americans)

51. Cleary, Brian P. (1996) *Jamaica Sandwich?* Lerner Publications. (Social Studies: Geography)

52. Climo, Shirley. (1989) *The Egyptian Cinderella.* HarperCollins. (Language Arts: Versions of Cinderella—Ancient Egypt)

53. Climo, Shirley. (1993) *The Korean Cinderella.* HarperCollins. (Language Arts: Versions of Cinderella—Korea)

54. Clinton, Catherine. (2005) *Hold the Flag High.* Illustrated by Shane W. Evans. HarperCollins. (Social Studies: Civil War—Massachusetts, Fort Wagner, Black Officer)

55. Coerr, Eleanor. (1993) *Sadako.* G. P. Putnam's Sons. (Social Studies: World War II)

56. Cole, Barbara Hancock. (1990) *Texas Star.* Orchard Books. (Mathematics: Patterns—Quilts)

57. Colman, Penny. (1995) *Rosie the Riveter.* Random House. (Social Studies: World War II)

58. Compestine, Ying Chang. (2003) *The Story of Kites.* Illustrated by Yongsheng Xuan. Holiday House. (Social Studies: China History) Three brothers find a solution to chasing birds from their family's rice fields. Compare to the development of scarecrows.

59. Compestine, Ying Chang. (2003) *The Story of Paper.* Illustrated by Yongsheng Xuan. Holiday House. (Social Studies: China History—Paper Making)

60. Coville, Bruce. (2003) *William Shakespeare's Twelfth Night.* Illustrated by Tim Raglin. Dial Books. This is a simplified prose

retelling of Shakespeare's comedy about shipwreck, mistaken identity, and misplaced love. Coville had similar retellings of *Macbeth*, *The Tempest*, and *Romeo and Juliet*.

61. Cowling, Douglas. (2002) *Hallelujah Handel*. Illustrated by Jason Walker. Scholastic Press. (Music: George Frideric Handel, History of London, Foundling Hospital). Handel bequeathed the score for his *Messiah* to the Foundling Hospital. This book makes the connection for students of Handel. Historical facts included.

62. Curlee, Lynn. (2003) *Capital*. Atheneum Books for Young Readers. (Social Studies: History of Washington, D.C.) Great introduction to travel and tourist sites. Write travel brochures.

63. Curlee, Lynn. (2005) *Ballpark: The Story of America's Baseball Fields*. Atheneum Books for Young Readers. (Sports history: Baseball stadiums—Map the location of the famous ballparks: Fenway Park in Boston, Yankee Stadium in New York City, Wrigley Field in Chicago, and others) Examine the cultural history, the food, and the significance of the differences.

64. Currier, Katrina Saltonstall. (2005) *Kai's Journey to Gold Mountain*. Illustrated by Gabhor Utomo. Angel Island Association. (Social Studies: Immigration—Angel Island, Chinese, San Francisco, Chinese) Actual experience of Albert Wong during his detainment at Angel Island.

65. Demi. (1997) *One Grain of Rice: A Mathematical Folktale*. Scholastic. (Mathematics: Geometric Progression)

66. Demi. (2003) *Muhammad*. Margaret K. McElderry Books. (Social Studies: World Cultures) Introduces Muhammad and the basic tenets of the Islamic faith.

67. Dooling, Michael. (1994) *Thomas Jefferson: A Picture Book Biography*. Scholastic. (Social Studies: American Revolution)

68. Dunlap, Julie, and Marybeth Lorbiecki. (2002) *Louisa May and Mr. Thoreau's Flute*. Illustrated by Mary Azarian. Dial Books for Young Readers. (Language Arts: Louisa May Alcott, Henry David Thoreau)

69. Edwards, Pamela Duncan. (1999) *The Wacky Wedding: A Book of Alphabet Antics*. Illustrated by Henry Cole. Hyperion. (Language Arts: Alliteration)

70. Erdrich, Liselotte. (2003) *Sacagawea*. Illustrated by Julie Buffalohead. Carolrhoda Books. (Social Studies: Lewis and Clark Expedition) Speculation about her life after the expedition completes this account of Sacagawea's life from age eleven, when she was kidnapped by the Hidatsa to the end of her journey with Lewis and Clark.

71. Evans, Freddi Williams. (2001) *A Bus of Our Own*. Illustrated by Shawn Costello. Albert Whitman & Company. (Social Studies: Segregation, 1950s, Mississippi) A black child finds a way to get a bus for her and other black children to ride five miles to school; based on real events in Mississippi in the 1950s.

72. Feder, Paula Kurzband. (1995, 2000) *The Feather-Bed Journey*. Illustrated by Stacey Schuett. Albert Whitman & Company. (Social Studies: World War II, Poland, Warsaw Ghetto, Jewish)

73. Fleming, Candace. (2003) *Boxes For Katje*, Illustrated by Stacey Dressen-McQueen. Farrar, Straus and Giroux. (Social Studies: Post-World War II, Holland, Kindness)

74. Frasier, Debra. (2000) *Miss Alaineus: A Vocabulary Disaster*. Harcourt Children's Books. (English: Vocabulary Building and Word Meaning)

75. Friedman, Aileen. (1994) *A Cloak for the Dreamer*. Scholastic. (Mathematics: Geometry, Puzzle to Solve)

76. Friedman, Robin. (2005) *The Silent Witness*, Illustrated by Claire A. Nivola. Houghton Mifflin. (Social Studies: Civil War, Battle of Bull Run, Appomattox 1865) This is a fictional account of the McLean family of Manassas, Virginia, and their eyewitness accounts of two important events. Pair with Candice F. Ransom's *Willie McLean and the Civil War Surrender*. illustrated by Jeni Reeves (Carolrhoda Books, 2004).

77. Fuchs, Bernie. (2004) *Ride Like the Wind: A Tale of the Pony Express*. Blue Sky Express. (Social Studies: American History— Pony Express) The book contains a *Storyteller's Note* and an epilogue with factual information about the Pony Express.

78. Gates, Phil. (1999) *The History News: Medicine*. Scholastic. (Science: Medical history)

79. Gerstein, Mordicai. (2003) *The Man Who Walked Between the Towers*. Roaring Brook Press. (Social Studies: Daring Events, World Trade Center, Philippe Petit.) Before the trade towers were completed, Petit walked, danced, and performed on a tightrope high above the street, a rope stretched between the two buildings.

80. Gerstein, Mordicai. (1999) *The Absolutely Awful Alphabet*. Harcourt Children's Books. (Language Arts: Alliteration)

81. Giovanni, Nikki. (2005) *Rosa*. Illustrated by Bryan Collier. Henry Holt. (Social Studies: Civil Rights) Rosa Park's experience during the bus boycott in Montgomery, Alabama, in 1955.

82. Granfield, Linda. (1995) *In Flanders Fields: The Story of the Poem by John McCrae*. Illustrated by Janet Wilson. Stoddart Kids. (Social Studies: World War I) The background for the famous poem by the Canadian medical officer who attended injured soldiers in Flanders Fields during World War I.

83. Granfield, Linda. (1999) *High Flight*. Canada: Tundra Books. (Social Studies: World War II)

84. Grimes, Nikki. (2008) *Barack Obama: Son of Promise, Child of Hope*. Illustrations by Bryan Collier. Simon & Schuster Books for Young Readers. (Social Studies: Government)

85. Halfmann, Janet. (2008) *Seven Miles to Freedom: The Robert Smalls Story*. Illustrated by Duane Smith. Lee & Low Books. (Social Studies: Civil War; Character Education: Perseverance, Persistence, Courage) Pair with Doreen Rappaport's *Freedom Ship*, a book that tells another version of the day in May 1862, when Robert Smalls sailed *The Planter* past three Confederate forts and into the arms of the Union fleet (Hyperion/Jump at the Sun, 2006) and became one of the Civil War's greatest heroes.

86. Hall, Bruce Edward. (2004) *Henry and the Kite Dragon*. Illustrated by William Low. Philomel Books. (Social Studies: Chinatown, New York City, 1920s, Kites) This book deals with racial tension.

87. Hall, Francie. (1998) *Appalachian ABCs*. Tennessee: The Overmountain Press. (Social Studies: West Virginia History)

88. Harshman, Marc. (1993) *Only One*. Cobblehill Books. (Character Education: Being Unique)

89. Heller, Ruth. (1987) *A Cache of Jewels and Other Collective Nouns*. Scholastic (English: Word Usage—Collective Nouns)

90. Heller, Ruth. (1990) *Merry-Go-Round: A Book About Nouns*. Grossett & Dunlap. (English: Word Usage—Nouns)

91. Heller, Ruth. (1988) *Kites Sail High: A Book About Verbs*. Grosset & Dunlap. (English: Word Usage—Verbs)

92. Heller, Ruth. (1989) *Many Luscious Lollipops: A Book About Adjectives*. Scholastic. (English: Word Usage—Adjectives)

93. Heller, Ruth. (1991) *Up, Up and Away: A Book About Adverbs.* Grossett & Dunlap. (English: Word Usage—Adverbs)

94. Heller, Ruth. (1995) *Behind the Mask: A Book About Prepositions.* Grosset & Dunlap. (English: Word Usage—Prepositions)

95. Heller, Ruth. (1997) *Mine, All Mine: A Book About Pronouns.* Grosset & Dunlap. (English: Word Usage—Pronouns)

96. Heller, Ruth. (1998) *Fantastic! Wow! And Unreal! A Book About Interjections and Conjunctions.* Grosset & Dunlap. (English: World Usage—Interjections and Conjunctions)

97. Hepworth, Cathi. (1992) *Antics!* G. P. Putnam's Sons. (English: Vocabulary) A book of word play, an alphabet of words with the syllable "ant."

98. Hesse, Karen. (2004) *The Cats In Krasinski Square,* Scholastic. Illustrated by Wendy Watson. (Social Studies: World War II, Poland, Warsaw Ghetto, Jewish, Holocaust) Two clever sisters figure out how to use cats to thwart an attempt by the Nazis to take food intended for the starving people of the Warsaw ghetto.

99. Hoestlandt, Jo. (1993) *Star of Fear, Star of Hope.* Allen & Son. (Social Studies: World War II, Holocaust)

100. Hoffman, Mary. (1991) *Amazing Grace.* Illustrated by Caroline Binch. Scholastic. (Character Education: Perseverance, Persistence)

101. Hoffman, Mary. (2002) *The Color of Home.* Illustrated by Karin Littlewood. Phyllis Fogelman Books. (Social Studies: Immigration—Somalia)

102. Hopkinson, Deborah (2001) *Under the Quilt of Night*. Illustrated by James E. Ransome. Atheneum Books for Young Readers. (Social Studies: Underground Railroad) A fictional account of a young slave girl's escape on the Underground Railroad.

103. Hopkinson, Deborah. (2003) *Girl Wonder: A Baseball Story in Nine Innings*. Illustrated by Terry Widener. Atheneum. (Sports: Baseball, Alta Weiss, Women in Sports, 1900s)

104. Hopkinson, Deborah. (2004) *Saving Strawberry Farm*. Illustrated by Rachel Isadora. Greenwillow Books. (Social Studies: Depression) A small boy helps neighbors ban together to save Miss Elsie's farm from being taken over by the bank. Author's note gives details about the effects of the Great Depression.

105. Hopkinson, Deborah. (2006) *Sky Boys: How They Built the Empire State Building*. Illustrated by James E. Ransome. Schwartz & Wade Books. (Social Studies: Construction, Empire State Building [1931]) Study the history of a significant building in your city/area.

106. Hummon, David. (1999) *Animal Acrostics*. Dawn Publications. (Science: Animals and Acrostic Poetry)

107. Hunt, Jonathan. (1989) *Illuminations*. Aladdin Books. (Social Studies: Middle Ages and Illuminated Text)

108. Innocenti, Roberto, et al. (1985) *Rose Blanche*. Creative Education. (Language Arts/Reading) Collaborative Title—*The Devil's Arithmetic* by Jane Yolen [Viking, 1988]; Social Studies: World War II, Holocaust)

109. Jaspersohn, William. (2000) *The Two Brothers*. Illustrated by Michael A. Donato. Vermont Folklife Center. (Social Studies:

Immigration—Prussia) Based on the story of two brothers, one who immigrated to the United States, and the other who stayed in Europe until their mother's death. They were reunited in America.

110. Johnston, Tony. (2004) *The Harmonica*. Illustrated by Ron Mazellan. Charlesbridge. (Social Studies: World War II, Poland, Warsaw Ghetto, Jewish) Music brings a young Jewish boy, in a concentration camp, some solace even during the worst of times.

111. Jordan, Martin, and Tanis Jordan. (1991) *Journey of the Red-Eyed Tree Frog*. Simon & Schuster Books for Young Readers. (Science: Rain Forest)

112. Jordan, Martin, and Tanis Jordan. (1996) *Amazon Alphabet*. Kingfisher. (Science: Rain Forest)

113. Karr, Kathleen, and Bonnie Christensen. (2005) *Mama Went to Jail for the Vote*. Illustrated by Malene Laugesen. Hyperion, 2005. (Social Studies: Women's Suffrage, 1913)

114. Keller, Laurie. (1998) *The Scrambled States of America*. Henry Holt & Co. (Social Studies: U.S. Geography)

115. Kerisel, Francoise. (2004) *Diogenes' Lantern*. Illustrated by Frederick Mansot. J. Paul Getty Museum. (Social Studies: Ancient Greece—Diogenes, 400 BCE)

116. Kerley, Barbara. (2004) *Walt Whitman: Words for America*. Illustrated by Brian Selznick. Scholastic Press. (Literature: An American poet who nursed soldiers during the Civil War and wrote of the nation's grief at Lincoln's assassination.)

117. Kimmel, Eric. (2005) *The Hero Beowulf*. Illustrated by Lee Fisher. Farrar, Straus and Giroux. (Literature) A brief retelling of Beowulf. A great introduction.

118. Kirk, Connie Anne. (2004) *Sky Dancers*. Illustrated by Christy Hale. Lee & Low Books. (Social Studies: Native Americans, Mohawk [Iroquois], Steelworkers, 1930–1940, New York City, Landmarks) Fiction, but the author's note details the history of the Mohawk steelworkers.

119. Kirk, David. (1995) *Miss Spider's Wedding*. Scholastic. (Language Arts: Vocabulary—Protagonists and Antagonists [and more])

120. Krull, Kathleen. (1995) *V is for Victory*. Alfred A. Knopf. (Social Studies: World War II)

121. Krull, Kathleen. (1996) *Wilma Unlimited: How Wilma Rudolph Became the World's Fastest Woman*. Illustrated by David Diaz. Harcourt Brace. (Sports) A tale of perseverance and determination. The biography of an African American woman who overcame crippling polio as a child to become the first woman to win three gold medals in track in a single Olympics.

122. Krull, Kathleen. (2003) *Harvesting Hope: The Story of César Chávez*. Illustrated by Yuyi Morales. Harcourt. (Social Studies: Labor) Story of union organizing among migrant workers.

123. Krull, Kathleen. (2008) *Hillary Rodham Clinton: Dreams Taking Flight*. Illustrated by Amy June Bates. Simon & Schuster Books for Young Readers. (Social Studies: Government)

124. Lach, William, ed. (2005) *Vincent's Colors: Words and Pictures by Vincent Van Gogh*. Metropolitan Museum of Art. (Art) Uses quotes by Van Gogh to describe colors in his paintings.

125. Landmann, B. (2006) *I Am Marc Chagall*. Eerdmans Publishing. (Art) Biography of Marc Chagall in first person; introduction to longer text *My Life* by Marc Chagall (classic title—various editions).

126. Langley, Andrew, and Philip De Souza. (1996) *The Roman News*. Candlewick Press. (Social Studies: Ancient Rome)

127. Lasky, Kathryn. (1994) *The Librarian Who Measured the Earth*. Illustrated by Kevin Hawkes. Little, Brown; Joy Street Books. (Mathematics: Measurement/Science) Describes the life and work of Eratosthenes, the Greek geographer and astronomer who accurately measured the circumference of the Earth.

128. Lasky, Kathryn. (1995) *She's Wearing a Dead Bird on Her Head*. Illustrated by David Catrow. Hyperion. (Social Studies: Audubon Society, Bird Protection, Harriet Hemenway, Minna Hall)

129. Lasky, Kathryn. (2003) *The Man Who Made Time Travel*. Illustrated by Kevin Hawkes. Melanie Kroupa Books. (Science: Inventions, John Harrison, Chronometer)

130. Lee, Jeanne. (2002) *Bitter Dumplings*. Farrar, Straus & Giroux. (Social Studies: China History—1405)

131. LeTord, Bijou. (1995) *A Blue Butterfly: A Story About Claude Monet*. Doubleday. (Art: Claude Monet's Life and Art)

132. Levitt, Paul M. (2009) *The Weighty Word Book*. University of New Mexico Press. (English: Vocabulary Building) Originally published in 1985.

133. Lewin, Ted. (2003). *Lost City: The Discovery of Machu Picchu*. Philomel Books. (Social Studies: World Geography) In 1911, a young Peruvian boy helps a Yale professor, Hiram Bingham, discovers a lost Incan city.

134. Lewis, J. Patrick. (2005) *Vherses: A Celebration of Outstanding Women*. Illustrated by Mark Summer. Creative Editions. (Social Studies: Women in History, Poetry)

135. Lied, Kate. (2002) *Potato: A Tale from the Great Depression.* Illustrated by Lisa Campbell Ernst. National Geographic Children's Books. (Social Studies: Depression; Language Arts: Writing Family Stories) This is the story of the eight-year-old author's grandparents, who survived the Depression by digging potatoes in Idaho and returned home to Iowa with a carload of potatoes. Connect to the Depression. (Read Karen Hesse's book *Out of the Dust* [Scholastic, 1997]) or connect to writing family stories.

136. Locker, Thomas. (2002) *Water Dance.* Harcourt. (Science) Discusses how storm clouds, mist, rainbows, and rivers are part of the water cycle.

137. Longfellow, Henry Wadsworth. (1990) *Paul Revere's Ride.* Illustrated by Ted Rand. Dutton. (Social Studies: American Revolution; Paul Revere)

138. Lorbiecki, Marybeth. (2006) *Jackie's Bat.* Illustrated by Brian Pinkney. Simon & Schuster Books for Young Readers. (Social Studies: Sports) Joey, the batboy for the Brooklyn Dodgers in 1947, learns a hard lesson about respect for people of different races after Jackie Robinson joins the team. Fictionalized.

139. Louie, Ai-Ling. (1982) *Yeh-Shen: A Cinderella Story from China.* Philomel Books. (Language Arts: Versions of Cinderella—China)

140. Macaulay, David. (2003). *Mosque.* Houghton Mifflin. (Social Studies: Architecture) Reveals the methods and materials used to construct a mosque in late-sixteenth-century Turkey.

141. Macauley, David. (2008) *The Way We Work.* Houghton Mifflin. (Science: Human Body) A lengthy (336 pages) illustrated look at the human body. Full of illustrations showing microscopic views from head to toe: skeletal structure, inner organs, joints, and all parts of the body.

142. Maltbie, P. I. (2005) *Picasso and Minou*. Illustrated by Pau Estrada. Charlesbridge. (Art: Picasso, Blue Period, Rose Period, Cubism)

143. Mann, Elizabeth. (1996) *The Brooklyn Bridge: The Story of the World's Most Famous Bridge and the Remarkable Family That Built It*. Illustrated by Alan Witschonke. Mikaya Press. (Social Studies: Construction, Brooklyn Bridge [1852–1883]; Roebling Family)

144. Mann, Elizabeth. (1996) *The Great Pyramid: The Story of the Farmers, the God-King and the Most Astounding Structure Ever Built*. Illustrated by Laura Lo Turco. Mikaya Press. (History: Egypt; Construction, Great Pyramid at Giza, Egyptian Civilization)

145. Mann, Elizabeth. (2001) *Hoover Dam: The Story of Hard Times, Tough People and the Taming of a Wild River*. Illustrated by Alan Witschonke. Mikaya Press. (Social Studies: Construction, Architecture)

146. Martin, Jacqueline Briggs. (1998) *Snowflake Bentley*. Illustrated by Mary Azarian. Houghton Mifflin. (Science) Biography that details the life and experiments of Wilson A. Bentley, who photographed hundreds of snowflakes and established the uniqueness of each snowflake. Compare to a fictionalized account of Bentley's life by Mary Bahr, *My Brother Loved Snowflakes: The Story of Wilson A. Bentley, the Snowflake Man*. (Boyds Mills Press, 2002). Discuss the color palette used by Laura Jacobsen for the Bahr title as compared to the palette chosen by Azarian for her Caldecott-Award-winning illustrations in Martin's biographical account.

147. Maruki, Toshi. (1982) *Hiroshima, No Pika*. HarperCollins. (Social Studies: Atomic Bomb) A powerful book about the bombing of Hiroshima during World War II.

148. McCain, Meghan. (2008) *My Dad, John McCain*. Illustrated by Dan Andreasen. Simon & Schuster Books for Young Readers. (Social Studies: Government)

149. McCann, Michelle, and Luba Tryszynska-Frederick. (2003) *Luba: The Angel of Bergen-Belsen*. Illustrated by Ann Marshall. Tricycle Press. (Social Studies: World War II, Germany, Jewish, Bergen-Belsen Concentration Camp.) Luba Tryszynska saved the lives of more than fifty Jewish children during the winter of 1944–1945.

150. McCully, Emily Arnold. (2004) *Squirrel and John Muir*. Farrar, Straus and Giroux. (Science: Environment, Nature) A fictional account of a friendship that was part of naturalist John Muir's life. A good introduction to the man who later was involved in establishing the Sierra Club and Yosemite National Park.

151. McCully, Emily Arnold. (1996) *Bobbin Girl*. Penguin Books. (Social Studies: Child Labor, Massachusetts, 1830) Based on the diary of a mill girl, this story describes the ten-year-old's life as a factory girl. Pair with the longer narrative about a twelve-year old working in the mills in Vermont in the early 1900s. It has the photography of Lewis Hine in his crusade against child labor. Also read *Kids at Work: Lewis Hine and the Crusade Against Child Labor* by Russell Freedman, photographs by Lewis Hine (Clarion Books, 1994).

152. McCurdy, Michael. (1998) *The Sailor's Alphabet*. Houghton Mifflin. (Science: Sailing—Parts of a Sailing Ship)

153. McGill, Alice. (1999) *Molly Bannaky*, Illustrated by Chris K. Soentpiet. Houghton Mifflin. (Social Studies: American History, 1893, Benjamin Banneker, Indentured Servant, Interracial Marriage)

154. McKissack, Patricia C. (2003). *Days of Jubilee: The End of Slavery in the United States*. Scholastic Press. (Social Studies: Slavery) Primary documents chronicle the end of slavery in the United States.

155. McKissack, Patricia. (2001) *Goin' Someplace Special*. Illustrated by Jerry Pinkney. Atheneum Books. (Social Studies: Segregation, 1950s, Tennessee, Public Library)

156. Mobin-Uddin, Asma. (2005) *My Name Is Bilal*. Illustrated by Barbara Kiwak. Boyds Mills Press. (Social Studies: Muslim Culture, School)

157. Mochizuki, Ken. (1993) *Baseball Saved Us*. Illustrated by Dom Lee. Lee & Low Books. (Social Studies: World War II; Japanese Americans in Internment Camps)

158. Mochizuki, Ken. (1997) *Passage to Freedom: The Sugihara Story*. Lee & Low Books. (Social Studies: World War II) Sugihara, a Japanese diplomat in Lithuania in 1941, issued thousands of visas to Polish Jews who, because of the visas, became "Sugihara survivors."

159. Mora, Pat. (2002) *A Library for Juana*: *The World of Sor Juana Ines*. Illustrated by Beatriz Vidal. Alfred A. Knopf. (Language Arts: Poet, Biography, Mexico) She was a seventeenth-century Mexican poet who became a nun later in life.

160. Morgan, Rowland. (1997) *In the Next Three Seconds*. Lodestar Books. (Mathematics: Math Extrapolations)

161. Morrow, Barbara. (2004) *A Good Night for Freedom*, Illustrated by Leonard Jenkins. Holiday House. (Social Studies: Underground Railroad, 1839, Levi Coffin.) Historical notes on the Underground Railroad and abolitionists Levi and Catherine Coffin. Bibliography.

162. Moss, Marissa. (2004). *Mighty Jackie: The Strike-out Queen*. Illustrated by C. F. Payne. Simon & Schuster Books for Young

Readers. (Sports: Baseball, Babe Ruth, Lou Gehrig, Jackie Mitchell, 1931, Women in Baseball) In 1931, seventeen-year-old Jackie Mitchell pitched against Babe Ruth and Lou Gehrig in an exhibition game. She became the first professional female pitcher in baseball history.

163. Mulhlberger, Richard. (1993) *What Makes a Monet a Monet?* Viking Penguin. (Art: Claude Monet's Life and Art)

164. Mullins, Patricia. (1993) *V for Vanishing: An Alphabet of Endangered Species.* Hamilton Books. (Science: Endangered Species)

165. Myers, Walter Dean. (2002) *Patrol: An American Soldier in Vietnam.* Illustrated by Anne Grifalconi. HarperCollins. (Social Studies: Vietnam War, 1970s, Point of View) From the author's own experience—a tragic tale. Pair with the author's *Fallen Angels* (Scholastic, 2008 anniversary edition).

166. Myers, Walter Dean. (2003) *Blues Journey.* Illustrated by Christopher Myers. Holiday House. (Music) Chronicles the origin of blues lyrics and the history of the African American role in the development of blues music.

167. Neuschwander, Cindy. (1997) *Sir Cumference and the First Round Table.* Charlesbridge. (Mathematics: Geometry, Word Play)

168. Neuschwander, Cindy. (1999) *Sir Cumference and the Dragon of Pi.* Charlesbridge. (Mathematics: Geometry, Word Play)

169. Nichol, Barbara, and Scott Cameron. (1994) *Beethoven Lives Upstairs.* Orchard. (Music: Ludwig van Beethoven)

170. Noble, Trinka Hakes. (1987) *Meanwhile Back at the Ranch.* Illustrated by Tony Ross. Dial. (Language Arts: Writing Patterns, Alternating Perspective Irony)

171. Noble, Trinka Hakes. (2006) *The Last Brother: A Civil War Tale*. Illustrated by Robert Papp. Sleeping Bear Press. (Social Studies: Civil War) Based on a true event that took place on July 4, 1863, at the Battle of Pickett's Charge. Friendship and loyalty are called into question.

172. Noyes, Alfred. (1990) *The Highwayman*. Illustrated by Neil Waldman. Harcourt. (Literature) An illustrated introduction to a well-known poem about the highwayman and his true love, the innkeeper's daughter.

173. Oppenheim, Shulamith Levey. (1992) *The Lily Cupboard*. HarperCollins. (Social Studies: World War II—German Occupation of Holland)

174. Pallotta, Jerry. (1991) *The Underwater Alphabet Book*. Charlesbridge. (Science: Oceans)

175. Pallotta, Jerry. (1997) *The Airplane Alphabet Book*. Charlesbridge. (Science: Airplanes)

176. Pallotta, Jerry. (1999) *The Jet Alphabet Book*. Charlesbridge. (Science: Airplanes)

177. Parsons-Yazzie, Evangeline. (2005) *Dzani Yazhi Naazbaa/Little Woman Warrior Who Came Home: A Story of the Navajo Long Walk*. Salina Bookshelf. (Social Studies: Native Americans, Navajo, Long Walk, Forced Resettlement)

178. Partridge, Elizabeth. (2001) *Oranges on Golden Mountain*. Illustrated by Aki Sogabe. Dutton. (Social Studies: Immigration—China, 1890s)

179. Patent, Dorothy Hinshaw. (1997) *Flashy, Fantastic Rain Forest Frogs*. Walker & Company, 1997. (Science: Rain Forest)

180. Pinczes, Elinor J. (1985) *A Remainder of One*. Houghton Mifflin. (Mathematics: Division)

181. Platt, Richard. (1999) *Castle Diary: The Journal of Tobias Burgess*. Illlustrated by Chris Riddell. Candlewick Press. (Social Studies: History England—1295 CE. Includes notes on noblemen, castles, and feudalism.)

182. Platt, Richard. (2005) *Egyptian Diary: The Journal of Nakht*. Illustrated by David Parkins. Candlewick Press. (Social Studies: Egypt 1465 BCE) A journal of life and a mystery in Memphis. Includes nonfiction information about Egyptian culture.

183. Polacco, Patricia. (2000) *The Butterfly*. Philomel Books. (Social Studies: World War II, Occupied France) A Jewish family is hidden in the basement of a young girl's family home. A butterfly is used as a symbolic sign.

184. Polacco, Patricia. (1994) *Pink and Say*. Putnam & Grosset Group. (Social Studies: Civil War/Slavery) Two young soldiers, one black, one white, are captured by Southern troops but meet different fates at Andersonville Prison.

185. Polacco, Patricia. (1998) *Thank You, Mr. Falker*. Philomel Books. (Character Education: Perseverance, Persistence; Reading Difficulties)

186. Polacco, Patricia. (2007) *The Lemonade Club*. Philomel. (Health) One of two friends develops leukemia. Use as a springboard to discuss symptoms of the disease, treatments, and how to support those who have a disease of this type.

187. Pomeroy, Diana. (1997) *Wildflower ABC*. Harcourt Brace. (Science: Wildflowers)

188. Potter, Beatrix. (1902; many editions) *The Tale of Peter Rabbit*. Warne. (Language Arts) Sequels: *The Tale of Benjamin Bunny*.

189. Potter, Beatrix. (1904; many editions) *The Tale of Benjamin Bunny*. Warne. (Language Arts) Sequel to *The Tale of Peter Rabbit*; companion books with *The Tale of the Flopsy Bunnies*.

190. Powell, Anton, and Philip Steele. (1997) *History News: The Egyptian News, The Greatest Newspaper in Civilization*. Candlewick Press. (Social Studies: Ancient Egypt)

191. Pratt-Serafini, Kristin Joy (2008) *The Forever Forest: Kids Save a Tropical Treasure*. Dawn Publications (Science: Rain Forest Animals—Biodiversity; Community Action)

192. Pratt, Kristen Joy. (1992) *A Walk in the Rainforest*. Dawn Publications. (Science: Rain Forest Animals—Alphabetical and Alliteration) Pratt includes fascinating facts about the lifestyle and habitat of each species illustrated.

193. Pratt, Kristen Joy. (1994) *A Swim Through the Sea*. Dawn Publications. (Science: Ocean Animals—Alphabetical and Alliteration)

194. Pratt, Kristen Joy. (1996) *A Fly in the Sky*. Dawn Publications. (Science: Environment, Flying Things, Alliteration)

195. Pringle, Laurence P. (2004). *Snakes!: Strange and Wonderful*. Illustrated by Meryl Henderson. Boyds Mills Press. (Science: Animals) Describes how snakes climb, swim, and move across the ground, discusses their hunting abilities and eating behaviors, and explains how they reproduce.

196. Pushker, Gloria Teles. (2003) *Toby Belfer Visits Ellis Island*. Illustrated by Judy Hierstein. Pelican. (Social Studies: Immigration—Poland, 1904, Flee) Story of when soldiers drove Jews from Poland.

197. Quezada, Juan, with Shelley Dale. (2004) *Juan Quezada/Asi Es Como Sucedio*. Norman Books. (Art: Pottery, Mexico; Community Culture) Juan revived the art of creating ceramics and rescued his village economically, and in the process became famous. Pair with Nancy Andrews-Goebel's *The Pot That Juan Built* (Lee & Low Books, 2002).

198. Raczka, Bob. (2003). *Art is ...* Millbrook Press. (Art) Introduces more than two dozen famous artworks from various time periods and mediums through quality photographs illustrating the diversity of art from a Picasso to a Greek vase to an African mask.

199. Raczka, Bob. (2003). *More than Meets the Eye: Seeing Art with All Five Senses*. Millbrook Press. (Art) Incorporates the five senses in exploring and appreciating art, from the taste of milk in Vermeer's "The Milkmaid," hearing the music in Tanner's "The Banjo Lesson," or smelling the fresh-cut stacks of wheat in Monet's "End of Summer."

200. Raczka, Bob. (2005). *Unlikely Pairs: Fun with Famous Works of Art*. Millbrook Press. (Art) Famous pairs of artwork join to create a story seemingly shown by the artwork. Rodin's *The Thinker* is paired with Klee's modernistic painting of a chessboard. The statue is positioned so it appears to be contemplating the next move. The boy blowing soap bubbles in Siméon-Chardin's painting seems to be creating Kandinsky's *Several Circles*. Invites readers to find their own stories in art.

201. Rand, Gloria. (2005) *A Pen Pal For Max*. Illustrated by Ted Rand. Henry Holt. (Social Studies: Chile, Community Culture, Aid to Earthquake Victims, Humanitarian Efforts) A pen pal in the United States arranges for aid to be sent to his pal and others affected by the Chilean earthquake.

202. Ransom, Candice. (2003) *Liberty Street*. Illustrated by Eric Velasquez. Walker & Company. (Social Studies: Underground Railroad; Fredericksburg, Virginia.)

203. Rappaport, Doreen. (2005) *The Secret Seder*. Illustrated by Emily Arnold McCully. (Social Studies: Nazi Occupation of France, World War II, Holocaust, Jewish Traditions)

204. Rappaport, Doreen. (2002). *Martin's Big Words: The Life of Dr. Martin Luther King, Jr.* Scholastic. (Social Studies: Civil Rights) Dr. Martin Luther King Jr.'s efforts to bring an end to segregation.

205. Rappaport, Doreen. (2006) *Freedom Ship*. Illustrated by Curtis James. Hyperion/Jump at the Sun. (Social Studies: Civil War) Based on an actual Civil War event that took place on May 13, 1862, when Robert Smalls, a wheelman for a Confederate ship the *Planter*, actually kidnapped the ship and sailed it past three Confederate forts and right into the arms of the Union fleet.

206. Raven, Margot Theis. (2002) *Mercedes and the Chocolate Pilot*. Sleeping Bear Press. (Social Studies: Post-World War II, Berlin Airlift, Chocolate Pilot.)

207. Raven, Margot Theis. (2004) *Circle Unbroken*. Farrar, Straus and Giroux. (Social Studies: African American Culture and History) A grandmother keeps alive the story of Gullahs and their beautiful sweetgrass baskets. The historical notes and bibliography in this book are invaluable.

208. Ringgold, Faith. (1996) *Dinner at Aunt Connie's House*. Hyperion (Social Studies: African American Women) Showcases twelve inspiring African American women.

209. Robertson, Bruce. (1999) *Marguerite Makes a Book*. Illustrated by Kathryn Hewitt. Getty Publications. (Literature: Bookmaking) In medieval Paris, Marguerite describes her father's preparation of an illuminated manuscript. Contains detailed information on the kinds of paper, inks, and colors that were used to make illustrated manuscripts.

210. Rubin, Susan Goldman. (2001) *The Yellow House: Vincent Van Gogh and Paul Gauguin Side by Side.* Harry N. Abrams. (Art: Vincent Van Gogh, Paul Gauguin, 1888, Paintings) Contains reproductions of Van Gogh and Gauguin and biography of the artists.

211. Rubin, Susan Goldman. (2007). *Edward Hopper: Painter of Light and Shadow.* Abrams Books for Young Readers. (Art) Includes Hopper's paintings and sketches—an introductory biography.

212. Ryan, Pam Muñoz. (1999) *Amelia and Eleanor Go for a Ride: Based on a True Story. Illustrated by Brian Selznick.* Scholastic. (Social Studies: Eleanor Roosevelt, Amelia Earhart) Fictional account of an event that did occur.

213. Ryan, Pam Muñoz. (2002). *When Marian Sang: The True Recital of Marian Anderson the Voice of a Century.* Illustrated by Brian Selznick. Scholastic Press. (Social Studies: Civil Rights) The story of Marian Anderson's encounter with the Daughters of the American Revolution, who refused to let her sing in their facility and how Eleanor Roosevelt invited her to sing on the steps of the Lincoln Memorial.

214. San Souci, Robert D. (1998) *Cendrillon: A Caribbean Cinderella.* Simon & Schuster. (Language Arts: Versions of Cinderella—Caribbean)

215. Say, Allen. (1991). *Tree of Cranes.* Houghton Mifflin. (Social Studies—Immigration) Investigate the back story of this book, share that information, and then read how a Japanese boy learns of Christmas when his mother decorates a pine tree with paper cranes; he learns of a holiday celebrated in his mother's childhood home in America.

216. Say, Allen. (1993). *Grandfather's Journey*. Houghton Mifflin. (Social Studies: Immigration) Allen interweaves his grandfather's immigration experience with his own to create this account of immigration.

217. Say, Allen. (2004) *Music For Alice*. Houghton Mifflin. (Social Studies: Japanese Internment, World War II, 1942) Based on the life of Alice Sumida who, with her husband Mark, established a large and successful gladiola bulb farm.

218. Schaefer, Carole Lexa. (2001) *Two Scarlet Songbirds: A Story of Anton Dvorak*. Illustrated by Elizabeth Rosen. Alfred A. Knopf. (Music: Anton Dvorak, New York City, 1892, *American Quartet*, Scarlet Tanager.)

219. Schnur, Steven. (1997) *Autumn: An Alphabet Acrostic*. Illustrated by Leslie Evans. Clarion Books. (English: Poetry; Acrostic Poetry)

220. Schwartz, David M. (1998) *G is for Googol: A Math Alphabet Book*. Tricycle Press. (Mathematics: Math Vocabulary)

221. Scieszka, Jon & Lane Smith. (1995) *Math Curse*. Viking Press. (Mathematics) Details math phobia, prime numbers, and other number concepts. Everything is a math problem. Use this text to stimulate student thinking about mathematics in their immediate environment.

222. Scieszka, Jon. (1994) *The Book That Jack Wrote*. Illustrated by Don Adel. Viking. (Language Arts: Writing) Innovation on a writing pattern ("The House That Jack Built"); parody, visual allusions.

223. Seuss, Dr. (1984). *The Butter Battle Book*. Random House. (Social Studies: Cold War) The Yooks and the Zooks are threatened by one another and each attempts to develop stronger and bigger weapons.

224. Seuss, Dr. (1954) *Horton Hears a Who*. Random House. (Language Arts, Social Studies) Parody on the post-World War II situation; symbolizes the Japanese people seeking democracy after World War II.

225. Seuss, Dr. (1958) *Yertle the Turtle and Other Stories*. Random House. (Language Arts; Social Studies: World War II) Parody on the Nazi regime under Hitler.

226. Seuss, Dr. (1971). *The Lorax*. Random House. (Science: Ecology) The Once-ler describes the results of the local pollution problem.

227. Shea, Pegi Deitz. (1995) *The Whispering Cloth: A Refugee's Story*. Illustrated by Anita Riggio and You Yang. Boyds Mills Press. (Social Studies: Vietnam War, 1970s, Hmong, Laos, Refugee Camp)

228. Sierra, Judy. (2000) *There's a Zoo in Room 22*. Illlustrated by Barney Saltzberg. Harcourt. (Science: Animals, Rhymed Couplets)

229. Sim, Dorrith. (1996) *In My Pocket*. Harcourt Brace. (Social Studies: World War II) A small girl's perspective of the Kindertransport that took 10,000 Jewish children from Nazi Europe to Britain from 1938 to 1939. Consider using this picture book with the novel by Olga Levy Drucker, *Kindertransport* (Henry Holt, 1992) or the stories of twenty-one other survivors told in *Ten Thousand Children: True Stories Told by Children Who Escaped the Holocaust on the Kindertransport* by Anne Fox and Eva Abraham-Podietz (Behrman House Publishing, 1998).

230. Simon, Seymour. (2006) *Stars*. HarperCollins (Science: Stars) Discusses the stars, their composition, and characteristics. Illustrated with photographs. Originally published in 1989, updated in 2006.

231. Simon, Seymour. (1991) *Galaxies*. HarperCollins. (Science: Stars) Identifies the nature, locations, movements, and different categories of galaxies, examining the Milky Way and other galaxies.

232. Simon, Seymour. (1996) *The Heart: Our Circulatory System*. HarperCollins. (Science: Heart; Circulatory System) A basic introduction to the heart, blood, and other parts of the body's circulatory system and explains how each component functions.

233. Simon, Seymour. (1997) *The Brain: Our Nervous System*. HarperCollins. (Science: Brain) A basic introduction to various parts of the brain and the nervous system and how they function to enable us to think, feel, move, and remember.

234. Simon, Seymour. (1998) *Muscles: Our Muscular System*. HarperCollins. (Science: Muscular System) Basic introduction to the work of muscles, the different kinds, and the effects of exercise and other activities on them.

235. Simon, Seymour. (1999) *Icebergs and Glaciers*. HarperCollins. (Science: Glaciers) Information on icebergs and glaciers, how they are formed and move, and the different kinds of glaciers and icebergs as well as their effect on the environment.

236. Simon, Seymour. (2002) *Destination: Space*. HarperCollins. (Science: Inventions) Discoveries made possible by the Hubble Telescope.

237. Simon, Seymour. (2005) *Guts: Our Digestive System*. HarperCollins. (Science: Digestive System) Presents a full-color illustrated study of how the digestive system works, how it turns food into energy, nutrients, and waste, how major organs move food through the body, and more.

238. Sis, Peter. (1996) *Starry Messenger: A Book Depicting the Life of a Famous Scientist, Mathematician, Astronomer, Philosopher, Physicist, Galileo Galilei*. Farrar, Straus and Giroux. (Mathematics/Science; Galileo) The life and work of Galileo, who changed the way people saw the galaxy.

239. Sis, Peter. (2003) *The Tree of Life: A Book Depicting the Life of Charles Darwin, Naturalist, Geologist & Thinker*. Farrar, Straus and Giroux. (Science; Charles Darwin) Presents the life of the famous nineteenth-century naturalist using text from Darwin's writings and detailed drawings by Sis.

240. Smith, Cynthia Leitich. (2000) *Rain Dancer*. Illustrated by Cornelius Van Wright and Ying-Hwa Hu. HarperCollins. (Social Studies: Native American Culture) A young girl is helped by her intertribal community to gather the items for her regalia to participate in a traditional dance. Use this book in conjunction with Simon Ortiz's *The People Shall Continue*, illustrated by Sharol Graves (Children's Book Press, 1998).

241. Spedden, Daisy Corning. (1994) *Polar, The Titanic Bear*. Little, Brown. (Social Studies: *Titanic*, 1900s) Pair with *Pig on the Titanic: A True Story* by Gary Crew (HarperCollins, 2005). *Pig on the Titanic* is another story of the *Titanic* in which a musical pig tells how he helped to save children when the ship sank. Both of these stories are told through the eyes of inanimate objects but reflect facts based on true stories.

242. Stanley, Diane, and Peter Vennema. (1994) *Cleopatra*. Morrow. (Social Studies: Ancient Egypt, Cleopatra)

243. Stanley, Diane. (1997). *Rumpelstiltskin's Daughter*. Morrow Junior Books. (Literature) An illustrated parody with lots of symbolism. Use this model to inspire parodies of other familiar pieces of folk literature.

244. Steedman, Scott. (1996) *The Greek News: The Greatest Newspaper in Civilization*. Candlewick Press. (Social Studies: Ancient Greece)

245. Stevenson, James. (1983) *The Great Big Especially Beautiful Easter Eggs*. Illustrated by Greenwillow. (Language Arts: Flashbacks)

246. Tobias, Tobi, and Peter Malone. (1998) *A World of Words: An ABC of Quotations*. Lothrop, Lee & Shepard. (English: Quotations, Famous Literary Quotes)

247. Tompert, Ann. (1990) *Grandfather Tang's Story*. Crown Publishers. (Mathematics: Tangrams, Geometry)

248. Towle, Wendy. (1993) *The Real McCoy: The Life of an African-American Inventor*. Scholastic. (Social Studies: Inventors) An African American inventor who not only contributed his inventions but was the basis for the phrase "The Real McCoy."

249. Tsuchiya, Yukio. (1951) *Faithful Elephants*. Houghton Mifflin. (Social Studies: World War II) This story has been publicized as true but it is not; it is purely fictional but does raise some interesting questions about war and animals in the throes of hostilities.

250. Turner, Ann. (1992) *Katie's Trunk*. Illustrated by Ronald Himler. Simon & Schuster. (Social Studies: Revolutionary War)

251. Van Allsburg, Chris. (1984) *The Mysteries of Harris Burdick.* Houghton Mifflin. (Writing) Each sepia-toned illustration begs for a story to accompany the drawings. If a paperback version is available, buy two copies and dismantle the book to present each student with just one image to write about.

252. Van Allsburg, Chris. (1986) *The Stranger.* Houghton Mifflin. (Science: Seasons, Changing to Autumn)

253. Van Allsburg, Chris. (1988) *Two Bad Ants.* Houghton Mifflin. (Science: Ants, Perspective in Art)

254. Van Allsburg, Chris. (1991) *The Wretched Stone.* Houghton Mifflin. (Social Studies: Television, Allegory) Pair with David Wisniewski's *Elfwyn's Saga* (Clarion Books, 1990) and Patricia Polacco's *Aunt Chip and the Great Triple Creek Dam Affair* (Philomel Books, 1996).

255. Van Steenwyk, Elizabeth. (2003). *One Fine Day: A Radio Play.* Illustrated by Bill Farnsworth. Eerdmans Books for Young Readers. (Social Studies: History) The story of the Wright Brothers' first successful flight.

256. Vander Zee, Ruth. (2004) *Erika's Story,* Illustrated by Roberto Innocenti. Mankato. (Social Studies: World War II, Nazi Death Camp, 1944) Rescued after being thrown from a train headed for a Nazi death camp, Erika was raised by those who risked their own lives to save hers.

257. Vander Zee, Ruth. (2004) *Mississippi Morning.* Illustrated by Floyd Cooper. Eerdmans Books for Young Readers. (Social Studies: Civil Rights, Ku Klux Klan, 1930s)

258. Vaughan, Marcia. (2004) *Up The Learning Tree*. Illustrated by Derek Blanks. Lee & Low Books. (Social Studies: African American History, Literacy)

259. Volavkova, H., ed. (1993) *I Never Saw Another Butterfly: Children's Drawings and Poems from Terezin Concentration Camp 1942–1944*. (Expanded Second Edition by the United States Holocaust Memorial Museum, ed.). Schocken Books. (Social Studies: Holocaust) A selection of children's poems and drawings reflecting their surroundings in Terezín Concentration Camp in Czechoslovakia from 1942 to 1944.

260. Waldman, Neil. (2003) *The Snowflake: A Water Cycle Story*. Millbrook Press. (Science: Snowflakes, Water) Follows a water droplet through the various stages of the water cycle, from precipitation to evaporation and condensation.

261. Wargin, Kathy-Jo. (2003) *The Edmund Fitzgerald; The Song of the Bell*. Illustrated by Gijsbert Van Frankenhuyzen. Sleeping Bear Press. (Social Studies: Historic Events, Sunken Treasure, Great Lakes) The *Edmund Fitzgerald*, the largest ship launched on the Great Lakes, sunk in 1958. This book presents evidence discovered thirty-seven years later (1975).

262. Wargin, Kathy-Jo. (2004). *M is for Melody: A Music Alphabet*. Illustrated by Katherine Larson. Sleeping Bear Press. (Music) Introduces instruments, terms, composers, and styles, each with additional information about the topic.

263. Warhola, James. (2003). *Uncle Andy's: A Faabbbulous Visit with Andy Warhol*. Putnam Juvenile. (Art) The artist's nephew provides a great introduction to his famous uncle, who felt that "art is everywhere."

264. Warhola, James. (2009). *Uncle Andy's Cats*. Putnam Juvenile. (Art) A follow–up to Warhola's earlier book about his eccentric artist uncle, Andy Warhol. This book features Warhol's twenty-five cats, all named Sam.

265. Weatherford, Carole Boston. (2002) *The Sound That Jazz Makes.* Illustrated by Eric Velasquez. Walker & Co. (Music: History of Jazz)

266. Weatherford, Carole Boston. (2004) *Freedom on the Menu: The Greensboro Sit-Ins.* Illustrated by Jerome Lagarrigue. Dial. (Social Studies: Segregation, 1960s, Civil Rights, Lunch Counter Sit-Ins, Woolworth, Greensboro, North Carolina)

267. Weitzman, David. (1997) *Old Ironsides: Americans Build a Fighting Ship.* Houghton Mifflin. (Social Studies: American History: USS *Constitution*)

268. Wells, Rosemary. (1996) *The Language of Doves.* Illustrated by Gary Shed. Dial. (Social Studies: World War I) The little-known story of the Italian Army and the messages these homing birds carried.

269. White, Linda Arms. (2005) *I Could Do That!: Esther Morris Gets Women the Vote.* Illustrated by Nancy Carpenter. Farrar, Straus and Giroux. (Social Studies: Women's Suffrage, 1869, Wyoming, First Woman in Public Office [United States]) Pair with Connie Wooldridge's *When Esther Morris Headed West* (Holiday House, 2001).

270. Wick, Walter. (1997) *A Drop of Water.* Scholastic. (Science: Molecules, Viscosity, Forms of Matter)

271. Wild, Margaret. (1991) *Let the Celebrations Begin!* Illustrated by Julie Vivas. Orchard Books. (Social Studies: World War II) Just before liberation, stuffed toys were made by a few women in the concentration camps for the meager number of children who were left in the camps. The compelling story of strong women putting aside their hunger, deprivation, and the inhumane conditions to care for the children in the camp.

272. Willing, Karen B., Julie B. Dock, and Sarah Morse (1996). *Cotton Now & Then: Fabric Making from Boll to Bolt.* Now & Then Publications. (Social Studies) Focuses on the history of cotton and its industry and technology. Use this book as a prototype for studying the history of other industries that are important in our culture.

273. Willard, Nancy. (1981) *A Visit to William Blake's Inn: Poems for Innocent and Experienced Travelers.* Illustrated by Alice and Martin Provensen. Harcourt (Language Arts) Introduce the poetry of William Blake.

274. Winnick, Karen B. (2005) *Cassie's Sweet Berry Pie.* Boyds Mills Press. (Social Studies: Civil War, Confederate, Mississippi.) Cassie tricks Union soldiers into leaving by creating a case of "measles" for her brothers and sisters.

275. Winter, Jeanette. (2005) *The Librarian of Basra.* Harcourt. (Social Studies: Iraq, Library) True story of Alia Muhammad Baker, chief librarian of Basra in Iraq, and how she protected the nation's books when the United States invaded in 2003.

276. Wyeth, Sharon Dennis. (1998) *Something Beautiful.* Bantam Doubleday. (Character Education: Community Service) Pair with *Miss Rumphius* by Barbara Cooney (Viking, 1982).

277. Yee, Paul. (2004) *A Song for Ba.* Illustrated by Jan Peng Wang. Groundwood. (Social Studies: Chinese Culture, Opera Singer)

278. Yin. (2001) *Coolies.* Illustrated by Chris Soentpiet. Philomel Books. (Social Studies: Transcontinental Railroad, Chinese)

279. Yolen, Jane. (1992) *Letting Swift River Go.* Illustrated by Barbara Cooney. Little, Brown. (Science: Environment)

280. Yolen, Jane. (1992) *Encounter*. Illlustrated by David Shannon. Harcourt Brace. (Social Studies: Columbus, 1492, Taino Indians, San Salvador) Tells of the landing of Columbus and his men from a Taino boy's perspective. Encourage readers to research the changing historical perspective surrounding Columbus's arrival in the Western Hemisphere.

Picture That!

General Index
(Authors, Titles, and Subjects)

Each of the sixty-two main entries in this book are fully indexed by title, author, and as much as practical by every subject that might stimulate a connection to some area of your curriculum. We did not however, list individual titles or authors of books associated with each main entry as collaborative reading or research titles. Those are cited completely in each of the booklists that appear at the end of the chapter for each main entry. So, if you turn to a page with information on a subject you wish to pursue further, page to the end of that particular chapter and you will find a list of books that we have connected to the main entry.

The index for *Picture This! Quick List ...* follows this index of the full entries.

Picture This!

Quick List Index
(Authors, Titles, and Subjects)

The additional two-hundred and eighty titles included in the quick list are fully indexed by title, author, and as much as practical by every subject that might stimulate a connection to some area of your curriculum.

Each entry in the quick list has been assigned a number that you might use as the folder number for keeping track and organizing additional information about this book and its curriculum connections. That quick list entry number is the number referred to here in this index—not the page number.

The brief annotations or quick suggestion of some curriculum connections are reflected in this index; however, creative users of the quick list and the index will be likely to identify additional connections for many of the titles. Browsing through the quick list will stimulate many of those ideas.

The index for *Picture That! General Index* ... precedes this index of the quick list.

About the Author

My life has been rather simple and uneventful to this point. I grew up in the heartland of the United States and found myself reading, over and over again, the stories of the Grimm Brothers and Hans Christian Anderson—those were the only two books I ever remember reading in any of the large farm homes where I lived. The nearby towns did not have libraries and our elementary school had but one bookshelf—far from filled and with all the books able to be facing out.

Years as an educator in elementary and secondary classrooms and libraries have brought many books into my life as I realized that success with children and young adults always involves books—readers do succeed. I have read books, shared them, and read them again. In addition to writing and speaking about books and the people who create them, I seek to find ways to surround others in literacy—acknowledging that to build a nation of readers requires us to do that one reader, one classroom, one school, one community at a time.

My family includes children (six spirited individuals) much like the Herdmans from *The Best Christmas Pageant Ever* by Barbara Robinson. And my grandchildren who would be very much at home in Serafina Sow's Waffery (*The Three Little Pigs* by Steven Kellogg) as they love waffles (and pancakes) as much as her large family. My house is filled with bookshelves and few have room for displaying the books face out, but there are always baskets of books ready for reading.

Our family home is nestled among tall stately trees, at the end of a long dirt lane, on the top of a hill where our acreage clings to the edge of a very small town—a little larger than the "population 100" town of my youth, but in the shadows of the second largest city in the state, Cedar Rapids.

It is here, and in borrowed classrooms, that I gather my inspiration for the dozens of books, columns, and articles that I've written. Up-to-date information about my writing and literacy activities can be found on my website at <http://www.mcelmeel.com>.

Sharron L. McElmeel